AMERICAN EXPLORATION AND TRAVEL

Up the Missouri with Audubon

The Journal of Edward Harris

Up the Missouri
with Audubon

The Journal of Edward Harris

edited and annotated by
JOHN FRANCIS McDERMOTT

UNIVERSITY OF OKLAHOMA PRESS

NORMAN

By JOHN FRANCIS McDERMOTT

Up the Missouri with Audubon, The Journal of Edward Harris (Editor)
(Norman, 1951)

*Travels in Search of the Elephant: The Wanderings of Alfred S. Waugh,
Artist, in Louisiana, Missouri, and Santa Fe, in 1845–1846* (Editor)
(St. Louis, 1951)

*Old Cahokia: A Narrative and Documents Illustrating the First Century
of Its History* (Editor) (St. Louis, 1949)

The Western Journals of Washington Irving (Editor) (Norman, 1944)

A Glossary of Mississippi Valley French (St. Louis, 1941)

Tixier's Travels on the Osage Prairies, translated by Albert J. Salvan
(Editor) (Norman, 1940)

Private Libraries in Creole Saint Louis (Baltimore, 1938)

Collected Verse of Lewis Carroll (Editor) (New York, 1929)

The Russian Journal and Other Prose of Lewis Carroll (Editor) (New
York, 1935)

Copyright 1951 by the University of Oklahoma Press
Publishing Division of the University
Composed and printed at Norman, Oklahoma, U.S.A.
by the University of Oklahoma Press

FIRST EDITION

TO MY GRANDSON
John Francis McDermott V

Preface

IN THE SUMMER OF 1843 Edward Harris accompanied Audubon on his expedition up the Missouri River to the Yellowstone. He kept a diary during this trip, and in 1850 Spencer F. Baird urged him to prepare it for publication by the Smithsonian Institution. For reasons unknown, no action was taken and the manuscript remained untouched until Stanley Clisby Arthur consulted it while writing *Audubon, an Intimate Life of the American Woodsman*. Probably the first public appearance of the Harris diary was at the Audubon exhibition held by the Academy of Natural Sciences of Philadelphia in 1938. Some portions of it were excerpted by Peter A. Brannon for his "Edward Harris, Friend of Audubon," a Newcomen Society paper published in 1947. The Harris journal is now made available for the first time in its entirety.

The account of the journey is contained in two books (now deposited in the W. U. Harris Collection of the Department of Archives and History at Montgomery, Alabama). The first is a pocket volume, 4 by 5¾ inches, with a printed title: "Diary for 1843 or Daily Register for the Use of Private Families and Persons of Business. . . . Published yearly by Hyman L. Lipman, 139 Chestnut St., Philadelphia." Alternately on right and left pages space was provided for entries for three days, with the opposite page left blank. Harris made his first entry on March 13. Once embarked on the journey up the Missouri River, he found that even his microscopic hand could not crowd in all the detail he had to report (see the reproduction below of the pages for May 25, 26, and 27). On May 28, therefore, he transferred his journal to folio sheets, 11 by 16¾ inches, bound in a heavy paper cover. This larger manuscript bears on its cover his name and address and a descriptive title:

Edward Harris

Moorestown

Burlington County   N. J.

Journal of a trip to the
Head waters of the Missouri
in the Summer of 1843. *Continued*

The last entry in the larger folio was that for August 12. On May 28 Harris had noted that he would still keep in the small diary "a list of Birds & Quadrupeds . . . and other etcetera." In this pocket volume he also made occasional entries relative to the return trip.

All of this material has been arranged in one chronological sequence. Some lengthy geological notations have been split into daily entries when they have been so dated in the manuscript. Date lines have been made uniform, since retention of the printed forms of the pocket diary would seem eccentric and inconsistent with Harris's procedure in the folio. The long *s* has been modernized. With these few exceptions, Harris's manuscripts have been reproduced exactly. It will be noticed that some words are spelled in more than one way: *chace* and *chase, prarie* and *prairie, Yellow Stone* and *Yellowstone;* these are the author's own variants.

In the notes no attempt is made to write a history of the fur trade, a topographical report on the Missouri River, or a study of the Indian tribes of the area in which Harris was traveling. The annotations are intended to point up the diarist's narrative, to fill in an occasional hiatus, and to clarify matters left vague in daily jottings.

I am, of course, particularly indebted to Mr. William U. Harris (grandson of Edward Harris) of Jackson, Alabama, for permission to print these manuscripts. Mr. Peter A. Brannon of the Department of Archives and History, Montgomery, Alabama, gave me access to the collection now under his charge;

he has been more than courteous and helpful during my work on this volume. The Graduate School of Arts and Sciences, Washington University, made it possible for me to devote the necessary months to the preparation of the manuscript by the grant of a Summer Research Fellowship. Mr. Stanley Clisby Arthur most generously let me examine his Edward Harris papers. Mr. John B. Ewers, associate curator of ethnology at the United States National Museum, Mrs. Venia T. Phillips, librarian of the Academy of Natural Sciences of Philadelphia, Mr. Phillips B. Street, and Mr. Isaac Sprague, Jr., have all been interested and helpful. To Mr. William A. Jackson, librarian of the Houghton Library, and to Harvard University, I am grateful for permission to examine and quote from letters in the Audubon collection of that library. And, as always, I am indebted beyond words to my wife.

JOHN FRANCIS McDERMOTT

St. Louis, Missouri
    August 3, 1951

Contents

Illustrations

Editor's Introduction

STRANGEST OF ALL ADVENTURERS in the decades before the Civil War were the naturalists who wandered through the forests and over the Great Plains cataloguing beast and bird and tree and flower, for they suffered pain and privation without the army officer's hope of promotion or the fur trader's hope of wealth. The lure of the unknown, the stimulating excitement of great difficulties overcome, the spice of danger, the sense of discovery, the exultation of survival as surely drew the botanist as the sportsman, the zoologist as the soldier, the ornithologist as the trader, from home and ease and a quiet life to a rigorous, harsh, rough, strange existence. Up distant rivers, away over the prairies, deep into the great mountains they pushed far beyond the frontier, these naturalists with their notebooks and their sketch pads, taking advantage of every military party or emigration train or fur-company expedition possible—indeed, even venturing alone and on foot where wiser frontiersmen did not choose to go.

Consider Henry Rowe Schoolcraft, a raw young man from New York state, whose interest in geology leads him on a walking tour in the Ozark Mountains with a single companion as ignorant of frontier forests as himself. For days at a time these brash, curious fellows do not see even the hut of a frontier squatter during that tramp in 1818–19. Prime example of the wandering naturalist is Thomas Nuttall (surely the prototype of Obed Battius) who in 1810 undertakes to make for Dr. Barton of Philadelphia a solo pedestrian jaunt west along the Great Lakes to Lake Winnipeg, thence to Minnesota, down the Mississippi, and back to Philadelphia by way of Illinois, Indiana, Kentucky, and Ohio. Actually he did get as far west as Michilimackinac where he made a change of plans that led to an even more extended "excursion," though a less solitary one. He and John Bradbury attached themselves to Wilson Price Hunt's Astoria party at St. Louis in 1811 and ascended the Missouri as far as the Arikaras, to return in the later summer with a small party of *voyageurs* being sent back by Manuel Lisa in charge of Henry Marie Brackenridge. Nuttall's travels up the Arkansas River in 1818–19, the botanical and zoological explorations of Say and other scientific members of Major Stephen H. Long's western and northern expeditions in 1819–20 and 1823, the two-year wanderings of Nuttall and John K. Townsend through the remote Northwest and to Hawaii in 1834–36 are a few among a hundred explorations being conducted during these decades by learned men far beyond the frontier.

Is it any wonder that John James Audubon, too, longed to penetrate the Far West in search of rare birds and quadrupeds? As a young man wandering up and down the Ohio Valley and the Lower Mississippi, he made marvelous use of his opportunities for bird-study. But from early days he had an overwhelming desire to see what lay beyond the frontier. In 1820 he was hoping to reach the Osage Nations: "My Intention is to Visit the country around New Orleans as far East as the Florida Keys, then ascend the Red River, and go to the Hot Springs—thence across to the Arkansas and Come down [it] to its mouth."[1] In 1831 he was proposing to traverse "the swamps of Florida—the wilds of Missouri—the snows of the Rocky Mountains—and, if possible, to reach the Pacific."[2] In 1838 he wrote from London to Thomas Brewer in Boston: "How would you like to trip it over the Rocky Mountains next spring in company with Ed. Harris, Townsend, and about forty others. . . . Harris tells me that such an expedition is now on *talk,* and that he feels anxious to join it."[3]

[1] *Journal of John James Audubon made during his Trip to New Orleans in 1820–1821,* ed. by Howard Corning (Cambridge, The Business Historical Society, 1929), 76.
[2] John Bachman to Mrs. J. J. Audubon, Charleston, Nov. 15, 1831 (C. L. Bachman, *John Bachman* [Charleston, 1888]), 96).
[3] London, May 26, 1838 (*Harpers Magazine,* Vol. LXI [October, 1880], 674).

Is it any wonder, either, that quiet, sedate, prosperous Edward Harris,[4] gentleman-farmer of Moorestown, New Jersey, should want to go beyond the frontier or that he should be the companion above all others whom Audubon wished to have with him on his longest and most difficult excursion into the wilds? The friendship between these men, the amateur ornithologist and professional bird-painter, had begun in 1824. In July of that year Audubon visited Philadelphia, portfolio under arm, hoping to find aid for the publication of his long-dreamed-of *Birds of America.* His beautifully delicate drawings won him more compliments than the practical encouragement he needed to keep alive. But on the nineteenth he met for the second time this amateur from New Jersey and was astounded by his behavior: "Young Harris, God bless him, looked at the drawings I had for sale, and said he would take them *all,* at my prices. I would have kissed him, but that is not the custom in this icy city." When Audubon was about to leave town some time later, the young ornithologist, as he was saying good-by, "squeezed

[4] Edward Harris, son of Edward Harris and Jane Ustick, was born at Moorestown, Burlington County, New Jersey, on September 7, 1799, and died there June 8, 1863. He was married twice: first to Mary Lang (1827) and second to Mary G. Ustick (1846) —both cousins. By his second wife he had four children, the third of whom, Edward III, had a son, William U., the donor of the Harris Collection. To sum up Edward Harris II in a sentence, we can say with Francis H. Herrick that "Edward Harris became a patron of science through his friendship with scientific men, and many besides Audubon were indebted to him for judicious advice as well as more substantial benefits." (*Audubon the Naturalist* [2nd ed., 2 vols. in 1, New York, D. Appleton-Century, 1938], I, 333.)

A brief appreciative sketch of Harris was published by George Spencer Morris, great-nephew of Harris's brother-in-law and close friend, Dr. John J. Spencer (*Cassinia,* Proceedings of the Delaware Valley Ornithological Society, VI [1902], 1–5). A much longer and more valuable account is the Newcomen Society paper (1947), "Edward Harris, Friend of Audubon," by Peter A. Brannon; it is based upon the W. U. Harris Manuscript Collection in the Department of Archives and History, Montgomery, Alabama. An interesting study of the remaining portion of Harris's bird collections has recently appeared by Phillips B. Street: "The Edward Harris Collection of Birds," *Wilson Bulletin,* Vol. LX (September, 1948), 167–84. Harris, of course, figures repeatedly in the published works of Audubon; much about him can be found in the two important lives of Audubon: Herrick, cited above, and Stanley Clisby Arthur, *Audubon, an Intimate Life of the American Woodsman* (New Orleans, Harmanson, 1937). For family background, travels, agricultural interests, and other such matters consult the Harris MSS.

a hundred-dollar bill into his friend's hand, saying, 'Mr. Audubon, accept this from me; men like you ought not to want for
money.' I could only express my gratitude [Audubon related]
by insisting on his receiving the drawings of all my French
birds, which he did, and I was relieved. This is the second instance of disinterested generosity I have met with in my life. . . .
And now I have in hand one hundred and thirty dollars to begin
my journey of three thousand miles."[5] From this day forth the
respect and affection of Audubon and Harris for each other
ever increased.

Edward Harris, now twenty-five years old, could afford to
indulge his scientific interests, for he had inherited a considerable
fortune and a large farm at Moorestown, New Jersey. An interested traveler, a well-informed bird specialist, a scientific agri-
culturalist, a careful businessman, he led an ordered and intelli-
gent life. From the day he met Audubon until Audubon's last
long illness, they were either together or in close correspondence,
and their relationship was one of personal liking as well as of
common interest. A hundred letters from Audubon to Harris
testify to their friendship, for it was not often possible for them
to meet. Occasionally we can read of typical meetings such as
the one in Philadelphia in September, 1836. Audubon was greatly
enthusiastic over the collection Nuttall and Townsend had
brought back to the Philadelphia Academy of Natural Science,
and Harris, noting this, offered to give Audubon five hundred
dollars towards the purchase of it. "Is not this a noble generosity
to show for the love of science?" asked Audubon.[6]

The first ornithological excursion the friends made together
was the one in the spring of 1837 to the coast of Louisiana and
Texas. The original plan, calling for an inspection of the Florida
coast via government cutter, was cancelled by the Seminole War.
Harris met his friend at Dr. Bachman's in Charleston, South

[5] Maria R. Audubon and Elliott Coues, eds., *Audubon and His Journals* (2 vols.,
New York, Scribners, 1897), I, 57 (this work will hereafter be cited as Audubon,
Journals); and Lucy Audubon, *The Life of John James Audubon* (New York, Put-
nam's, 1871), 103–104.

[6] Lucy Audubon, *Life of Audubon*, 387.

Carolina. About ten days later they went by railroad to Augusta, Georgia, and thence to Montgomery, Alabama, by mail coach. The next stage was by steamer to Mobile. They spent some time in Pensacola before going to New Orleans and by and by hunted birds as far down the Gulf Coast as Galveston, visiting that town and Houston before returning to New Orleans. It was during this trip that Audubon wrote to Dr. Bachman of Harris: "He is in facto one of the finest Men of Gods Creation—I wish he were my Brother."[7]

Nothing came of the far western trip that was "on talk" in 1838. It was not until four years later that mere words and wishes turned into active planning for, at last, *the* great trip that Audubon had so long wished to make and on which he must have the companionship of his "friend Harris."

By midsummer, 1842, Audubon had fully decided on the western trip.[8] Going to Washington, D. C., in July to obtain subscriptions for the *Birds* and the *Quadrupeds,* he visited "the different Departments of State where it was my duty to call, preparatory to my next coming Great Western Journey."[9] He had already suggested to young Spencer F. Baird (who was to become the second secretary of the Smithsonian Institution) that the young man accompany him on such a trip as his secretary, and he now wrote to him from New York on July 30 that

[7] For a detailed account of this trip consult Lucy Audubon, *Life of Audubon,* 400–15; and Arthur, *Audubon, an Intimate Life,* 433–41. A fragment of a journal kept by Harris is now in the Harris Collection at Montgomery. For a list of birds seen or procured at this time see Street, "The Edward Harris Collection of Birds," 172–77.

[8] Spencer Fullerton Baird's letter to Audubon from Washington, D. C., dated July 27, 1842, seems to contain the first specific reference to this trip: "One thing I wanted to ask you about, was respecting your proposed trip next Spring. In the first place the expense. . . . Nothing would delight me more than to go, if I can afford it." (William Healey Dall, *Spencer Fullerton Baird, a Biography* [Philadelphia, Lippincott, 1915], 76.)

[9] At this time he obtained letters of introduction from President Tyler, Secretary of State Webster, Secretary of War J. C. Spencer, General Winfield Scott, and Lord Ashburton, British diplomat serving on the Maine Boundary Commission (*Auk,* Vol. XXV [April, 1908], 170–73.)

he was pleased Baird was "favorably disposed to accompany me on this long thought-of and contemplated Tour."[10]

During the autumn, plans were ripening. Audubon talked with the Chouteaus in New York and with the Scottish sportsman, Sir William Drummond Stewart. On the twenty-ninth of November he wrote again to Baird: "It is now determined that I shall go towards the Rocky Mountains at least to the Yellowstone River, and up the latter Stream four hundred of miles, and *perhaps* go across the Rocky Mountains. I have it in my power to proceed to the Yellowstone by Steamer from St. Louis on the 1st day of April next; or to go to the *'Mountains of the Wind'* in the very heart and bosom of the Rocky Mountains in the company of Sir William Drummond Stewart, Baronet, who will leave on the 1st of May next also from St. Louis."

With the new year we discover that Audubon has made up his mind to ascend the Missouri rather than ride out over the plains. There was even a possibility of combining the advantages of both parties. "On the 1st of April next," he now wrote to Baird, "I *must* be at St. Louis, *ready* to *embark* on board my friend's Mr. Chouteau's Steamer leaving for the Yellowstone River." It would be a trip of at least eight months' duration. Passages of the party from St. Louis to the Yellowstone would be free. When they turned back, Audubon declared, "It is my intention to join the party of Sir William Drummond Stewart, Bart., on his return from the Central part of the Rocky Mountains, and to come back with him and his 100 followers to St. Louis next Octr or early in November."

He had already proposed that Harris join the expedition. In this letter to Baird he expressed the hope that "our friend Harris will be one of the party." On January 30 Audubon wrote to Harris that he had "engaged Bell to accompany me" and asked his friend to let him know quickly "what you have determined respecting your going with me to the Yellow Stone River."[11]

---

10 Dall, *Spencer Fullerton Baird,* 78. The quotations which immediately follow appear on 85, 88–89, and 88.

11 Audubon MSS, Houghton Library, Harvard University.

Harris had been ready enough until he heard about Bell. "I had made every preparation to join you on your expedition," he answered the next day. "I have rented my farm and made such arrangements that I shall be able to command funds enough for the journey by the time you are ready to start." But he was disturbed over the arrangements made with Bell. Was he to have liberty to make a collection of birds for himself? If so, the younger ornithologist thought the taxidermist "would be appropriating to himself all that would be most valuable to me, for I *cannot* skin," he reminded Audubon.[12] However, the difficulty was resolved: Bell[13] was to travel with them "to our sole use and benefit" and they would split his $500 salary between them.

Two other members were to be attached to the party, a secretary and an artist. Young Baird was being subjected to pressures from his family. "I wish you would assure your good mother," Audubon wrote from New York on February 10, "that to go to Yellow Stone River, in a good Steamer, as passengers by the courteous offers of the President of the American Fur company who himself will go along with us, that the difficulties that existed some 30 years ago in such undertakings are now rendered as Smooth and easy as it is to go to Carlisle and return to New York."[14] In the long run it was not his lack of money nor the fears of his family, but an attack of palpitations of the heart that stopped Baird from going to the Rockies.[15] On receipt

[12] Herrick, *Audubon the Naturalist,* II, 251.

[13] John G. Bell was born at Sparkhill, New York, July 12, 1812, and died there is 1879. Consult Brannon, "Edward Harris, Friend of Audubon," and the Missouri River journals of both principals. According to an entry in Audubon's journal, Bell too kept one, but it has not yet been discovered. Bell's expenses on this trip were paid by Audubon.

[14] Dall, *Spencer Fullerton Baird,* 90–91.

[15] Dall, *Spencer Fullerton Baird,* 92. On his return Audubon wrote Baird from Minnie's Land (New York), November 3, 1843, a letter which must have made the young man realize all he had missed: "You may well regret the difficulties thrown in your way through the fears of your good friends. Why, only think that *I* saw not one Rattlesnake and heard not a Word of Bilious fever, or of anything more troublesome than Muschietoes and of those by no means many! No, our Trip was a pleasant one. Abundance of the largest Game was killed, and much more could have been procured had we wished for it; but when a fat buffalo weighing some 1500 pounds or

of Baird's letter declining to go, Audubon informed him, "I have concluded to take a Young Gentleman in your stead who is a Neighbour of ours, but who alas is no naturalist, though a tough, active, and very willing person."[16] This was Lewis M. Squires, whom he described to Harris a few days later as "strong, active ... and will do well."[17] The artist chosen for the expedition was Isaac Sprague of Hingham, Massachusetts, "some of whose drawings I believe you [Baird] have seen, and who will assist me when wanted, but who will especially draw plants and Views for backgrounds to our present work [the *Quadrupeds*]." Audubon had met him three years earlier in his home town and had been much impressed with his bird drawings.[18]

Now the talk is all of preparation for travel beyond the frontier. Provisions and ammunition will be bought in St. Louis. Harris must get himself *"a good strong large Musquito Bar ...* 2 Good Blankets ... Bullet moulds for your Guns. ... *a good large life preserver* made expecially for yourself. ... a good large Butcher Knife or 2. ... I have bought several pairs of 6 barrelled

---

upwards is dead and the camp is prepared and the beast is roasting by large Juicy pieces, who could have the heart to kill more for the sake of the Tongue, or for that of the Wolves? Why, not I, I assure you. I have brought home alive a Deer which we thought may prove new. A Swift Fox and an American Badger. All these are doing quite Well; 15 *New* Species of Birds, and a Certain Number of Quadrupeds. We met with many of the Birds procured on the Western side of the Big Rocky Hills by Nuttall and Townsend. Yet I feel that much remains to be done, and all I regret is that I am not what I was 25 years ago, Strong and Active, for willing I am as much as ever." (*Ibid.*, 93.)

[16] Audubon to Baird, New York, February 23, 1843, in Dall, *Spencer Fullerton Baird*, 92.

[17] Audubon to Harris, Minnie's Land (New York), February 3d 1843, Audubon MSS, Houghton Library, Harvard University. Concerning Squires almost nothing is known beyond what Audubon and Harris have reported in their journals. In a letter dated Minnie's Land, November 30th 1843, Audubon informed Harris that "Squires is about going to China, where he may make money." (Audubon, MSS, Houghton Library, Harvard University.)

[18] Audubon to Baird, New York, Jany. 31, 1843 (Dall, *Spencer Fullerton Baird*, 89–90). Isaac Sprague was born at Hingham, Massachusetts, about 1811 and died in 1895. Showing ability for draughtsmanship as a boy, he was apprenticed to a carriage painter. Among his important work as a botanical illustrator were the plates for Gray's *Botany*. His best-known landscape work has been preserved in a set of sixteen views of White Mountain scenery which were lithographed by Bufford and Thayer and published by William Oakes in Boston in 1848. Sprague too kept a diary of which the editor has a copy and which he hopes presently to publish.

8

revolving pistols and one pair of these is for yourself.—John Bell showed me one he had, and shoots it with as much accuracy as if it was a first rate rifle! . . . I will use nothing but old clothes myself.[19] . . . I have not been able to find any India rubber beds and I would advise you to purchase the 2 you spoke of. . . . add to your list of wants a good common Spoon or 2 as well as forks. . . . Trudeau [has promised] to lend me his double barrelled Gun. . . . I will be sure to purchase the 4 Boxes of James' Pills and take them with me to you—Do have the arsenic put up in Canisters and placed in a Common Hair trunk, as *Boxes* always pay in Cart or in Coaches. . . . I wish you could come to us [in New York] so that I might introduce you to old Mr. Chouteau and Major Sandford."[20]

The time of departure is still uncertain. On the tenth: "I cannot positively say on what day we will have to leave Phila. but will let you know in good time as soon as I have seen Mr. Chouteau, *who goes with us to the Yellow Stone!*"[21] Two weeks later: "We are to leave New York on the 10th of March, and Phila. on the 11th as Mr. Chouteau says that it will be best for us to have a few days to Spare at St. Louis previous to the departure of the Steamer, which *must* leave from the 25th of

[19] Someone who saw Audubon in St. Louis noted that "he wore a dark frock coat, velvet vest, and blue hunting shirt." (From an unsigned letter in the *Buffalo Courier,* August 22, 1843, as reprinted in the *Auk,* Vol. XXXIV [April, 1917], 239-40.)

[20] Audubon to Harris, Minnie's Land, Feby 10th 1843 and New York, Feby 26th 1843, Audubon MSS, Houghton Library, Harvard University. These two men were Pierre Chouteau, Jr., and his son-in-law John F. A. Sanford. "Old Mr. Chouteau" was some four years younger than Audubon; the epithet was probably used to distinguish him from his twenty-three-year-old son, Charles Pierre, whom Audubon also knew. It should, perhaps, be added that the "American Fur Company" had ceased to exist in 1842. It was succeeded by Pierre Chouteau, Jr., and Company; the old name, however, remained in popular use.

[21] There is some uncertainty concerning the party traveling to St. Louis. In his journal Audubon mentions only the five of his own party, although he had written to Harris earlier that "Mr. Chouteau" (which one?) was going west with them. Harris names as fellow passengers, in addition to the five, "Mr. Fellows of Louisville" and "Mr. Howell of Louisiana opposite Natchez." Sprague mentions only their own party. It is clear, however, from Clapp's letter to Chouteau (St. Louis) Monday Evening, 28 March 1843, that Charles Gratiot had started west with the Audubon party: "Mr. Audubon states that General Gratiot was left ill at Cumberland—that his party waited for 4 days at Louisville, where the General was to join them, but he had not been heard from when they left." (Chouteau-Maffitt Collection, Missouri Historical Society.)

March to the 1st of April." Finally, on March 4: "Now we have positively concluded to leave this [New York] on *Saturday Next, the 11th* instant, and will reach Phil[a]. that night, and stop at Sanderson's as you desire, and where I do hope we will all meet you.—I have a letter this day from my Brother in Law William Bakewell of Louisville Ky. he cannot go with us I am sorry to say, for he is in fact the very Nimrod of the West; but he says that 'the Ohio is and will be in good order' at the time we reach that stream, that it takes 3 to 3½ days to reach Louisville, and 3½ to 4 to reach S[t]. Louis from Louisville, and unless we meet with delays or accidents We can reach S[t]. Louis on the 23[d] or 24th of this month, which would give us a Week to turn about and lay in our Provisions, ammunition, &c. &c."[22]

On March 11 the party of five did meet at Sanderson's in Philadelphia. Audubon arrived at 11:00 P.M. with his son Victor. Harris, "old John G. Bell, Isaac Sprague, and young Lewis Squires"[23] were already there. On Sunday they called on Philadelphia friends, among others Dr. Samuel G. Morton, with whom they discussed the possibility of making geological observations along the Missouri.[24] Victor turned back to Minnie's Land on Monday morning, and the others took the cars for Baltimore. They ate dinner there and visited together. The next morning—Tuesday, the fourteenth of March—they "entered the cars for Cumberland" and about six that evening changed at that place to coaches for Wheeling. "The weather has been bad ever since we left Baltimore," Audubon wrote. "There we en-

[22] The letters from which the quotations in this paragraph have been taken are all in the Audubon MSS, Houghton Library, Harvard University.

[23] Audubon, *Journals*, I, 453.

[24] In the minutes of the meeting on March 14, 1843, of the Academy of Natural Science (of which Harris was a member), it was noted that Audubon and his party had departed "yesterday." Professors Rogers and Johnson and Dr. Morton were named a committee "to transmit to Messrs. Audubon and Harris a series of inquiries relative to the geology of the country which will be traversed by them." On March 21 Rogers "submitted a report embracing seventeen queries" (which must have been mailed to Harris at St. Louis, for the original list, dated March 21 and signed by the committee, is in the Harris Collection in Montgomery). See *Proceedings of the Academy of Natural Sciences, Philadelphia*, I, 252–54. Harris's report, published in the *Proceedings*, II (1845), 235–38, is reprinted in the appendix to this volume.

countered a snow-storm that accompanied us all the way to this very spot [St. Louis] and at this moment the country is whitened with this precious, demi-congealed, heavenly dew. As to ice!— I wish it were all in your icehouse when summer does come, should summer show her bright features in the year of our Lord 1843.[25] We first encountered ice at Wheeling, and it has floated down the Ohio all around us, as well as up the Mississippi to pleasant St. Louis."[26]

At Wheeling, where they arrived seven hours late, they took passage on the steamboat *Eveline* to Cincinnati. Two days later at Cincinnati they transferred to the mail steamer *Pike* for Louisville, arriving there at half-past nine at night on the eighteenth. Audubon stayed with his brother-in-law, William G. Bakewell; the others stopped at the Scott House. On the twenty-second they went aboard the steamboat *Gallant* which made an abortive attempt to pass the Falls. The next morning with some difficulty they were actually once more on their way to St. Louis. Listen to Audubon:

"And such a steamer as we have come in from Louisville here!—the very filthiest of all old filthy rat-traps I ever travelled in; and the fare worse, certainly much worse, and so scanty withal that our worthy commander could not have given us another meal had we been detained a night longer. I wrote a famous long letter to my Lucy on the subject,[27] and as I know you will hear it, will not repeat the account of our situation on board the 'Gallant'—a pretty name, too, but alas! her name, like mine, is only a shadow, for as she struck a sawyer one night we all ran like mad to make ready to leap overboard; but as God would have it, our lives and the 'Gallant' were spared—she from sinking, and we from swimming amid rolling and crashing hard

[25] The Millerite destruction of the world predicted for this year. St. Louisans had the advantage of reading William Miller's proofs in detail, for the *Daily Evening Gazette* on March 11, 14, and 16, 1843, reprinted his pamphlet.

[26] Audubon to James Hall (brother-in-law of John W. Audubon), St. Louis, March 29, 1843 (*Journals,* I, 450).

[27] What a book his letters to Lucy would make! Only a few of them, alas, are known today and those only by excerpts.

ice. THE LADIES screamed, and the babies squalled, the dogs yelled, the steam roared, the captain (who, by the way is a very gallant man[28]) swore—not like an angel, but like the very devil —and all was confusion and uproar, just as if Miller's prophecy had actually been nigh. Luckily, we had had our *supper,* as the thing was called on board the 'Gallant,' and every man appeared to feel resolute, if not resolved to die.

"I would have given much at that moment for a picture of the whole. Our *compagnons de voyage,* about one hundred and fifty, were composed of Buckeyes, Wolverines, Suckers, Hoosiers, and gamblers, with drunkards of each and every denomination, their ladies and babies of the same nature, and specially the dirtiest of the dirty. We had to dip the water for washing from the river in tin basins, soap ourselves all from the same cake, and wipe the one hundred and fifty with the same solitary one towel rolling over a pin, until it would have been difficult to say, even with your keen eyes, whether it was manufactured of hemp, tow, flax, or cotton. My bed had two sheets, of course, measuring seven-eighths of a yard wide; my pillow was filled with corn-shucks. Harris fared even worse than I, and our 'state-room' was evidently better fitted for the smoking of hams than the smoking of Christians. When it rained outside, it rained also within, and on one particular morning, when the snow melted on the upper deck, or roof, it was a lively scene to see each person seeking for a spot free from the many spouts overhead."[29]

Whatever their discomfort, the voyage to St. Louis did come to an end on the morning of the twenty-eighth—only for them to discover that the Fur Company steamer would not be leaving for several weeks. The *Omega*—the last word in Missouri River steamboats?—had been in dry dock since March 15,[30] and there was no date in sight when it would be ready for duty. The St. Louis office of the Fur Company had been alerted concerning

[28] His name was Gildea, according to newspaper steamboat notices.
[29] Audubon to James Hall (*Journals,* I, 450–51).
[30] Benjamin Clapp to Pierre Chouteau Jr. and Company, Saint Louis 15 March 1843) Chouteau-Maffitt Collection, Missouri Historical Society).

the Audubon party, and Captain Sire of the *Omega* had written back to Pierre Chouteau in New York on March 20: "Mr. Audubon and his companions shall have all the attentions you have made them expect on my part. I shall do everything . . . to render their stay on board as comfortable as possible excepting however if the demands of these gentlemen should delay the progress of the boat for as to that I shall be inexorable and everything will be well understood before their departure." Sire's postscript then informed the main office that "the Omega is still in dock—no one works there because the workmen have not been paid. Judge Wash and Thomas promise every day to begin."[31] On Monday evening, the twenty-eighth, Benjamin Clapp informed Chouteau that "Mr. Audubon & party arrived to day, and handed your letter of introduction, to which due attention will be paid—The Omega is still in Dock, and owing to the cold Weather & some little difficulty with the workmen about wages, nothing as yet has been done to her—She will however require but little to be completed when a beginning is made."[32]

Audubon, for his part, was "extremely kindly received and treated by Mr. Chouteau and partners. Mr. Sire, the gentleman who will command the steamer we go in, is one of the finest-looking men I have seen for many a day, and the accounts I hear of him correspond with his noble face and general appearance."[33] The travelers put up at first at the Glasgow House.[34] Audubon wrote, however,

"[We] will leave it the day after tomorrow [the thirty-first], as it is too good for our purses. . . . The markets here abound with all the good things of the land, and of nature's creation. To give

[31] Chouteau-Maffitt Collection, Missouri Historical Society. In French.
[32] Chouteau-Maffitt Collection, Missouri Historical Society.
[33] Audubon to Hall (*Journals*, I, 452).
[34] This sixty-room hotel was located on the corner of Second and Olive Streets. According to the *Missouri Republican* (March 29, 1843), "This new and commodious edifice was completed and opened for the reception of transient and permanent boarders on the 2nd instant. The interior arrangements of the building, in point of comfort and convenience, [are] not surpassed by any similar establishment in the Valley of the Mississippi."

you an idea of this, read the following items: Grouse, two for a
York shilling; three chickens for the same; Turkeys, wild or
tame, 25 cents; flour $2.00 a barrel; butter, sixpence for the best
—fresh, and really good. Beef, 3 to 4 cents; veal, the same; pork,
2 cents; venison hams, large and dried, 15 cents each; potatoes,
10 cents a bushel; Ducks, three for a shilling; Wild Geese, 10
cents each; Canvas-back Ducks, a shilling a pair; vegetables for
the asking, as it were; and only think, in the midst of this abundance and cheapness, we are paying at the rate of $9.00 per week
at our hotel, the Glasgow, and at the Planters we were asked
$10.00."[35]

The reporters called at the Glasgow House. "Although an
old man[36] with silver locks and the weight of years upon him,"
the *Daily People's Organ* informed its readers on April 4, Audubon "retains all the freshness, elasticity, and energy of youth, and
is as ready to endure the toils and deprivations of long and tedious
journies through savage wilds and uninhabited territories, for the
purpose of pursuing his favorite study, as he ever was in his
juvenile days." The *Missouri Republican* on the following morning announced that he "intends starting about the 20th inst., in
the boat of the American Fur Company, for the mouth of the
Yellowstone. He will proceed from thence to the Rocky Mountains in company with several gentlemen who are with him. He
will also be joined by Sir William Stewart, of Scotland, who is
also in the city. His object in visiting the mountains and the
prairies of the far West, is to add to his splendid collection such
specimens of birds, &c., as he may find there. Mr. Audubon is
quite an aged man, but his active and hardy life has given a vigor
and strength to his constitution which renders him far more
active than the generality of men of his years."

On the fourth, Harris, Sprague, Bell, and Squires went off to
Edwardsville, Illinois. Audubon moved in with his friend Nicolas
Berthoud, who had just begun housekeeping, though his wife
(Lucy Audubon's sister Eliza) had not yet arrived from Pitts-

[35] Audubon to Hall (*Journals*, I, 451–52).
[36] Audubon was then in his fifty-eighth year.

burgh.[37] "My time at St. Louis would have been very agreeable to any one fond of company, dinners, and parties; but of these matters I am not, though I did dine at three different houses."[38] His time was well taken up buying and packing supplies for the coming voyage. There was, too, conversation with Stewart about their plans. The Scottish sportsman had arrived at St. Louis on the first of April, after suffering shipwreck near Commerce, Missouri, about 142 miles below St. Louis. The naturalist wrote to his wife, "Sir W^m is so desirous that we should accompany him & party, that he offered me 5 Mules and a Waggon for ourselves; but we shall not Change my plans!" Later: "Sir W^{am} Stewart goes off in about a week to Independence with his 70 followers of all Sorts.—. . . He has done all he could to persuade me to Join his party, but it was no go."[39]

In the meantime Harris and the others were hunting near Edwardsville. From a letter of Audubon's we learn that they were "cheaply settled" but that game was scarce. "I have enquired from several persons, but all of them say that they do not know of any better place and that in fact, the season is to far advanced to do much." There is news of progress in St. Louis: "There are a great number of hands at work on the Omega, and she will be ready to go off dry Dock on Friday or Saturday next, but Mr Sire says we cannot start before the 22^d to 25th inst."[40] On Thursday, April 13, Harris returned to the city, while the other three went on to Bunker Hill, Illinois. Saturday afternoon he took the packet boat to Alton and the next day drove over the prairie in a buggy to join his companions.[41] The entire party

---

[37] At the beginning of this year, Berthoud had established himself as doing a general commission business at No. 68 Water Street (*Missouri Reporter*, January 4, 1843).

[38] Audubon, *Journals*, I, 454.

[39] Arthur, *Audubon, an Intimate Life*, 454–55.

[40] Audubon to Harris, April 10th 1843 (Audubon MSS, Houghton Library, Harvard University).

[41] "One day our friend Harris came back, and brought with him the prepared skins of birds and quadrupeds they had collected, and informed me that they had removed their quarters to B———'s. He left the next day, after we had made arrangement for the party to return the following Friday, which they did." (Audubon's *Journals*, I, 455.)

was reunited in St. Louis on the evening of the twenty-first, since at any moment Sire might announce that he was leaving.

At half-past eleven on the morning of April 25, the *Omega* steamed away from the levee at St. Louis. "At last we are off on our long talked of expedition," Harris wrote in his little pocket diary. "The captain had great difficulty in getting the trappers on board, they were nearly all drunk and it was about noon before we got under way, amid the shouts and yellings and firing of guns from our drunken trappers."[42] The boatmen struck him as "the very offscouring of the earth, worse than any crew of sailors I ever met with." The *Omega* moved slowly up the Mississippi to the Missouri and made its way to St. Charles. On this first day's run Harris had forebodings that the passage would be tedious: "Our boat makes a very poor attempt at stemming the current of this great river." Indeed, Captain Sire's log is a record of the difficulty of Missouri River navigation: battling the current and adverse winds and stopping three or four times a day to wood, forced often to use driftwood, the last fuel desirable.

With the beginning of May, Harris has more of interest to report in his diary. They reached Independence on the second and Fort Leavenworth the next day, but Harris was not taking a long journey to write notes about the appearance of towns. On the third the boat went aground and the captain snapped a cable in the effort to get her free. Eventually he worked her off, but the sandbar and the strong, unfavorable wind caused a loss of twenty-four hours. On the fifth they reached Black Snake Hills (the first lots in the city of St. Joseph were to be offered for sale in the autumn of that year). All this time Harris has his eye out for birds. Paroquets he has seen since the twenty-ninth, near Boonville. Now he mentions Lincoln's Finch and Townsend's Finch. Near the Great Nemaha agency he is interested in the jack rabbit. At Fort Croghan on the ninth they pass the last army

---

[42] All quotations hereafter not specifically acknowledged are from Harris's Missouri River journals.

John James Audubon

from the oil painting by John W. Audubon, November, 1843

Edward Harris

from a daguerreotype
in the W. U. Harris Collection, Montgomery, Alabama

post. There the boat is searched, as is customary, for liquor, which is contrabrand in the Indian country (but Mr. Audubon has been allowed a few bottles for medicinal purposes). The garrison is in rather a bad way, for it has been flooded out of its quarters. The daily entries now are filled with references to the birds that so interest Harris as well as Audubon. The chief annoyance is that "our opportunities for shooting do not come up to our expectations," Harris notes on the twelfth. "Instead of stopping two hours before night to cut wood as we had been led to believe, they stop whenever they can find that which is suitable no matter what time in the day."

On May 14 and 15 they were held up by a heavy storm. At least that gave the naturalists an opportunity to go hunting. Harris and his dog Brag and the others all wore themselves out struggling through the mud trying to reach the prairies on the bluffs. The trappers "are very much in our way on our shooting excursions.... We find these men (who are scarcely any of them old trappers) to be the worst shots we have ever met, with either a rifle or shot gun, and how they are to subsist in the woods after they are turned loose to shift for themselves is not easy to conceive."

The next day they reached the Vermillion Post of the Fur Company. Now a new kind of trouble overtook the *Omega*. They had gone on their way but three miles when one of the boilers burned out. Not until the nineteenth were they able to move. On that day Harris began a long letter to his brother-in-law:

"Missouri River May 19th 1843[43]

"My dear Doctor

"I wrote you a few hasty lines yesterday by M[r] Laidlaw the

[43] Harris to Dr. John J. Spencer, Harris Collection, Montgomery. The omitted portions of this letter are merely passages extracted word for word from his diary. A few excerpts from this letter were published by George Spencer Morris, "Notes and Extracts from a Letter of Edward Harris," *Auk*, Vol. XII (July, 1895). The most interesting passages were merely summarized by Morris: one could not guess the value and fascination of the letter from its presentation in the *Auk*.

Company Superintendant at Fort Pierre who was on his way to St. Louis with 4 Mackinaw boats loaded with hides. I now commence a letter to be sent by the Trapper from Fort Pierre which we hope to reach in 6 to 8 days. . . .

"Our last accident, the burning out of two plates in one of our boilers, which I mentioned in yesterday's letter, detained us three days, we only got off this morning. . . .

"20th It rains this morning and our prospect for the day is rather dull. Our mode of life is rather tiresome to us, who are impatient for something to do, and you may see by the tremor in my hand that it is difficult to write while the boat is in motion, and yet when we compare it to a voyage at sea, we think we have no right to complain, there is no seasickness, no bilgewater, and several times a day we have the glorious privilege of putting our feet on *land,* I was going to say dry land, but we cannot as yet boast of a superfluity of that article. Instead of whales, porpoises and dolphins to relieve our eyes from the monotony of the scenery, we are occasionally called on deck to see a bear or a deer swimming the river or a dead Buffalo, deer or Antelope floating down it. By the by this reminds me that we have four Indians on board of the Puncah tribe, a branch of the Sioux nation, we took them in at Vermillion River, they are going 60 to 70 miles up the river to hunt for their village, like Stephens for the government of Central America,[44] their costume is that of Adam & Eve immediately after the fall with the exception of a miserable blanket thrown over their shoulders. These Natures noblemen as Catlin would make you believe they are, were busily employed during our three days detention, in searching the driftwood along the shore, for the chance of a dead Buffalo lodged among it. Fortunately for our olfactories they did not find any. Our Captain and every one who has been up the river

[44] The reference must be to John L. Stephens, *Incidents of Travel in Central America, Chiapas and Yucatan* (2 vols., New York, Harper and Brothers, 1841), or his *Incidents of Travel in Yucatan* (2 vols., New York, Harper and Brothers, 1843). In spite of their almost identical titles these were separate works, each reprinted a number of times. It is interesting to note that the newer work was reviewed in the *Daily Evening Gazette* (April 20, 1843) while Harris was in St. Louis.

assure us that we shall very soon have ocular demonstration of the fact of their eating such food.

"21st Since writing the above we have got into the Buffalo Country. Yesterday we saw a small gang of 5 or 6 at a long distance, just as they were crossing one of the knolls of the prarie. This morning while I was dressing about half past 5 o'clock, I was called out to see a large gang of about 38 about a mile distant, they were feeding on a bottom prairie just under the hills and were not disturbed by the boat, we saw five others feeding on the hills at the same time. A short time before dinner[45] we saw two buffalo take the river about 200 yards ahead of the boat, the noise of the boat alarmed them and they put back and scrambled up the bank again, and went off for the hills at a smart gallop which they kept up as far as we could see them, about 3 miles. It is unusual to find Buffalo so far down the river, but it has been caused by the severity of the winter. On the 5th of May snow fell here to the depth of two feet, and it is said that thousands of Buffalo calves were killed by it. We are also informed that they are so poor as not to be worth killing. We were stopped for a few hours today by a high wind, on an island, Bell shot a deer, and several others were seen, also three Elks, the first that we have seen. 3 Antelopes were seen this evening just before we stopped for the night. Another rare bird Say's Flycatcher has been added to our list, also *Pipilo arcticus,* the new Towhee Bunting, which you will find figured in Mr Audubon's small work.[46] We passed this evening the Running River or *L'eau qui court* as it is called by the French, It is quite a large stream which rises in the Rocky Mountains, if you can find it on the map it will give you some idea of our whereabouts, it is above the Great Sioux and Jacque Rivers which are on the East side. We find that our Captain and Pilots know little about the distances since we have left the settlements. They think that 8 days

[45] "Talking of dinner makes me think of giving you the hours, usually, of our meals. Breakfast at half-past six, dinner at half-past twelve, tea or supper at seven or later as the case may be." (Audubon, *Journals,* I, 476.)

[46] The octavo edition of *The Birds of America,* of which the seventh and last volume was to be published in 1844.

fair work will bring us to Fort Pierre, but allow themselves ten, and the Captain assures us that he has never been more than 12 days from that place to Fort Union at the Yellowstone. We have now been 26 days, and if we reach the Yellowstone in 23 days more we shall make the trip in 7 weeks and shall feel very well satisfied. For the last few days we have seen immense quantities of the nests of the cliff Swallow in the limestone rocks, which compose the base of the High prarie hills, and where they jut upon the river are perpendicular cliffs. But there are no birds to be seen and we fear that they have all been killed by a severe gale we had on the 14th when the thermometer fell from 76 to 43. Since that gale we have seen very few swallows of any kind.

"22ᵈ We continue creeping along slowly, not having made more than 35 miles to-day, we are moored for the night at Cedar Island which is covered with Red Cedar. We shall not leave it in the morning until we get as much of the wood as we can carry, probably it will occupy about an hour and a half after daylight, and while the men are chopping we will ransack the Island for birds and beasts. We have now got into a country where the Buffalo are plenty, particularly on the West Bank of the River, we have not seen less than 200 to-day, and at one time this afternoon there were at least 100 in sight at once, feeding in several gangs. The Captain sent out four men this evening and one of our party has gone with them (Squires). They are to walk up the river several miles, build a fire and camp until daylight, and then start after the Buffalo, and if successful bring the meat to the river to meet the boat. We saw a small war party of Santee Indians to-day on the East Bank. They were very anxious for us to stop but we did not gratify them.[47] They live on the Mississippi River and frequently wander over to this. Our stoppages for wood to-day have been short and we have not cut much. We have seen to-day the Arkansaw Flycatcher and a Meadow Lark which must prove to be a new one, it[s] note is so entirely different from ours, though as far

[47] Actually, the *Omega* was fired on by the Indians, although no one was injured. Cf. Harris's journal of this date.

as we have been able to observe it the markings and habits are very similar. Antelopes have been seen for two or three days by some one on board of the boat, but not [*sic*] of our party have had that pleasure until this evening just before we stopped we had a fine view of 10 of these beautiful animals on the summit of a hill, they started suddenly and came down the hill towards us at full speed, it was really a beautiful sight. You would be surprised to see how the whole country here is trodden up by the feet of the Buffalo, and we see their deeply worn paths in all directions, they are now shedding their coats which they leave on every bush, their appearance is exceedingly shabby and we have been near enough to them to see that they are very poor. We fear that the report is true that the calves have all been killed by the snow of the 5th as we have not yet seen one of the dear little creatures."

On the morning of the twenty-third they picked up the hunters who had been set ashore, but though they had killed four buffalo little fresh meat was provided for the *Omega* because there was not enough water to land where the meat was waiting and the men, having to walk two miles farther on, were able to carry only a small portion of their kill. The boat went aground again in the afternoon, and here the next day Audubon began a letter to his friend Dr. Gideon B. Smith in Baltimore.[48]

"Missouri River, May 24, 1843
"My dear Friend: As it happens that we are now fast on a bar, about 150 miles below Fort St. Pierre, one of the many establishments of the American Fur Company, I have taken it into my head to bore you with another letter, and you must make the best of it. I will, however, try to give it some interest as far as I can. Since my last to you dated May 18, the country has assumed a different aspect, and for the worse. The river has become more contracted between the hills through which it passes, and has also become more straight; we meet with less water,

[48] *Niles National Register,* Vol. LXIV (July 8, 1843), 297–98. It was also reprinted in the St. Louis *Missouri Reporter* on August 17, 1843.

fewer snags, and many more sand bars. The bluffs have become more abrupt and more picturesque in their forms, for as the effects of cold and thaws take place, their upper portions lose their softer parts, and the harder parts assume the shapes of battlements, towers, etc., and when viewed from a distance look not unlike curiously built cities. The trees are becoming scarcer, and of extremely stunted growth, and in the ravines, that wind their way between the hills, the growth is principally red cedar. The hills themselves which gradually ascend to plains of immense extent, are one and all of the very poorest description, so much so that one can scarcely conceive of how millions of buffaloes, antelopes, deer, etc. manage to subsist, and yet they do so, and grow fat between this and autumn. Then, my dear friend, we have reached these wild, and, to my eye, melancholy looking districts on which those countless multitudes of monstrous sized animals live, and die, more by the arrow and rifle bullet than even by drowning whilst attempting to cross the rapid Missouri. The shores are strewed with their carcasses, on which the wolf, the raven, and the vulture gorge themselves at leisure and unmolested, for hunters rarely if ever shoot at any of these. We have seen many elks, abundance of deer, antelopes, buffaloes, wild cats, wolves, and one bear. Our folks have shot buffaloes, but I have not done so, simply because they are worthless through poverty, and when killed only display a mass of bones and skin, with a very thin portion of flesh; and if you shoot a bull the rankness of its better parts is quite enough to revolt the stomach of all but starving men.

"The winter has been so very severe that buffaloes have been 3 or 400 miles lower down the river than they had been for twenty years. The calves have been nearly all destroyed. In the way of plants, we have seen some Cactuses unknown to us previously, and intend to take plenty of specimens home with us. We have also found a beautiful dwarf sweet-scented Pea, that perfumes the whole atmosphere. It grows over all the sandy and gravelly dreary plains and hills, of which I have spoken. There exists a root called here the white apple, which is farinaceous, and makes a good mush when dried and pounded fine. Of these, also, we shall take specimens. We have collected every thing that was in bloom, and shall continue to do so, when in seed and ripe, for all our friends, far and near. In Zoology, we have done pretty fair, in Ornithology better, as we have already four *new birds,* and will, no doubt, find more. We have felt all the transitions of weather that we have at the eastward, the thermometer ranging from 44° to 92° in the same day. We are sadly annoyed by heavy and almost constant winds that retard our progress, more or less, almost daily. We have caught only a few cat fish, and these I do not much relish. No otters, beavers, muskrats, or even minks, are found in or about the turbid waters of this all-mighty stream, the water of which looks more like that of a hog puddle than any thing else I can compare it to. About one-tenth of its bulk forms a deposite in half an hour. Springs of magnesia abound in many of the ravines. Sulphur, and oxide of iron show themselves frequently. Immense bluffs of white, blue, and yellow sandstone, are also found, as well as banks of granite, even to the tops of the highest hills. But not a single specimen of fossil remains as yet, although we were assured that they abounded along these bluffs. We were equally assured we should see no small birds, and we have seen millions of them, including almost every species we find in the eastern states."

Harris had broken off his letter to Spencer on the twenty-second; six days later he resumed it and made up for the missing days by extracting interesting passages from his diary. Chief among the events of recent days was the landing of the Audubon party on the twenty-sixth to walk a couple of miles across the Great Bend while the boat went miles around by water. They found their first prairie dog village this evening and presently camped out under six cottonwoods. One of the hunters brought in a yearling black-tailed buck: "we all agreed it was the best Venison we had ever tasted." That night, Harris tells us, their "beds were soon blown up[49] and wrapped in our blankets with

[49] Toward the close of the entry for the twenty-sixth in his letter of May 19 to Dr. Spencer, Harris wrote: "we blew up our Indian rubber mattrasses."

our guns at our sides, we were soon asleep." On May 28 the
Omega passed Fort George, an establishment of the Opposition
fur company, some thirty miles below Fort Pierre. Since the
boat had to be lightened in order to cross a bar, Audubon walked
back to the fort, and the next day Harris, too, visited the place.
There they met James Illingworth, who was in charge of that
post, and who volunteered to get them a buffalo calf, which was
procured the next day.[50] It was not until 4:00 P.M. on the thirtieth
that the *Omega* was ready to proceed, and just before they departed Messrs. Honoré Picotte and F. A. Chardon arrived from
Fort Pierre especially to meet them.[51] That evening the boat
pushed on to within seven or eight miles of their first port.

Harris now has more to tell us about the events of the last
days of the month in the journal-letter to Spencer begun on
May 19:

"31st We have at last reached Fort Pierre after a passage of
36 days, which we now learn is the shortest passage they ever
made, and 10 or 12 days earlier in the season than it was ever
reached before, although they have sometimes started before the
first of April. It certainly requires time and patience to ferret

---

[50] One more paragraph of Audubon's letter to Gideon Smith was published in
Niles Register. Dated May 29, it may well be entered in the record here: "We are now
at Fort George, not more than 20 miles from Fort St. Pierre, but may have to put
ashore one-half of our cargo, as the water is as low now as it was high when we left
St. Louis. This is a great disappointment to us all, as Fort St. Pierre is the place where
one-half of our cargo has to be delivered. No one can form an idea of the quantity
of buffaloes we have seen since writing the above [the paragraphs dated May 24, with
which this letter was begun]. The prairies, the hills, and the ravines are all dotted with
these heavy looking animals. We had a pleasant excursion across the *Great Bend,*
where the river runs 26 miles, and our walk exceeded not three and a half. We encamped one night, and fed entirely upon the best venison I ever ate—it was of that
species of deer called the black-tailed or mule deer. We saw, the next day, upwards of
5000 buffaloes feeding in the prairies around us, but they are too poor at present to
eat, and for this reason none, or few, were killed.—I have met with an opportunity
for forwarding this to St. Louis, quite unexpectedly, and will take it—therefore excuse
further details at present."

[51] In the letter to Spencer begun on May 19, Harris noted on the thirtieth: "Mr
Picot the superintendent of Fort Pierre, Mr Chardon the head of the establishment at
Fort Clark at the Mandan Village, and several others from Fort Pierre came down to
us in the yawl of the Trapper."

out truth in this world, and more particularly I think in this far western world. Our Captain is a very good fellow, but to hear his daily complaints you would suppose that all nature was conspiring to retard our progress and that we should never reach our destination. Heretofore they have frequently been obliged to take part of the cargo out of the boat and after passing the obstruction return for it and they have in one instance been detained 20 days at one place, whereas we have not lost more than 5 or 6 days in this worst part of the river. It is now reduced to a certainty that if the Company will build such a boat as experience has demonstrated to be proper for the navigation of this river, they may always make their trip to the Yellowstone in as short a time as we have done to this place, doing away with the liability to such a misfortune as occurred last year by being obliged to leave the Trapper at this place. It will then be in their power to carry the Spring Fresh all the way up and start to return at the commencement of the June rise. We reached here about 2 P.M. and for want of water immediately at the Fort we are discharging the freight ab [MS torn] miles above. I must walk down and see the place and endeavour to ascertain how long we are likely to remain here. Evening. I have not been down to the Fort this afternoon. Mr Audubon reports it worth looking at and I shall go down in the morning with him and Sprague who are going to make some sketches of Buffalo calves of different ages, which they have there. Mr A. has received from Mr Picot a splendid Indian dressed Elk Skin of the largest Elk ever known to have been killed in this part of the country, the Captain also presented him with the horns of the same animal which are enormous. Since we found the first Buffalo berry tree which I think I noticed in one of my letters we have seen them constantly along the Banks of the river and in the ravines of the Praries. We have not yet seen any flowering trees or shrubs that would be worthy of a place in our collections, excepting perhaps a very pretty Dwarf Wild Cherry of which I shall bring the seeds and a Cornus with a red bark and rather pretty flower, and is the plant the bark of which is smoked by the Indians instead of

25

tobacco, and which Catlin rather stupidly calls a Willow. There is an edible root growing on the lower part of the river and is found to the mouth of the Mississippi which grows in strings on the root an[d] which is invariably called the Wild Potatoe[52] and as universally affirmed by the settlers to be the origin of the common potatoe, and that in a few years of cultivation it will grow in clusters like the common potatoe and rapidly improve in quality. But as I have not seen this fact recorded and as I have many times known popular belief to be very wide of the truth I want to try the experiment before I give full credit to the statement. The Pomme blanche[53] or Turnip of the Praries is another root worthy of attention. It is evidently neither an Apple nor a Turnip, but the substance under the bark of the root, as I must call it, is of a very pleasant taste and appears to be highly farinaceous and although it might not be worth cultivating to make bread, still it may make an excellent substitute for Arrow Root, or perhaps it may improve by cultivation, so as to be valuable for the feeding of stock, a result not at all improbable if it should increase much in size and the cuticle become thinner. I have no doubt that one of these roots in its wild state contains more Farina than a large Ruta baga. It is about the size of a hen's egg and the form of a rather elongated Turnip Radish and very much the appearance of a Black Radish, it is covered with a very thick woody cuticle, the eighth of an inch in thickness, as hard as an Oak bark, and the interior portion is when dried about the consistence and appearance of [illegible] Root. The Captain thinks that we shall get off tomorrow by twelve o'clock. I have my doubts however as the wind has just commenced blowing violently directly up the river and I know the Omega well enough to be satisfied that she will not stand driving. If it does not storm in the morning, after visiting the Fort I intend paying a visit to the Prarie Dog

---

[52] Commonly called *pomme de terre* by the Canadian and Mississippi Valley French. Consult John Francis McDermott, *Glossary of Mississippi Valley French* (St. Louis, Washington University Studies, 1941), 125.

[53] McDermott, *Glossary of Mississippi Valley French,* 124–25.

village about a mile distant, it is said to be quite a City covering at least a square mile of the Prarie. I shall leave my letter open until the last moment.

"June 1st My dear Doctor—The Captain assures me he will leave this place at about 12 o'clock ... I will close this letter.... poor Brag would be glad enough to be back to the old homestead, he has been in a continual fright ever since he left home. Indians and trappers are his utter abomination, in fact he is a miserable traveller and I heartily wish he was safe at home again."

Harris's diary for the next two months is very full and there will be little point here in summarizing the occurrences he set down. Arriving at Fort Clark on the seventh, the travelers had time enough to look at the old Mandan village and visit some of the lodges of the Arikaras who now occupied the place—another opportunity for Harris to call into question the accuracy of Catlin's presentation of Indians. On the twelfth of June at 7:00 P.M. they reached Fort Union after a voyage of "17 hours less than 7 weeks and arrived here earlier in the season by one day than has ever been done before and made a quicker passage than any other boat by about 15 days." The next day Captain Sire spent cleaning his boat and readying it for the return trip. The following morning the *Omega* was headed for home, and the travelers remained as the honored guests of Alexander Culbertson, superintendent of this greatest post of the fur company.

Their days were now filled with many hunting experiences which Harris has recorded in his diary. We are constantly with Culbertson and Owen McKenzie, half-blood son of the famous Kenneth McKenzie, once styled "King of the Upper Missouri"; we are introduced to Edwin Denig, chief clerk of Fort Union (today recognized as an important authority on the Indian tribes of that region); we meet the Indian wife of Culbertson; we roam with famous hunters such as Etienne Provost, Bonaventure Le Brun, and Boucherville; we attend a dog feast; we have glimpses of fur-trade activities and life around the forts; we see Fort Mortimer, local post of the rival company; we look through

Harris's eyes at squalid parties of Indians at Fort Union; but always, whatever else may be happening, we take part in the search for birds and beasts. All this culminates in the two exciting buffalo hunts that took place on the sixteenth and the twentieth of July. Let us listen to Edward Harris as he tells his brother-in-law what happened on those days:

"New Orleans Dec. 1, 1843

"My dear Doctor

"I wrote you a long letter yesterday in which I promised to turn-to, some of these rainy days, and give you [a] long yarn about Buffalo hunting. As the storm continues to-day I proceed at once to fulfil my promise. I will first give you an account of the first chase I saw, and then proceed with the first in which I was an actor. On the 15th of July Mr. Culbertson the superintendant of Fort Union, Mr. Audubon and all our party except Sprague started up the Yellowstone by land to look for Elk, Beaver & Bighorns. We took a skiff on a cart drawn by two mules, in order that some of the party might descend the River to find the Beaver & Bighorns. I will not enter into full particulars of our first days proceedings. We took an early breakfast before leaving the Fort and took no provisions with us excepting about a dozen hard buiscuits and some coffee. We encamped on the bank of the River about 25 miles from the Fort, and three of us started off immediately to the *Point of Woods* near our camp to hunt Elk and Deer for our supper and Mr. Audubon took his line and sent [set?] to fishing. Towards evening when we were expecting the Elk and Deer to begin to walk, the Mosquitoes became so abundant as actually to drive us out of the Woods. Even our old guide and hunter could not stand it, and we all bundled into Camp at a quick step, and without an ounce of meat for our suppers. Mr. Audubon had caught four small Cat-fish. Our supper was not likely to give us the nightmare so we cut sticks and erected our mosquito bars outside the tent as soon as possible as the night was very warm, and we were soon sleeping soundly. About 12 o'clock we were awakened by the noise of an approaching Thunder gust, which was upon us in savage fury before we could get all our fixings into the tent, where we stowed away heels and points as well as we could. I had the misfortune to be placed near the opening of the tent and was obliged to hold on to the corners of the tent to prevent the wind from getting under it and carrying the whole into the River.

"In something less than an hour the wind died away and I was released from my uncomfortable position, but completely drenched. I wrapped myself in my blanket and passed the night as well as the Mosquitoes would permit. We were up at early dawn. Two hunters started for meat. There were no more fish to be caught as we had nothing for bait, and our search for frogs proved unsuccessful. Owen M'Kenzie our half-breed hunter was started off on his Buffalo horse to run the first Wolf he could find and bring it in for bait and for our sustenance if we could get nothing better. He found one within a quarter of a mile of the Camp, but the Dog had like to have proved to[o] fleet for his horse and it was not until he had chased him between three and four miles and fired some seven or eight shots that we saw him returning with the Wolf slung across his saddle in front of him. Just before we saw him returning Mr. Culbertson had discovered a single Buffalo at a very long distance. His Blackfoot mare was soon saddled and he started in pursuit, he made signals to Owen who joined him. They proceeded slowly to give Owen's mare time to breathe after her long chase, while we mounted the cart and carryal and watched them with great anxiety. It was nearly an hour before we saw them in Chase of the Bull which passed into a ravine from which I could see that they did not emerge until I saw Mr. C. standing on the edge of it. I then felt sure that the Bull was killed, although the distance was so great that we could neither see the flash nor hear the reports of their guns. We ordered the cart to go for the meat and Bell and I put a horse to the carryal and drove to the spot. It proved to be a fine specimen and we went to work at once to skin it for Mr. A. We had just commenced when another Bull was discovered coming slowly across the Prarie directly toward us. Mr.

Culbertson had returned to Camp and Owen had shot away all his balls. I gave him my gun and balls and he walked his horse leisurely towards the Bull while Bell and I placed ourselves on an eminence to view the chase.

"The Bull either did not see him or took him for another Buffalo and they continued to approach each other until within 70 or 80 yds., when the Buffalo started at full speed. It was with difficulty that Owen's mare from having had two severe runs, could overtake him, when a shot from the first barrel so disabled him that he was quickly along side and put the second ball through his shoulder and lungs, which brought him to a stand precisely in the position represented in Catlin's work of the Wounded Bull. Bell and I ran as fast as we could to the scene of action and as soon as we were within speaking distance called to Owen not to shoot again. The Bull did not appear to be much exhausted yet, but he was stiffened by the shot through the shoulder blade which made it difficult for him to turn. As we approached him he would turn himself slowly round until he faced us, when he would pitch at us with great force, then we would jump aside and discharge our six-barreled pistols at his side with little more effect than increasing his fury at every shot. His appearance was now one to inspire terror had we not felt satisfied of our ability to avoid him. I came however very near being caught through my own imprudence, I placed myself directly in front of him and as he advanced I fired at his head and turned and ran ahead of him, not supposing he was able to overtake me, but casting my head over my shoulder, to my great surprise and consternation I saw Mr. Bull within three feet of me, with his head lowered, in that peculiar knowing position which says so plainly "now I'm into you, stranger." Not much relishing the taste of Bull's horns, although it was long past noon and I had not yet broken my fast—I flew the track with a desperate spring and the poor beast passed on, unable to turn quick enough to avenge the gross insult I had put upon him. We now came to the wise conclusion that he was a rather dangerous customer to play with. Bell took the Gun from Owen and sent an-

other ball through his lungs which soon brought him to the
ground. He proved to be very poor and a bad skin and we left
him for the wolves and birds of prey.

"We returned to the first Bull and I took a horse, on which
a messenger had arrived from Mr. Audubon, and leaving the
man to assist in skinning I returned to Camp, and found that
Mr. A. had been successful in catching fish with the liver of the
Wolf. I made a light meal of some boiled catfish and drank
some of the broth which I found very palatable. We got back
to the Fort that night without procuring any of the game we
went after, and without anything further of interest occurring.
I will now give you some account of my first Buffalo chase, as I
have just given you one of the first time I was chased by a Buffalo
—but not the last.

"It was on the 20th of July that we started on our first Buffalo
hunt, well equipped. Mr. Audubon, Bell and I riding in the
Carryall driven by Mr. Culbertson, with the horses in tandem,
followed by two carts carrying our tent and baggage, with a
man sitting behind each cart leading two Buffalo horses, and
Squires riding in one of the carts. We crossed the Missouri in
the Scow early in the morning and took a middle road between
the two Rivers. About noon we reached the Valley of the Fox
River which runs into the Yellowstone when there is any water
to run, but at this season it was quite dry. We had just crossed
the bed of the river when Mr. C. happened to look back and
discovered four Bulls quietly feeding about a mile from us and
about a quarter of a mile from the path we had come, but hidden from us by some intervening elevations. Our hunters were
soon saddled, powder horns slung, ten or twelve bullets in our
pockets, our belts drawn tightly around us and we set off with
the whole of our equipage directly for the herd, covered by a
small eminence, behind which we left the vehicles with Mr.
Audubon so that he could, from its summit, have a good view of
the chase, while we filed off to the right, keeping out of view
of the game so as to come upon them in such a way as to oblige
them to run into the Valley of the Fox river, thereby assuring

ourselves of a fine view and at the same time give to Mr. Audubon a chance to see the fun. We made a good approach, and as soon as the Buffalo started Mr. C. gave the word to follow.

"There was a Bull for each horseman and we agreed not to interfere with each other. They divided two and two. Squires and I attacked the right wing and Mr. C. and Bell the left. Squires had the fleetest horse and I let him take his choice. He fired into his Bull before I came up, and as I was crossing his track, he again approached the animal who suddenly turned upon him, the horse, as in duty bound, shied off to avoid the attack, and Squires being unprepared for the movement, lost his seat and came to the ground, he was soon on his feet and singing out at the top of his voice "Stop my horse," "Stop my horse." Taking this as pretty strong evidence that neither his mental or physical powers were much damaged by his fall, (The Bull had passed on without making the threatened attack) and seeing my services no longer needed for Squire's safety, I pushed on after my own Bull, which I soon overtook and firing my first barrel struck him in the thigh and riding a little closer I gave him the second through the lungs. He kept on and I rode alongside of him reloading my gun, which I had just accomplished when I saw the blood gushing from his mouth and nostrils in such a way as satisfied me that he was a gone Bull. Without waiting to see him fall I galloped after poor Squire's horse which I soon caught and took back to him. On looking round I saw my Bull was down. Squires was soon remounted, and as his Bull had halted at the distance of a few hundred yards to look after the fate of his companions, we started in pursuit, full of the most deadly intentions. We had not proceeded far before Squires discovered that in falling the muzzle of his gun had become stopped with earth. I exchanged with him one of my barrels being loaded, and on we pushed at a rattling pace. Squires fired into him but struck him so far behind as not to arrest his progress, we kept up the chase, but through some difficulty in reloading he did not get another shot, and complaining of pain and weakness from his fall he gave up the chase. We had now a long ride, and from the time lost the Bull had gained on us nearly a quarter of a mile, still I could not bear to give up the chase. I took my gun and laid whip to the horse and Squires went back. I had almost overtaken the Bull when he tumbled headlong down a steep bank of about 15 feet, I was fortunately far enough behind to check my horse and walk him down. This prolonged the race—at last however I got alongside of the ugly monster. As I raised myself in the stirrups to fire leaning towards him, and just as I was on the point of pulling the trigger, he turned and made a rush at my horse—forgetting poor Squire's mishap and all the cautions I had received on this head, in the excitement of the chase, I was unprepared for the shying of the horse, and as a matter of course down I came within twenty feet of the Bull, who stood looking at me. I was on my feet in an instant, having received no injury, and levelling my gun, with deliberate aim at his vitals, had the mortification to have both barrels snap! Fortunately for me Mr. Bull not understanding how decidedly the odds of the fight were in his favour left me to recover my wind after a very long chase and a pretty hard fall and was soon out of sight. On examining my gun I found that the head of the hammers had become filled with earth as the gun fell to the ground and consequently made no impression on the caps. My noble hunter was waiting for me at a short distance and I caught him without difficulty, and mounting, walked slowly back to the place of starting. I found that Mr. Culbertson and Bell had each killed their Bull and I also found that my last race had been more than three miles. Two of the Bulls were soon butchered and the meat put on one of the carts and dispatched for the Fort, while we pushed further out in the Prarie to find a good camping ground, determined to have another chase before returning to the Fort. On reaching a small pond of water, suitable for camping purposes, we saw a small head of Buffalo a short distance beyond it. We all thought we had glory enough for one day excepting poor Squires, and we left it to him to say if we should run them at once or take the chance of finding them in the neighbourhood in the morning. His voice was for war, and we buckled to for the fight. These cattle being on an eminence it was impossible to conceal our approach. After getting within about 600 yards of them we formed into single file, Mr. C. in advance and we were directed to follow all his motions, as we got nearer we leaned our bodies forward as much as possible, and whenever a Bull would stop grazing and look up at us, we stopped our horses until he went to feeding again. In this way we got within 300 yds. of them before they took to their heels. We were soon alongside and discharged our pieces, but as we had become a little more wary of Bull's horns (at least Squires and I) our shots were not so effective and our Bulls kept up with the Herd (there were 8) at a rattling pace down the hill, which was a long slope of a couple of miles, giving greatly the advantage to the Buffalo who run with remarkable speed down hill, while the speed of a horse is sensibly checked, during this time I fired two more shots into him, when he came to a place of rising ground and finding himself too closely pushed he turned and gave chase to me, but I was prepared for the manoeuvre and easily avoided him. He now began to fail and turned off from the herd and came to a stand in a ravine and stood with the blood gushing from his mouth and nostrils at the same time showing a strong disposition for fight. I levelled at him once more and my [blank in MS] snapped, and seeing that he was about falling I did not fire again. Bell's Bull had dropped about 100 yds behind mine, and Squires passed us in pursuit of his and was soon out of sight, he returned ere long complaining that his side hurt him so much in consequence of his fall that he could proceed no further. It was after dark when we reached our Camp. We slept well after the fatigues of the day and returned to the Fort the next evening. I am almost ashamed to tell you that we left our Bulls, and fine fat ones they were, on the ground for the Wolves, carrying away nothing but the tongues, and novices as we were in this sort of murder, we were weak enough to feel more depressed than exalted at our triumph, and even ventured to utter some such treason as this, that Buffalo hunting was no better than the chasing a Wild Steer. But ere long our consciences became pretty well scar[r]ed and

we had no more feeling at the death of a Buffalo Bull than at
the demise of a Towhee Bunting, such you know is human nature all the world over. You will be somewhat surprised that
after another hunt or two, Bell and I were pronounced the best
Buffalo debutantes that had made their first hunt from Fort
Union. I assure you I was surprised at my own success not on
account of the shooting, but the riding. You know that I never
straddle a horse at home, and the only fear I had when I commenced was that I should fail in horsemanship. But the moment
the first Bull started before me I forgot everything but the game
before me, and through this very absence of fear I soon became
a better rider than I should have done in a year at a riding
School. A few words will perhaps be necessary to give you a
better idea of a Buffalo hunt. Before starting all unnecessary
clothing must be thrown aside, belt drawn tight, a common
powder horn slung under the right shoulder, and a sufficiency of
bullets placed in one of your pockets. You start with your gun
loaded and when you are sufficiently near to prepare for shooting, you throw the reins upon the horses neck and leave them
there until you have killed or lost your Buffalo, at the same time
putting a couple of bullets in your mouth. Your horse if well
trained soon places himself on the right side of the Buffalo at
the distance of 15 or 20 feet, you raise yourself a little in your
stirrups, depressing the muzzle of your gun so as to point just
behind the shoulder (without bringing your gun to the shoulder)
and fire. Whether your gun takes effect or not you proceed at
once to reload by throwing your gun into your left arm and
proping it against your body to retain a firm hold of it then
pour a charge of powder into the palm of your left hand, closed
around the mouth of the powder horn, drop the powder horn
without waiting to restop it, draw back your gun with your right
hand, at the same time advancing your left toward the muzzle
throw in the charge of powder elevate the muzzle and shake
down the powder, take a wet ball from your mouth at the same
time and throw it into the gun with your left hand and you are
loaded with the exception of your cap. I should have said strike

35

your gun once or twice with your right hand to ensure the ball's going down. The wet ball gathers enough of the powder around it to prevent its falling out when the gun is depressed to fire.

"In this way a first rate Buffalo hunter will fire from 8 to 12 shots while his horse is running a mile and kill three or four Buffalo from a band in the same distance. If you think your horse is too near or not near enough to the animal, you have only to incline your body the way you wish him to go, and he obeys it as well as he would the reins. At the same time he keeps his eye sharply on the Buffalo, and at the least disposition shown by the animal to turn upon him he shies off to the right as he also does to a short distance when you have fired. He never loses sight of the animal you have fired at however large the herd may be, and the moment you are reloaded, a signal to go ahead brings you again alongside for another shot. The process of cutting up a dead Buffalo would rather astonish our butchers. The skin is split down the back and the upper side turned over on the ground, a knife is run alongside the spine the whole length and then inserted on the top of the ribs is carried at right angles to the first incision taking out the whole of the thick meat on the top of the ribs and along the spine, this piece is called the fleece, or by the Canadian voyageurs, the dupuy.[54] The shoulder is then disjointed and with the foreleg makes another piece, then the thigh, unless they do not wish to take the whole of the meat, in which case they turn the knife down the thigh when cutting out the fleece and lengthen it by taking a piece of the same width and thickness, the meat from the thin part of the ribs and the flank [blank in MS] into another piece. The ribs are then jointed at their connection with the brisket—and cut through when they join the spine, this makes the second best piece from the Buffalo, although a novice would be disposed to leave it, there appears to be so little meat upon it. The body being now open the paunch is taken out, emptied and saved, also the coecum with some of the fat and coagulated blood to make a pudding, tender loins and kidneys are cut out, and if the hunters

[54] *Depouille.* Consult McDermott, *Glossary of Mississippi Valley French*, 66.

36

have been long fasting, they regale themselves with pieces of raw liver and of the manifold washed in the warm blood of the animal, which they profess to consider most dainty morsels, though I never could be induced to taste them. The animal is now turned and the same operation performed on the other side, the hump ribs as they are called are then chopped off at their base and constitute the prime piece, there are ten or twelve remarkable elongations of the spinal processes which form the hump or bosse, the first one, or rather the second one, being sometimes 19 inches in length, they decrease gradually until they reach about the middle of the back, the remainder of the processes to the end of the tail being about the same as in the common ox. The brisquet and the tongue are taken, the brains are frequently taken out and eaten raw by the hunters and sometimes the head is taken home that their squaws may enjoy that dainty morsel. When there are plenty of hands, to cut up, the Buffalo is raised upon his knees and the fore and hind legs spread out, so that both sides may be worked upon at once. Poor Squires never became a Buffalo hunter—anxious to retrieve his character (he had counted largely on his superior horsemanship, and gave us to understand that he should show us no quarter, but run in and take a shot from us whenever opportunity offered) he made one more effort—a single Bull was found, Squires was mounted flanked by Mr. Culbertson and Owen to see fair play. He fired too soon and only wounded the Bull sufficiently to enrage him and when he approached to fire again, the beast turned upon him and pursued him so closely that he was compelled to throw away his gun and to seize the horse's mane to save himself from falling. I was following without my gun, and at one time thought Squires would certainly lose his seat and be gored and trampled to death by the monster. It took 20 balls to bring this Bull to the ground. Squires could never again be induced to chase a Buffalo, and I assure you he did not hear the last of it very soon. We were lolling about the Fort one sultry afternoon, when 4 bulls made their appearance on the brow of the Cliff about 17 miles back of the Fort (no Buffalo had been seen within several miles of the Fort for 18 months). Mr. C., Bell and I saddled our horses, and in about 20 minutes after we commenced the chase they were all down.

"Mr. C. killed 2 and Bell and I each one. This race was over ground that I should a few weeks before have dismounted from my horse and walked over, had there been no Buffalo in view. The first hunts were all after Bulls, and it was only about two weeks before we left that any Cows were to be found, perhaps fortunately for us, as we should have been more likely to have failed had we commenced on the Cows, which are far swifter than the Bulls, and keep the Indian horses very busy to over-take them, in fact they go ahead of the Bulls at once, the heifers, yearling Bulls and calves keeping with them. We had seven hunts and Bell and I each killed seven Buffaloes—4 Bulls and 3 Cows. The whole of our hunting was during the rutting sea-son, which lasts from beginning of July to last of August—it afforded us a fine opportunity of observing their habits, and is the only time when you can hear them bellow, a strange un-earthly noise they make. The hunting is most dangerous at this season. On two occasions I have known a Bull to stop with a wounded cow urging her on with his horns, and when she could no longer run we were under the necessity of shooting the Bull before she could be approached. I believe I have given you the sum and substance of our Buffalo hunting. On my return you shall see the particulars of the whole in my Journal."[55]

By the middle of August, Harris was ready for the return trip. He had noted on August 2 that he had lost nearly twenty-five pounds and though his health was "perfectly good" he found himself "weak and unable to endure the fatigue that [he] could at the commencement of the expedition." Anyway, it was time

[55] This very long letter exists in typescript in the Harris Collection, Montgomery. The copyist regularized the spelling, and was occasionally confused by the handwriting. The editor has made a very few obvious corrections. The remaining portion of the letter, omitted here, includes a quotation from Harris's diary for July 26 and some paragraphs dated December 13, 15, and 21 in which Harris discusses home business matters.

to start, for they had a two-months' voyage ahead of them. Accordingly, the twelfth found them busy making preparations for departure. The mackinaw boat built for them was ready and loaded on the sixteenth. Farewells were said and the travelers turned their faces toward home. Harris made a few notes of the trip down-river. They reached the Mandans on August 25, Fort Pierre on September 8, changed to a larger boat there, and set out again on the fourteenth. On the sixteenth they were once more in the Grand Detour; the twenty-first found them at Cedar Island. They arrived at Fort Croghan on October 5—just in time to see the evacuation of that post by the dragoons who had been ordered back to Fort Leavenworth.

St. Louis they reached about 3:00 P.M. on the nineteenth of October, and three days later Audubon, Bell, Sprague, and Squires boarded the *Nautilus* for Cincinnati and Pittsburgh. Harris, however, had other plans. He remained in St. Louis a week longer and then went to Louisville where he thought of arranging for a trip to Santa Fé, but an attack of asthma led him to change his mind. On November 5 he left Louisville for New Orleans, arriving six days later. There he presently drew up for Audubon the account of expenses for which he was responsible as cashier of the expedition. He now wrote to Audubon:

"New Orleans Nov. 16th 1843
"My dear friend
"You will be somewhat surprised to see me date from this place, but my dear Sir I have had nothing but sickness since we parted. I was first attacked with the Hemmerhoids very violently, and being anxious to be speedily rid of them I placed myself under the care of a Physician and threw myself on my back. The consequence was that the piles were soon checked—but—as soon as I got about I barked my shin against a Coal Scuttle—so badly that I had to lie by again for a few days, as soon as I was able to walk I started in the Belleaire for Louisville, I had been there one day when I took cold (owing to my previous confinement) and had a violent attack of Asthma. This

39

determined me at once to turn my steps towards the South and I took passage in the Jos. H. Daviess for N. Orleans, for three days and nights after I started I could not lie down and I arrived here on Monday 13th not much better than when I started. I have *now* got rid of the asthmatic Symptoms, but retain a very bad cough and a great weakness of the chest with unpleasant expectoration. I fear that I shall be under the necessity of moving farther South, perhaps to Havanna. I had made up my mind to return home and make preparations to go out in the spring with the Santa Fe traders, a route which it seems to me opens the widest field for the ornithologist which as yet remains unexplored within the limits of our Fauna. I must however abandon the idea for the present. I send you the account of Exps. and my a/c current which I hope you will find to your satisfaction. I also send you a draft on Dr Spencer for $391.58 for the Balance of that a/c due you. Please acknowledge the receipt as early as possible Make my best regards to each one of the family

Yours sincerely
Edward Harris

The fever has entirely abated."[56]

Here we will leave Edward Harris recuperating from his strenuous excursion to the wilds of the Upper Missouri, enjoying the "remarkably mild" weather in New Orleans, and considering—not very energetically—whether he shall go on to Mobile and Pensacola with his friend Frazer or sail to meet his brother-in-law in Havana. "It would be a fine climate [in New Orleans] were it not for the fogs and rains, in spite of which I have had no return of Asthma. We have had green peas ever since I have been here. Havanna fruits are abundant and fine, as they are brought by the Steamer. Yellow fever too is quite abundant in spite of the Frosts, and the newspaper announcements that Yellow Jack was dead. No less than 43 deaths by that disease were announced for the last two weeks (officially) and there have been

[56] Draft in the Harris Collection, Montgomery. The original is in the Audubon MSS, Houghton Library, Harvard University.

about 150 deaths since I have been here, Imagine the same number to have died in the same time in Ohio and what a noise it would have made,—here it is thought nothing of. . . . If you will write me word that you will meet me in the Havanna I will go there at once. . . ."[57]

[57] Harris to Spencer, New Orleans, December 1, 1843, Harris Collection, Montgomery. These passages are dated December 13 and 15.

MARCH

[1843]

Monday, March 13th.[1] Left Philadelphia[2] for the Rocky Mountains via Baltimore, Wheeling, & St. Louis——Party

> J. J. Audubon
> Edwd Harris
> J. G. Bell
> Lewis M. Squires
> Isaac Sprague

Tuesday, March 14th. Left Balt[imore] 7 A. M. for Cumberland[3] & Wheeling. Arrived at Cumberland at ½ past 6 P. M. took Coach in the National road line[4]—the baggage of our party weighed 1120 lbs—250 lbs deducted, allowance for 5 persons left 870 lbs to be paid for at 4 cts=$34.80, compromised at $30.[5] Our

[1] The only entry in the 1843 diary preceding this date is a paragraph opposite the blanks for January 10–12: "Mr Audubon's father was an officer in the French Navy during the revolutionary War. Came over with Count Rochambeau, quitted the Navy and entered the Army and fought at Valley Forge and several of the Revolutionary battles, afterwards received a new commission in the Navy and died an admiral at upwards of 90 years of age, an active man to an extreme age, his wife died upwards of 80 years old—"

[2] The party met in Philadelphia on the evening of Saturday the eleventh and stayed two nights at Sanderson's. On Monday morning they "took the cars" for Baltimore (Audubon, *Journals,* I, 453). See "Expense Accounts" in the appendix for notations opposite March 11–13 and 29.

[3] By train.

[4] Probably the National Road Stage Company, for which see Archer B. Hulburt, *The Cumberland Road* (Cleveland, Arthur H. Clark Co., 1904), 124 ff.

[5] "A first-rate piece of robbery" (Audubon, *Journals,* I, 454).

party with Mr Fellows of Louisville Ky & Mr Howell of Louisiana opposite Natchez, our own and their baggage made a very heavy load for 4 horses.

[*Memo on opposite page*] Mar 14   Started from Baltimore with

        9 Trunks   ⎫
        1 Box   ⎬
        2 Gun Cases ⎬ Ticketed
        4 Bags   ⎬
        1 Carpet Bag ⎭
        1 Cloak
        4 Guns
        1 Dog[6]

Indian Rubber composition to mend beds &c. Apply it with a brush around the rent and on the inside of the patch, leave it ab[ou]t an hour to become somewhat stiff, renew the application 4 or 5 times in the same way before the patch is applied to the rent.

Wednesday, March 15th. We have had snow on the ground since leaving Elicotts Mills[7] near Balt. On the highest mountains it lies about one foot deep. Dis[tance] Cum[berland] to Wheel[ing] 131 miles, promised to set us down in Wheel[ing] in 24 hours   we are 7 hours behind the time.[8]

Thursday, March 16th. Arrived at Wheeling 3 o'clock A. M. Embarked for Cincinnati in Steam Boat Eveline at ½ past 1 P. M. —Passage to Cin[cinnati] $5 ea. Continued to snow all day—excessively cold Wind N. W. Wild geese and Ducks in river, not very abundant. Wrote to Dr Spencer.[9]

    6 "I shall take my pointer with me," Harris to Victor G. Audubon, Philadelphia, Feby 8 1843 (Harris Collection, Montgomery). This is Brag, who will appear a number of times in the narrative.
    7 On the Baltimore and Ohio Railroad, about twelve miles west of Baltimore, now Ellicott City.
    8 Audubon wrote: "We went on now by coaches, entering the gap, and ascending the Alleghanies amid a storm of snow, which kept us company for about forty hours, when we reached Wheeling." (*Journals,* I, 454.)
    9 Dr. John J. Spencer, of Moorestown, New Jersey, brother-in-law of Harris. Of

Friday, March 17th. Excessively cold this morning, continues cloudy with wind at North West. This boat has her wheel in the stern, makes about 12 knots with the Current distance to Cinn. ab^t 380 miles.

Saturday, March 18th. Arrived at Cinn. at 3 A. M. removed to Stm^r Pike, mail boat to Louisville—Started at 11 A. M. arrived at Louisville 9½ P. M.[10]
   Passage $3 ea
   Wrote to D^r S[pencer]

Monday, March 20th. White fronted Goose in the market— here called Brant.[11]

Tuesday, March 21st. Shot the White Crowned Sparrow, and Shore Lark—both very abundant. Saw the Tree Sparrow.

Wednesday, March 22nd. Went on board the Gallant[12] for St Louis at 12 M. the afternoon proved so squally from the N. W. that we could not get over the falls.
   Fare to St Louis $5 each.

Thursday, March 23rd. Started this morning at 9 A. M. and got safely over the falls, rubbing pretty hard on entering them.

the many letters from Harris to Spencer written on this trip only two are to be found in the Harris Collection at Montgomery—those dated Missouri River, May 19th 1843, and New Orleans, Dec. 1st 1843. They have been reproduced in great part in the introduction above.

   [10] According to Audubon, they arrived before daylight on the nineteenth (*Journals,* I, 454). Audubon stayed with William G. Bakewell; the others went to the Scott House.

   [11] The birds mentioned in the entries for March 20 and 21 are described by Audubon in *Ornithological Biography, or An Account of the Habits of the Birds of The United States* (5 vols., Edinburgh, 1831–39), III, 568–70 (Plate 286); V, 24–29 (Plate 391); II, 88–92 (Plate 114); II, 570–75 (Plate 200); II, 511–14 (Plate 188). Attention is called to the fact that the *Ornithological Biography* was issued as text without plates and intended to accompany the 435 folio plates of *The Birds of America.*

   [12] The *Gallant* (Gildea, master) ran regularly in the St. Louis-Pittsburgh trade; on this trip it was carrying to St. Louis sixty-six cabin and eighty-four deck passengers, as well as fifteen horses and considerable freight. Audubon, writing to his wife from St. Louis, said: "Harris and I have one *State Room,* he sleeps on 3 boards and I on 4, our meals are none of the best, all is greasy and nasty . . . a first rate initiation for the trip to the Yellow Stone." (Quoted in Arthur, *Audubon, an Intimate Life,* 453.) For other comment by Audubon, see introduction, 11–12.

Saturday, March 25th. Mouth of the Ohio Cairo 8 A. M. Canada[13] & White-fronted Goose abundant in the Mississippi.

Tuesday, March 28th. Arrived at St Louis 10 A. M.

Wednesday, March 29th. Squires D^r to Cash from fund $5.
  E. Harris D^r to Cash from fund $6.
  Wrote to Dr Spencer

Friday, March 31st. E. Harris D^r to Cash from fund 0.75

[13] *Ornithological Biography,* III, 1–19 (Plate 201).

APRIL

[1843]

Saturday, April 1st. Sir William Stewart[1] arrived today on the Julia Chouteau, he started from N. Orleans on the J. M. White, the finest boat and the fastest on these waters, about 12 miles below this place, at the Grand Chain, a ledge of rocks which crosses the river, she struck and sunk in 4 minutes in deep water, the passengers and crew were saved and most of the baggage, boat a total loss.[2]

Wrote to Dr Spencer.

Tuesday, April 4th. Started[3] from St Louis for Edwardsville, Ill[inois], 8½ A.M., and from Ill[inois] City[4] 9½ A.M. changed horses 10 miles, 2½ P.M., and arrived at Edwardsville[5] 5¾ P.M. Roads very heavy—day fine.

[1] For the earlier American adventures of Stewart see Bernard DeVoto, *Across the Wide Missouri* (Boston, Houghton Mifflin Co., 1947).

[2] About 142 miles below St. Louis. The *J. M. White* left New Orleans on the twenty-fifth and sank in three minutes on the twenty-eighth (according to the St. Louis *Daily Evening Gazette,* April 3, 1843). The boat was a total loss, but all the passengers were saved except one Negro girl.

[3] That is, Harris, Bell, Sprague, and Squires. Audubon remained in St. Louis to oversee preparations for the upriver trip. The others went to Illinois to hunt specimens.

[4] Now East St. Louis. For a contemporary view see J. C. Wild and L. F. Thomas, *The Valley of the Mississippi Illustrated* (St. Louis, 1841–42), 111–14.

[5] For Edwardsville, Alton, and the countryside in which Harris and his companions were hunting during this three-week period, see Edmund Flagg, *The Far West* (vol. XXVI of R. G. Thwaites [ed.], *Early Western Travels* [32 vols., Cleveland, Arthur H. Clark Co., 1904–1907]), 180–229. The town, named in honor of Ninian Edwards, was laid out in 1816 (*History of Madison County Illinois* [Philadelphia, 1882], 333–47).

[Memo on opposite page]   St Louis[6]

Mr Berthoud

Mr Sarpie ⎤
Mr Clapp ⎬ A. F. C.
Capt Sears ⎦

Mr Fitzpatrick

" Campbell

" Sublette

" Keemle

" Snyder

" Woodruff

Dr Johnson

" Brown

Mr Glasgow

Major Lee

Mr Hopkins of Boston

Mr Davenport

" Hoffman

Major Mitchell

Dr Sykes

Sir Wm Stewart

[6] Probably this list is one of persons whom Harris met in St. Louis during the first days of April. They were, briefly: Nicolas Berthoud (brother-in-law of Audubon, recently settled in St. Louis); John B. Sarpy (cousin of Pierre Chouteau, Jr., and a principal partner in the American Fur Company—or, more properly, Pierre Chouteau, Jr. and Company); Benjamin F. Clapp (a principal official in the St. Louis office of the fur company); Joseph A. Sire (captain of the *Omega;* see note 24, p. 54); Thomas Fitzpatrick (shortly to leave St. Louis as guide on Frémont's second expedition); Robert Campbell (partner in the firm of Sublette and Campbell); William L. Sublette (also partner in the firm of Sublette and Campbell, presently to guide Stewart's party to the Wind River Mountains); Charles Keemle (veteran of the fur trade as well as veteran newspaperman who was to found the *St. Louis Reveille* a year later); probably George Snyder of the firm of Engelmann and Snyder; possibly either A. D. Woodruff, attorney-at-law or James E. Woodruff, commission merchant; either Dr. George J. or Dr. J. B. Johnson; Dr. B. B. Brown (dentist and a founder of the Western Academy of Science at St. Louis in 1837); William Glasgow (merchant); Major Richard B. Lee (in charge of commissary at St. Louis); Col. George Davenport (who was murdered two years later); possibly Dr. Herman Laidley Hoffman; Major D. D. Mitchell (superintendent of Indian Affairs at St. Louis); Dr. James Sykes; Sir William Drummond Stewart, Bart.; the Rev. Mr. William Greenleaf Eliot (although Harris clearly wrote "Episc," the only St. Louis cleric of this name at this time was the Unitarian minister who ten years later founded Washington University); and Judge Bryan Mullanphy.

Harris' Finch

1. Adult Male   2. Young Female

from Audubon's *Birds of America*, Vol. VII (1844)

Sprague's Missouri Lark (Male)

from Audubon's *Birds of America*, Vol. VII (1844)

Rev^d Mr. Elliot Episc
Judge Melanfé

Wednesday, April 5th. Hunted grouse today on the Ridge Prairie 4 miles E. of Edwardsville, found them scarce and exceedingly wild, killed 2. Males have the bare skin on the side of the neck extremely loose, and extended, colour bright orange (it is now the blowing season)   it is capable of being enormously distended by blowing into the mouth in the same manner as is practiced with the Pouting Pigeon, the ovaries of the female, a young one, were not enlarged. Sprague fell in the creek and lost Trudeau's gun[7] in 10 feet of water

[Memo on opposite page]   Saw grouse—Cranes—Canada Geese —Snow Geese—Ducks—Curlews—Golden Plover[8]

Thursday, April 6th. Sprague, Squires and Bell went after the Gun and fished it up. I walked a mile or two up the Cohoes [Cahokia] Creek but found nothing. Bell shot one of the Foxy Squirrels[9] of this region— Afternoon—Bell skinned the Prairie hens. Took Trudeau's Gun to pieces and gave it a thorough cleaning.

[Memo on opposite page] Female Foxy Squirrel killed 6th weighed 2 lbs 1 oz

Length to end of tail bone	23	inches
" hair beyond tail bone	2¾	"
Extreme length	25⅜	"
Tail	10½	
Length, end of fore to hind feet	19¼	

[7] Audubon wrote to Harris from Minnies Land, March 4th 1843: "Trudeau who did promise to lend me his double barreled Gun has not yet done so, and if I should not get it *tomorrow* I must try my luck in another quarter." (Audubon MSS, Harvard University.) Obviously Trudeau did make good his promise. For much about James De Berty Trudeau, see *Tixier's Travels on the Osage Prairies,* ed. by John Francis McDermott (Norman, University of Oklahoma Press, 1940).

[8] Snow Geese: See *Ornithological Biography,* IV, 562–66 (Plate 381); Golden Plover, III, 623–28 (Plate 300).

[9] John James Audubon and John Bachman, *The Quadrupeds of North America* (3 vols., New York, V. G. Audubon, 1851–54), II, 132–38 (Plate 68). This work will hereafter be identified as *Quadrupeds.*

Width of tail	3
Ear to nose	2½
Eye to nose	1¼
Length of Ear	1⅛
Breadth of Ear	¾
Width between Ears	1¼

Friday, April 7th. This morning Bell went to a large Lake,[10] about 5 miles to the N. W. to look for Cranes & Geese. I followed about 12 o'clock and shot a Snow Goose, Prairie Hen & 5 Lark finches.[11] Sprague & Squires, after squirrels—did not find any. Evening Bell skinned 1 Lark finch & Grey Squirrel.[12]

[Memo opposite April 6] Male Grey Squirrel weighed 1 lb 7 oz

Length to end of tail bone	19½ inches
" hair beyond tail bone	2⅞
Extreme length	22⅜ "
End of fore to hind feet	18
Tail	9
Width of tail	3
Eye to nose	1⅛
Length ear	1⅛
Breadth of ear	⅝

5 Grey Squirrels weighed 5½ lbs

Saturday, April 8th. Bell [skinned] Red Squirrels[13]—Snow

10 Now known as Smith Lake; about one and one-quarter miles long, it lies in the American Bottom, east of the town of Wood River.

11 *Ornithological Biography,* V, 17–18 (Plate 390). However, this may possibly be Smith's Lark Bunting, for in *The Birds of America from Drawings Made in the United States and Their Territories* (octavo ed., 7 vols., Philadelphia and New York, 1840–44) Audubon recorded the discovery by Harris and Bell of this bird near Edwardsville. He quoted Bell as saying, "We found these birds very abundant on the low prairie, near a lake in Illinois, about seven or eight miles distant from Edwardsville." (VII, 336–38 [Plate 487]).

12 Probably the Migratory or Northern Gray Squirrel (*Quadrupeds,* I, 265–76, [Plate 35]).

13 Audubon to Harris, S[t] Louis, April 10th 1843 (Audubon MSS, Harvard University): "The Squirrel you have shot, is the Sciurus macrouresus of Say. I have received a very fine one from M[r] Sublette, and have made two outlines of it." For the *sciurus macrourus* see *Quadrupeds,* II, 274–76 (Plate 89).

Goose, Male; Grous, Male. After dinner Bell and I rode to the Lake. Bell shot one young Snow Goose, and three White fronted Geese. Going out about 2 miles from the town saw 3 wild Turkeys[14] and immediately afterwards 4 deer crossed the road. Squires went down the Am[erican] bottom[15] 7 miles and sent home two Sandhill Cranes.[16]

Tuesday, April 11th. Bell & I went again to the Lake. Shot 17 Lark Finches, 2 Sprig-tailed ducks and some Snipe.[17]

Wednesday, April 12th. Shot a few Gray Squirrels about the town.

Thursday, April 13th. I took the Alton Stage at 2 P. M. reached here at 6 and found the Steamer Macedonian starting for St. Louis—arrived at 8½ P. M.—The rest took the stage for Bunker Hill 17 miles N. W. from Edwardsville—I expect to join them on Monday.[18]

[Memo opposite April 14th] E. Harris D^r to Cash from fund Hat $3.00

Saturday, April 15th. To go to the Paul House when we return on Friday the 21st. Corner Second and Elm. Left at 4 P. M. for Alton 25 miles up Miss[issippi] in the Eagle. Sent 1 Trunk—1 Gun Case—1 cap—1 pair of boots to Messrs. Chouteau's Store. Slept at Alton House.[19]

---

[14] *Ornithological Biography*, I, 1–17, 33–34 (Plate 1, 6).

[15] The low ground on the east bank of the Mississippi from about Alton to Kaskaskia in the latter part of the eighteenth century was called the American Bottom to distinguish it from the Spanish area on the west bank.

[16] *Ornithological Biography*, III, 202–13 (Plate 226).

[17] Possibly Red-breasted Snipe or American Snipe. See *Ornithological Biography*, IV, 284–89 (Plate 335); III, 322–29 (Plate 243).

[18] "One day our friend Harris came back, and brought with him the prepared skins of birds and quadrupeds they had collected, and informed me that they had removed their quarters to B——'s. He left the next day, after we had made arrangement for the party to return the Friday following." (Audubon, *Journals*, I, 455).

[19] The first Alton House, built in 1832, burned and was replaced by a three-story brick building in 1837; Calvin Stone was the proprietor. For a view of Alton about this time consult Wild and Thomas, *The Valley of the Mississippi Illustrated*, 47–51.

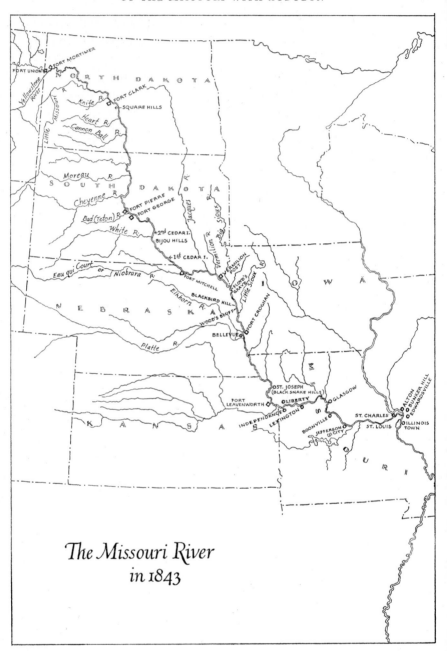

The Missouri River
in 1843

[Memo on opposite page] E. Harris D^r to Cash from fund Boots $11.50

Sunday, April 16th. Hired a buggy to Bunker-hill,[20] 19 miles.

Wednesday, April 19th. Bell & I hired a horse and Yankee Wagon to go a Grouse shooting—Killed 17, principally from the Waggon as they were *blowing* and courting the females. When thus engaged they will suffer themselves to be approached by a horse, and frequently several may be shot before the rest will fly away. One bird had its leg broken by the first shot and waited for the second without making an attempt to fly.

Friday, April 21st. Mr Nutter of Bunker Hill house carted us to Alton where we took the steamer Annawan and reached St. Louis before dark.[21]

[Memo opposite April 22nd]

E. Harris D^r to cash from fund (to gunsmith)		4.50
E. Harris D^r to cash from fund for Hats		1.87½
Bell D^r to Cash from fund	"	1.25
Squires D^r to cash from fund	"	1.25
Sprague D^r to cash from fund	"	1.25

[Memo opposite April 24th]

E. Harris D^r to Cash from fund	2.75
J. J. Audubon C^r by his due bill to Pierre Chouteau J^r & Co for Cash & Sundries per bill rendered (included in last A/C rendered by Chouteau Octr 21	368.30
J. J. Audubon C^r by Cash paid N. Berthoud's 120.—	

[20] Bunker Hill is about twelve miles north of Edwardsville and about sixteen miles northeast of Alton. It was laid out in 1836 on the route between St. Louis and Springfield (*The History of Macoupin County, Illinois* [Philadelphia, 1879], 143–47).

[21] It is probable that Harris went to the Glasgow House rather than to the Paul on his return to St. Louis. A notation on the rear flyleaf of the small diary reads: "St. Louis April 21 Glasgow House 1 shirt 1 flan d^o 2 pr drawers 2 pr stockings 2 Hdfs"—presumably a list of purchases.

Tuesday, April 25th. At last we are off on our long talked of expedition.[22] The captain had great difficulty in getting the trappers on board, they were nearly all drunk and it was about noon before we got under way, amid the shouts and yellings and firing of guns from our drunken trappers.[23] Yesterday one who had enlisted for the trip was arrested for counterfeiting and murder. How many more of like character we have among us would be difficult to know, all we do know is that they appear to be the very offscouring of the earth, worse than any crew of sailors I ever met with. Our boat makes a very poor attempt at stemming the current of this great river, now more filled with water than it has been for many years—We look for a tedious passage. Our boat is called the Omega, commanded by Capt. Joseph A. Sire.[24]

[22] The packing account (Harris Collection, Montgomery) for the Audubon party is worth quoting as an indication of what travelers had to provide for themselves on such a journey, including food supplies and presents for Indians, as well as hunting equipment: "10 lbs. Blue Beads, 10 lbs. White beads, 10 lbs Vermillion, 4 Gros finger rings, 2 gros Indian awls, 1 Gros Gun worms, 3 dozen Crambo Combs, 4 dozen Wilson Butcher Knives, 500 Gun flints, 100 lbs Bar Lead, 10 Musk Rat Traps, 10 House Rat Traps, 10 Boxes Claret Wine, 1 Box Tobacco, 1 Box Tea (6 lbs), 1 Barrel N.O. Sugar, 1 Barrel Sup^r Flour, 4 Barrels Pilot Bread, 1 Barrel Mess Pork, 1 half Barrel Rice (25 lbs), 1 Keg Coffee (25 lbs), 1 Bundle 3 Bacon hams (*sic*), 4 Bottles Best Table Olive Oil, 2 lbs Gro Ginger, 2 lbs Epsom Salts, 5 Boxes Claret, 2 Kegs powder, demiJohn 5 Gls Brandy, 30 Bags Shot, 1 Barrell Cornmeal, 10 dressed deerskins, 5 belts & Scabbards, $100." The last four items are not in the packing account, but do stand charged to Audubon on P. Chouteau, Jr. and Company Ledger FF, 407–408 (Missouri Historical Society).

[23] "We left St. Louis at 11:30 A.M. with . . . a hundred and one trappers of all descriptions and nearly a dozen nationalities, though the greater number were French Canadians, or Creoles of this State. Some were drunk, and many in that stupid mood which follows a state of nervousness produced by drinking and over-excitement. . . . The men came in pushing and squeezing each other, so as to make the boards they walked on fairly tremble. The Indians . . . had already seated . . . themselves on the highest parts of the steamer, and were tranquil lookers-on. . . . As the boat pushed off from the shore, where stood a crowd of loafers, the men on board had congregated upon the hurricane deck with their rifles and guns of various sorts, all loaded, and began to fire what I should call a very disorganized sort of a salute, which lasted for something like an hour, and which has been renewed at intervals, though in a more desultory manner, at every village we passed." (Audubon, *Journals*, I, 455–57.) The number "one hundred and one" is intended to be accurate, not fanciful.

[24] Joseph A. Sire, born in La Rochelle, France, in 1799, came to St. Louis from Philadelphia in 1821 and died there in 1854. He married Victoire Labadie and was therefore a cousin by marriage of Pierre Chouteau, Jr., and John B. Sarpy. During the eighteen forties he commanded the annual supply boat of Pierre Chouteau, Jr., and Company on its annual trips up the Missouri. This was the only year that the *Omega*

[Memo on opposite page]   Shot purchased at St. Louis

Buck Shot No. 3		1	Bag
Buck Shot No. 0		5	Bags
Patent Shot No. 000		3	"
"	" No. 0	1	"
"	No. 1	3	"
"	No. 3	6	"
"	N. 6	3	"
"	N 8	2	"
"	N 10	2	"
"	N 11	4	"

Letters to be sent to S. C. Owens & Co. at Independence to remain until our return.[25]

Saturday, April 29th.[26] Write to Dr Spencer at Boonville.[27] Saw the first paroquet today.[28]

[Memo opposite April 30th]
Red Squirrel shot 220 miles up the Missouri[29]

Extreme length	23¼ inches
Fore to hind feet	18½
Weight	1 lb 8 oz

made the trip. The logbook of this voyage was published in translation by H. M. Chittenden, *The American Fur Trade of the Far West* (new ed., ed. by Stallo Vinton, 2 vols., New York, The Press of the Pioneers, 1935), II, 956–73. The original (in French), together with logs of other trips from 1841 to 1847, is preserved among the papers of the American Fur Company in the Missouri Historical Society. References here will be merely to the Sire *Log*.

25 Samuel C. Owens, a Kentuckian who had settled in Independence in 1827. For twenty years he was a leading frontier merchant.

26 According to Audubon (*Journals*, I, 458), on the twenty-eighth, above Jefferson City, Harris saw a Peregrine Falcon. For this bird, the Great-Footed Hawk, see *Ornithological Biography*, I, 85–90 (Plate 16).

27 Audubon said they reached Boonville at 9 A.M. and added an interesting statement which cannot be confirmed by any other source: "We found here some of the Santa Fé traders with whom we had crossed the Alleghanies." (*Journals*, I, 459.)

28 *Ornithological Biography*, I, 135–40 (Plate 26).

29 Probably taken when the *Omega* stopped to wood above the Chariton. Audubon, Harris, Bell, and Squires went ashore to hunt after breakfast. "Bell, Harris, and myself shot running exactly twenty-eight Rabbits, *Lepus sylvaticus*, and two Bachmans, two *Sciurus macrourus* of Say, two *Arctomys monax*, and a pair of Tetrao umbellus. . . . Harris shot an Arctomys without pouches." (*Journals*, I, 461.)

MAY
[1843]

Monday, May 1st.. Saw a few Paroquets today.
[*Memo on opposite page*] J. J. Audubon C^r by Cash advanced
Fund $25

Tuesday, May 2nd. Arrived at Independence this morning and
took in 144 lbs of Tow which we had written for—We paid
25 cts per lb for it!!!^{1} Saw abundance of Parroquets today. Bell
shot two at the first stopping place. Sent letter from Independence to Mrs Lang—Dr Spencer & Mrs Vansittart.^{2}

Wednesday, May 3rd. Stopped at Fort Leavenworth to take in
some cargo. Saw abundance of Parrokeets but did not procure
any. Got aground a few miles above and after working several
hours parted the cable which was carried to a snag some two
or three hundred yards ahead of the boat, and were obliged to
remain all night. In the morning carried the cable ashore and
made it fast to a tree and got her off, but the wind blew so strong
up stream that the boat would not steer, we had to lie by until

---

1 According to Audubon they reached Independence at 1 P.M.; he records the
tow as weighing 148 pounds, "for which we were charged no less than 12½ to 25 cts
per pound" (*Journals*, I, 467). For a picture of Independence in 1845–46 see John
Francis McDermott (ed.), *Travels in Search of the Elephant: The Wanderings of Alfred
S. Waugh, Artist, in Louisiana, Missouri, and Santa Fe, in 1845–46* (St. Louis, Missouri Historical Society, 1951).

2 Mrs. Lang was an American cousin of Harris's, Mrs. Vansittart, an English cousin.

nearly night—We lost by the sand-bar and the wind just 24 hours.[3]

Thursday, May 4th. Missouri R. below black-snake Hills shot a finch supposed to be new, it has a black head and throat, with a large patch of ash color on the cheeks and loral space running back into the neck. Shot a number of Paroquets to-day.[4]

Friday, May 5th. We find Lincoln's Finch[5] very abundant. Saw Henslow's Bunting.[6] Stopped at Black Snake Hills on the Missouri side of the river.[7] This is the last Post Office and I wrote to Mrs Gamble.

Saturday, May 6th. Shot another Finch of the same species as that of Thursday in better plumage—both Males—It corresponds in measurements with Townsend's Finch, *F. Townsendii,*[8] which was described from a female bird and does not correspond —possibly this may be the male of that bird. We hope to find the female soon. Landed our Indians today at their settlement. Mr Richardson the agent met us there.[9] He came up in the John

[3] After running all night (which was not usual) the *Omega* reached Fort Leavenworth at 6 A.M. and left at 8 A.M. (Sire *Log*). The breaking of the cable took place on the fourth, according to Sire. Audubon (*Journals*, I, 469–70) also makes clear that Harris crowded into his May 3 entry the difficulties that occupied Sire and the *Omega* through much of May 4.

[4] Seventeen, according to Audubon (*Journals*, I, 470); in the Harris Bird Collection, Phillips B. Street has found two paroquets dated May 4 ("The Edward Harris Collection of Birds," 182). More interesting than the mention of paroquets, however, is Audubon's remark: "Friend Harris shot two or three birds, which we have not yet fully established": these proved to be *Fringilla harrisii*, of which more in the next few days.

[5] *Ornithological Biography*, II, 539–41 (Plate 193).

[6] *Ornithological Biography*, I, 360–61 (Plate 70).

[7] Sire noted that they reached Black Snake Hills at 1 P.M.; this was Robidoux's Post, destined very soon to become the city of St. Joseph. Audubon on this day wrote: "On examination of the Finch killed by Harris yesterday, I found it to be a new species." (*Journals*, I, 472.) In a note to this passage Coues declares that Nuttall had previously discovered this bird in 1834; however, it is today known by Harris's name. For its description see *The Birds of America*, VII (1844), 331–32 (Plate 484). On May 17 Audubon wrote in his journal: "I am truly proud to name it *Fringilla Harrisii*, in honor of one of the best friends I have in this world."

[8] *Ornithological Biography*, IV, 183–84 (Plate 400).

[9] W. P. Richardson, subagent for the Ioways and the Sacs and Foxes. This was the Great Nemaha Sub-Agency. Audubon said he "appears to be a pleasant man" (*Journals*, I, 474).

Auld[10] to Independence where we met him, he put his baggage aboard and we started, he expected the John Auld to overtake us, but we saw no more of him until we reached the Ioway village, he started the same day on horseback and reached the village the next day, after sleeping out on the Prairie.— Saw a Hare[11] today when we stopped to cut wood. At Fort Leavenworth the officers told us there were no hares, and Mr Richardson at the Ioway village only 45 miles distant by land says there are no rabbits there, and hares very abundant. It must have been near the line of separation of the species that I saw the hare as I saw a rabbit at the same place.

Grey Squirrel Shot on the Missouri R. in the Country of the Sac Inds.

Length of Head & body	9½ inches
Length of tail (vertebra)	8⅛
D° to the tip	10¾
Height of ears from Scull	¾
Length of ear	1⅛
Breadth of ear	⅝
Tip of Nose to eye	1¼
Width between ears	1½
" between eyes	1⅜
[Palm?] to end of middle claw	1¹¹⁄₁₆
Heel to end of middle nail	2⅜
Breadth of tail with hairs extended	4⅛

Monday, May 8th.[12] Shot another of the rare Finches.

Tuesday, May 9th. Wrote to Dr Spencer from Bellevue. We ar-

10 The *John Aull*, a new boat this season in the Missouri River trade between St. Louis and Weston, had left St. Louis the day after the *Omega*. The Audubon party had seen the *Aull* near Glasgow on the twenty-ninth, at Lexington on May 1, and at Independence on the second.

11 *Lepus townsendii*, the Rocky Mountain Hare, better known as the Jack-rabbit of the Great Plains (*Quadrupeds*, I, 25–30 (Plate 3). Harris mentions it again on May 24, June 8, and later.

12 On the seventh, according to Audubon (*Journals*, I, 475–76), they went ashore between 11 o'clock and noon while Sire wooded: "Harris killed another of the new Finches, a male also."

rived today at Bellevue, Mr. Sarpie[13] was absent, there were a large number of Ottoe Indians on shore and some of the chiefs came on board. They are like all the Indians we have met, in a state of great distress for want of food, in consequence of the long winter. Moved on a few miles to Fort Croghan, discharged our freight, and not finding the officers or the Indian agent[14] here to examine the cargo, which is always done here to prevent the introduction of Whiskey into the Indian Country, we moved on a few miles to lie by for the night. While at Fort Croghan Bell shot a small sparrow which we could not make out, in consequence of his having shot the tail off. I went on board and got my cane gun and succeeded in shooting another, when we ascertained it to be the *Emberiza pallida* of Swainson.[15] We have now made about 800 miles by the river, in a few hours over 14 days, and as we shall leave about half our cargo & 45 men at Fort Pierre, 700 miles above, we hope to be able to accomplish the whole distance in 6 weeks from the time of starting. The officers at Fort Croghan, in consequence of the Fresh[et] had been obliged to abandon their quarters and encamp on the hills about 4 miles distant.[16] The soldiers informed us that the Prairie Wolves are so abundant that they came within the camp at night.

Wednesday, May 10th. Started this morning by daylight, but had proceeded but a few miles when we were halted by an officer and four soldiers who had ridden after us from the fort, and ordered to stop. Lieut. Noble[17] came on board and insisted on an examination of the cargo.[18] This gave us a few hours for

13 Pierre Abadie Sarpy, brother of John B. Sarpy, had been in charge of the Bellevue post for a number of years; at this moment he was 300 miles away on the Platte, according to Audubon (*Journals*, I, 477).

14 Daniel Miller, who was with Sarpy at this time. On the return trip Audubon met him and described him as "a good man for this place" (*Journals*, II, 172).

15 The clay-colored bunting. See *Ornithological Biography*, V, 66–68 (Plate 398).

16 Fort Croghan was established in May, 1842, by Captain Burgwin who had been sent from Fort Leavenworth to prevent hostilities between the Sioux and Potawatomis and to stop whisky smuggling into the Upper Missouri. On their return trip in October, Audubon and his friends reached Fort Croghan just as the post was being abandoned.

17 Lieutenant Patrick Noble from South Carolina.

18 Sire wrote in his *Log*: "We progressed finely as far as Hart's Bluffs, where,

hunting. We did not succeed in getting any more of the E. pallida. Sprague shot another of the new Sparrows, still a male. M[r] Audubon took one of the horses of the soldiers and one of them for a guide and rode over to the Hills about three miles distant to call upon the officers, he brought back with him Capt. Burgoyne[19] the commandant and Doctor Madison,[20] they expressed great disappointment that we could not stop a week or two and said that if we would stay they could go about 80 miles where we could kill Buffalo & Elk.[21] Mr. Audubon found at the encampment the Yellowheaded Troopial,[22] very abundant, he shot several, he also saw 2 Yellow-crowned herons and several bitterns. The Magpie is found here in the winter season, and is easily caught in snares. They had two tame ones at the camp, caught last winter. Nearly 30 miles above we passed the old site of Council Bluffs.[23] Two years ago the river passed close to it, but it has cut itself a new channel and left this splendid situation near two miles from its present channel. The bluff is one of the level prairies of which we have seen so many within the last few days and which we have called bottoms praries but it appears to be elevated 30 or 40 feet above the present state of the waters

---

at 7 A.M., we were summoned by an officer and four dragoons to land. I received a polite note from Captain Burgwin, informing me that his duty obliged him to make an inspection of the boat. We put ourselves to work immediately, while Mr. Audubon goes to call upon the Captain. They return in about two hours. I compel, as it were, the officer to make the strictest possible inspection, but on the condition that he would do the same with the other traders." The editor finds nothing in the available accounts to justify E. Coues's statement (in Audubon, *Journals*, I, 479, note 1) to the effect that Sire used these two hours to shift his cargo so that illegal whiskey could be concealed. The inspection was quite apparently made by the lieutenant during Audubon's absence— not by the captain on Audubon's return.

19 John H. K. Burgwin of North Carolina.

20 Coues tentatively identified him as Thomas C. Madison of Virginia, appointed assistant surgeon, United States Army, February 27, 1840 (Audubon, *Journals*, I, 481, note 1).

21 "Last July the captain sent twenty dragoons and as many Indians on a hunt for Buffaloes. During the hunt they killed 51 Buffaloes, 104 Deer, and 10 Elks, within 80 miles of the camp." (Audubon, *Journals*, I, 481). Carleton also mentioned this hunt (J. Henry Carleton *The Prairie Logbooks*, ed. by Louis Pelzer [Chicago, The Caxton Club, 1943], 139).

22 *Ornithological Biography*, V, 6–8 (Plate 388).

23 That is, Lewis and Clark's Council Bluffs.

which have fallen some 8 or 9 feet, and seems to be of great extent, perfectly level and running back to the real Bluffs which are crowned by the great Prarie running to the Rocky Mountains. We have stopped for the night a few miles above the Bluffs. I regret very much that we have had no opportunity to examine the Geological character of this country. The Stratified secondary limestone, so nearly horizontal, that no dip can be detected by the eye, and which has faced the hills between the mouth of the Ohio and Bellevue on this river, appears to dip below the surface of the river, and nearly opposite Council Bluffs a chain of rocks cross the river which I take for granted is the last of the immense ridge which appears above the surface. At Fort Croghan, on the East Bank, we were informed that there was no stone except water worn pebbles of the size of paving stone, I had no opportunity of securing any or ascertaining their character. Bell found a large piece of scoria or pumice which had been transported from above by the current of the river in a freshet. There is no apparent difference in the diluvium here from that which overlies the limestone rock below. I have seen no boulders on this river. I saw a small one of granite at Bunker hill in Illinois, they are also found in the neighborhood of St. Louis.

Thursday, May 11th. But little of interest seen today excepting that we saw a Deer for the first time and a Wolf, it appeared to be the common Wolf[24] and was walking on a sand-bar. We landed on the same bar to cut up some drift wood for fuel, and Wolfy scarcely raised a trot to get out of our way. We are now frequently obliged to depend on drift-wood for fuel, the timber is now becoming so scarce that it is difficult to meet with any which is suitable to burn green. The cottonwood is fast giving way to the willow. Ash is the only wood we have used green.[25] We are now passing one of the bottoms or level praries on the west side of the river which the Captain says extends 60 miles

[24] According to Coues, this should be read as the common large wolf of North America, not the prairie wolf (*Quadrupeds*, II, 126–31 [Plate 67]).

[25] Although supplies were irregular, Sire mentioned cutting *liard* (cottonwood) all the way to Fort Union. Necessity, however, frequently forced them to make use of driftwood.

above, in a straight line and that we shall follow it by the sinuosities of the river about 150 miles. I forgot to mention yesterday that the horse which Mr. Audubon rode yesterday is eleven or twelve years old, has been a dragoon horse for many years, and has never learned to stand fire, but actually grows more afraid of a gun as it grows older.

Friday, May 12th. Reached this evening Blackbirds Grave[26] at the end of the 60 miles prairie. We saw today 4 deer which Mr. Audubon supposed to be black-tailed Deer.[27] One of the Pilots who has travelled up the river by land says that this Deer is found before reaching this part of the river on the high prairies, but it is not often seen so low down on the river. At a place where we wooded today on the east bank of the river Elk tracks were seen. Wild geese (*canadensis*) are seen in great numbers every day, all in pairs, they breed on the whole course of this river. At Wood's Bluff[28] we saw vast numbers of Bank Swallows flying about their holes in the Bluff, we supposed them to be *serripennis*.[29] It is rather singular that we have seen what we have supposed to be this bird ever since we have left St. Louis, and not one of us has yet had an opportunity to shoot them. Our opportunities for shooting do not come up to our expectations. Instead of stopping two hours before night to cut wood as we had been led to believe, they stop whenever they can find that which is suitable no matter what time in the day. We have seen nothing like rocks since we left Bellevue, until we reached Wood's Bluff, ten or twelve miles below this place, here there is every appearance of stratified rock as we pass the Bluff in the boat, but it is impossible to tell without landing, we think it must be either indurated clay or exceedingly soft sandstone. The swallows have

26 The death and burial of the Omaha chief Washinga-Sabba was related by every Missouri River traveler; probably the first account of it in print was that of Henry Marie Brackenridge in his *Journal of a Voyage up the River Missouri in 1811* (2nd ed., Baltimore, 1816), 86–88.

27 The mule deer: *Quadrupeds*, II, 206–12 (Plate 78).

28 Wood's Bluff was *below* Blackbird's Hill. It was so called "because a man of that name fell overboard from his boat while drunk" (Audubon, *Journals*, I, 485).

29 *Ornithological Biography*, IV, 584–92 (Plate 385).

holes in it, which I should think was conclusive against it being rock. This shows the utter impossibility of ascertaining the Geological character of the country while passing on the river in a Steamer. We hope to do better in returning. We have seen a considerable number of Yellow-headed Troupials to-day and expect to find them all the way up.

Saturday, May 13th. Bell shot t[w]o Lark Buntings (*Emberiza grammaca*[30]) on the top of a Bluff before breakfast in the morning while we were detained by a fog. Soon after starting we passed bluffs the substratum of which was evidently sandstone and to judge from the appearance of the dip inclined to the North West. We saw holes of the common bank swallow or serripennis in it and also nests of the Cliff Swallow. We stopped again to wood before dinner, and Mr. Audubon shot down a fine turkey hen, she ran off so fast that she was soon out of sight. I happened to be near with Brag, he took the track and soon came to a point. I saw it squatting under a bush and shot it with No. 10 shot, it weighted 11¾ lbs. Saw 11 Indians of the Omaha Tribe   they appear to be in a miserable condition, were very anxious for us to land   one of them ran after the boat at least 2 miles until he was stopped by a Bluff.[31] Passed the Bluff on which the grave of Sergeant Floyd one of the companions of Lewis and Clark, on the East Bank of the river. Saw to-day the frame of an Indian Canoe made of Willow sticks, over which hides of animals are stretched while green, making a watertight boat when dry.

Sunday, May 14th. Rain with thunder and lightning in the night. A large Black Bear[32] was discovered crossing the River just as he came opposite the bow of the boat the men ran for their rifles and several shots were fired without effect. Bell fired a load of large shot which must have tickled his hide a little,

---

[30] See *Birds of America*, III (1841), 63.

[31] "They made signals for us to land, but our captain never heeded them, for he hates the redskins as most men hate the devil." (Audubon, *Journals*, I, 487.) Sire made no mention of this episode in his *Log*.

[32] *Quadrupeds*, III, 187–97 (Plate 141).

when he reached the opposite bank which was very steep it was amusing to see him scramble up the bank until he was on the point of gaining the top, when the earth would give away, and poor Bruin would dive backwards into the water again, after several such attempts he came to a place where the roots were pretty strong and he landed safely on terrafirma, and the way he galloped off rather astonished us after seeing him perform such a rapid and fatiguing transit of the river. He seemed to be fully aware of the blood-thirsty nature of the crew he had left behind him. A dead Buffalo floated down to-day. We stopped to cut wood and I discovered a Heronry of 20 to 30 nests of the large Blue Heron.[33] Saw also where the wolves had been digging up the ground in search of roots on which they feed when hard pressed for animal food. When we started from our wooding place the wind was so high that we were obliged to put ashore again about one mile further up the river. The wind increased to a very severe gale, our fires were put out and the trappers set to chopping wood, at which they continued all the afternoon. The thermometer which was at 76 in the morning fell to 46 during the gale.

Monday, May 15th. The wind continued to blow a severe gale all night, and in the morning although it had about abated there appeared to be little prospect of our getting away this day. We took our guns and struck through the heavily timbered bottom to endeavor to reach the Prarie Bluffs,[34] which we could not see for the timber, after going for a couple of miles and getting deeper in the mud as we proceeded, we turned back pretty well jaded with our walk and very interesting figures to look at, in particular poor Brag who walked close behind me all the way and was completely coated with my splashings.[35] Saw a dead Elk

[33] *Ornithological Biography*, III, 87–97 (Plate 211).

[34] Not a place-name, but merely the prairies on the bluffs.

[35] "Bell, Harris, Mr. La Barge—the first pilot—a mulatto hunter named Michaux, and I, started at nine. We first crossed through tangled brush-wood, and high-grown rushes for a few hundreds of yards, and soon perceived that here, as well as all along the Missouri and Mississippi, the land is highest nearest the shore, and falls off the farther one goes inland. Thus we soon came to mud, and from mud to muddy water, as *pure* as it runs in the Missouri itself; at every step which we took we raised several

24th

While aground last evening, two boats landed on the shore near us and we sent our barge for the men. We found they were from Fork Pierre with Furs, these boats were in the form of scows and covered with Buffalo hides. They were 8 days from the Fork. We passed to day a Bluff which was said to have been burning for two years but is now extinguished, it has the appearance of containing much Sulphur. The fire appeared to be internal as only smoke appeared.

From the Great Bend as seen from the Hills.

26th

and greasy that it was with difficulty we kept our feet. The Geological character of this country must receive more of our attention in descending, there are said to be exceeding interesting fossil remains of fishes and shells on the tops of these hills. About this band the Strata of Limestone which we have carried from Council Bluffs appear to lose themselves under the bed of the River and at the turn of the bend there is a chain of rocks across the river. The upper stratum of Yellow Stone (which appears to be tinged with Iron) now only shows itself in fragments thickly strewed on the bank superimposed by the Black shale which is found to the summit (whereas lower down it only formed a portion of the summit) Started 4 Blacktailed Deer in crossing the hills, Bell shot but did not stop any of them. We struck our camp on the River shore under 4 Cotton Wood trees growing in a clump, and after making a good fire Michaux and one of the Frenchmen started after the Deer, having still an hour or more of daylight, we had hardly had time to refresh ourselves with a little bread and cheese, before they brought in a fine young doe, back of this one arrived to us. It was not long before some of the choice morceaux were roasting before the fires impaled on sharp sticks stuck in the ground. We all agreed it was the best Venison we ever tasted, and every one failed to do ample justice to the repast. Our beds were soon blown up and wrapped in our blankets with our guns by our sides we were soon fast asleep. Saturday the 27th. A light rain in the night only made us hug our blankets the closer, and by the peep of day we were all stirring. We did not wait to break our fast but started off with our guns, while the venison was cooking. I was out about an hour but met with nothing, Bell and the two hunters were gone 4 hours and walked several miles after Buffalo. They discharged their guns into an old Bull at about 30 paces but he would not stop. We made no addition to our larder and by the time we had eaten again of the Deer most heartily and redoubled our praises of its superior quality, it came on to rain quite hard and we went to work to build a regular camp of cedar boughs, fearing the boat might meet with obstructions and leave us out another night or two, particularly as our hunters had reported having seen here from the little tops (whence the whole course of the river around the bend is visible) not more than two miles ahead of where we left her at 5 P.M. yesterday. The Marie Dog & Arctomys Ludovicianus worth the eats and the Black tailed or mule deer (from the great size of its ears) were the only animals we saw that were new to us on this trip and we got no birds that we had not procured before. At 3 o'clock we left our camp and carried our effects down the river a few hundred yards as we saw the Boat approaching and we knew she would stop there to cut wood. As soon as the wood was on board we started but had not gone more than a mile and a half before we met with difficulties from sand bars and

Thursday, May 25th, 1843.

We have had a dull cold rainy day and have not been ashore with our guns, and scarcely out of the cabin. Thermometer 50 to 53. The day before yesterday at 92. Met three Mackinaw Boats laden with Furs belonging to the opposition Company. Expected to reach Great Cedar Island to-night but were obliged to stop short where there is no wood, but any quantity of dead Buffalo calves. The men found 2 Specimens of the young of the Wood Rat _Neotoma floridana_ in a hollow tree.

Friday, 26th.

Bazil River

We put 3 Men ashore at _____ Creek, about 60 miles by land & 150 by water from Ft. Pierre to make their way to that post with Despatches from Capt. Sire. We proceeded very slowly encountering numerous obstructions, until we reached the Great Bend, where all of our party (with the exception of Squires who is employed in taking the course of the river) went on shore about 5 o'clock P.M. to walk across the Bottoms and encamp for the night on the other side and await the arrival of the Boat to-morrow or whenever she may happen to arrive. We took a good teamsters with us to carry our baggage, act as guides, &c. &c. The distance is between two and three miles across and 26 miles around. We started on a beautiful and very extensive level prairie, lying just above the highest freshets, and reaching about half way across, the rest was steep and rugged hills, of several hundred feet in height. On the prairie we found a Village of Prairie Dogs, the first we have seen. We diverged a little from our path but did not succeed in shooting any not having time to wait for them to come out of their holes to reconnoiter after their first alarm. We found the ascent of the hills extremely fatiguing from the peculiar nature of the soil, it is a stiff clay mixed with shale which appears to have undergone the action of fire (the shale) and so moist

Saturday, 27th. begins on the other page.

Wrote to Dr. Spencer for in Boonville

had to send our Yawl out to sound, while performing this duty the report spread through the boat that they had been fired upon by Indians, we ran out to see but soon found that the Indians had only fired to induce them to stop, and then they had found a channel we soon came up to the Indians, they were on horse back 4 of them, fine looking well dressed fellows, they alighted and fired off all their guns ahead of the boat. Capt. Sire who understands the Sioux Language told them he could not stop them, but if they would follow us on we would soon stop for the night, when they could come on board. They mounted their horses, sitting on a Buffalo skin and we soon had them aboards; their horses are the best we have yet seen among the Indians, they are of the Yanctonan tribe, a part of the Sioux Nation. One of them who is a chief showed a treaty made with Genl. Black. They proved great beggars and after we had given them some powder they wanted lead, as they said that powder was of no use to them without balls. They staid on board until about 12 o'clock.

which had been principally consumed by the wolves. Elk tracks have been seen at every landing place, and to-day more numerous than ever. Saw a fresh bear track. After dinner walked down the river to the Heronry which I discovered yesterday, we shot four of them and a Raven which came to feast on their eggs when they found the herons absent. The trappers who are very much in our way on our shooting excursions had been shooting all the morning at them and had only killed one. We find these men (who are scarcely any of them old trappers), to be the worst shots we have ever met, with either a rifle or shot gun, and how they are to subsist in the woods after they are turned loose to shift for themselves is not easy to conceive. Doubtless many of the poor creatures will perish from hunger, and many more will meet their death from the hand of the ruthless savage. It was nearly night before the wind would permit us to start again, and we made but 7 or 8 miles. Vermillion River where the company have a station is about 17 or 18 miles ahead of us and we hope to be there sometime in the course of the morning. The river is rising quite fast, it is supposed to have risen at least two feet[36] since we stopped yesterday, this makes our running quite slow. Our Captain fears this rise is caused by the melting of snow in the mountains, and that it is the beginning of the freshet which usually comes in June and is called the June Fresh. Another dead Buffalo floated down today. Found a dead Bank Swallow. Fear they have been killed by the storm. Temperature was 43 this morning.

Tuesday, May 16th. Started as usual about 3 o'clock A.M. Stopped at the Vermillion River estab. of the Company, took in wood and discharged the freight we had for them, stayed but a short time,[37]

pounds of mud on our boots. Friend Harris very wisely returned, but the remainder of us proceeded through thick and thin until we came in sight of the prairies. But, alas! between us and them there existed a regular line of willows—and who ever saw willows grow far from water? Here we were of course stopped, and after attempting in many places to cross the water that divided us from the dry land, we were forced back, and had to return as best we could. We were mud up to the very middle." (Audubon, *Journals,* I, 492.)

[36] Fourteen inches, according to Sire.

[37] From 11:30 to 12:30 (Sire, *Log*). Audubon treated this stop a little more fully: Pascal Cerré, "the agent of the Company at this post, a handsome French gentleman,

learned that the country abounds in Elk & hares— About 3 miles above found that one of our boilers was burned out and stopped with a prospect of lying by two or three days.[38] Took our guns and walked out, some of the party reached the hills in about 3 miles, saw some deer but did not kill any. I shot another of my finches which proved to be a female and resembling in markings exactly the male, only rather fainter. Several Buffalo floated by to-day, one cow with her calf by her side. (The Vermillion Fork [Fort] is ten miles below the mouth of the River) Killed a yellow-headed Troopial. Bell & Michaux saw a number of Deer.

Wednesday, May 17th. Bell & Michaux started on a hunt at 4 A.M. Breakfasted at 5 & Mr. A. and one of the Pilots[39] followed after breakfast. I started as soon as I could get through attending to my various patients,[40] taking a lunch in my pocket. On reaching the top of the hills I was hailed by Squires (who had gone out in the mean time) from the top of a distant knoll in the Prarie, where I found him watching a deer which Michaux had killed. I passed on to meet the hunters and found Bell and Mr A. in pursuit of some finches which we had not seen before, we succeeded in killing two, which we found to be the Chestnut collared lark Finch of Townsend.[41] We also shot a lark Bunting.

Thursday, May 18th. The Captain called us at ¼ before 4 this morning, 4 Mackinaw boats[42] having stopped on their way

---

of good manners . . . dined with us. After this we landed, and walked to the fort, if the place may so be called, for we found it only a square, strongly picketed, without portholes. It stands on the immediate bank of the river, opposite a long and narrow island, and is backed by a vast prairie, all of which was inundated during the spring freshet. . . . We left as soon as possible, for our captain is a pushing man most truly." (*Journals*, I, 493–94.)

38 Audubon located this forced stop at "about ten miles below the mouth of the Vermilion River" (*Journals*, I, 494).

39 La Barge (Audubon, *Journals*, I, 495).

40 As early as May 9, Audubon, referring to one of the trappers' having cut his foot very badly with an axe, mentioned that "Harris, who is now the doctor, attended to it as best he could." (*Journals*, I, 477.)

41 *Ornithological Biography*, V, 44–45 (Plate 394).

42 Named the *War Eagle*, the *White Cloud*, the *Crow Feather*, and the *Red-Fish* (Audubon, *Journals*, I, 499).

down from Ft. Pierre, Mr. Laidlaw[43] the superintendent at that post and Major Cripps [*sic*] the Indian Agent[44] offered to carry any letters for us and we were soon all busy with our pens.[45] I wrote a short letter to D[r] Spencer. These gentlemen inform us they have had a severe and long winter, and that on the 5th of May while we were near Fort Leavenworth and had a severe storm of rain, they had 2 feet of snow which killed thousands of Buffalo calves which now strew the Praries. They mention a rumor that one of their clerks at the Fort at the upper falls of the Missouri had killed a Blackfoot Chief.[46] I trust this will not produce an outbreak and interfere with the prosecution of of our enterprise. The Mackinaw boats are long and broad flat-bottomed craft, carrying about 25 packs of Buffalo hides, 10 hides in a pack, these are covered with bent saplings over which are stretched Buffalo hides, those we examined had been sewed together and used for Indian lodges.[47] We did not do much work

[43] William Laidlaw, born in Scotland, became a chief figure in the Upper Missouri Outfit of the American Fur Company. See Annie Heloise Abel, *Chardon's Journal at Fort Clark 1834–1839* (Pierre, South Dakota, 1932).

[44] Andrew Drips, of course, although both Harris and Audubon wrote it as given. Drips was born in Ireland in 1789 and went to St. Louis in 1817, where he was associated with the fur trade on the Upper missouri. In 1842 he left the service of Pierre Chouteau, Jr., and Company to accept the post of Indian agent for the tribes of the Upper Missouri; four years later he was back with the fur company. The best brief account of his life and his career as Indian agent is that of Abel, *Chardon's Journal*, 259–63, note 247, which is based largely on the Drips MSS of the Missouri Historical Society. It was western custom to give every Indian agent the honorary title of Major.

[45] According to the *Baltimore Patriot* as quoted in *Niles National Register*, LXIV (June 10, 1843), 233–34, one letter Audubon wrote at this moment informed Dr. Gideon B. Smith "that the party are all well, in excellent spirits, and that they have procured specimens of several new quadrupeds and birds. A defect in the boiler of the steamboat had caused them to stop for a few hours [*sic*], but the repairs were just completed, and they would proceed immediately on their voyage."

[46] Alexander Harvey was responsible for this trouble at Fort McKenzie. See Chittenden, *The American Fur Trade* (1935), II, 685; and Charles Larpenteur, *Forty Years a Fur Trader on the Upper Missouri, The Personal Narrative of Charles Larpenteur*, ed. by Elliott Coues (2 vols., New York, Francis P. Harper, 1899), I, 217–19. Our travelers will meet with further rumors about this affair as they move upriver.

[47] "These boats are strong and broad; the tops, or roofs, are supported by bent branches of trees, and these are covered by water-proof Buffalo hides; each has four oarsmen and a steersman, who manages the boat standing on a broad board; the helm is ten feet long, and the rudder itself is five or six feet long." (Audubon, *Journals*, I, 500.) Audubon said the boats were carrying 10,000 robes (*Journals*, I, 499). Obviously someone was wrong.

to day, having worked hard enough to take a day's rest. Sprague shot today one of Bell's new Vireos[48] and one of my Finches, again a female but shot too badly to skin.

Friday, May 19th. Our accident is repaired at last and we got off at 3 A.M. We have had a dull day[49]—Stopped three times to wood but our stay was so short that we procured nothing—Saw a deer swimming the river. The last rise in the river has subsided very much and we saw fewer dead animals afloat. At the mouth of the Vermillion River we got aground and lost a couple of hours before we could find the channel. From the information received from Mr. Laidlaw we expect to see Buffalo by Sunday morning. They are much lower down the river than usual in consequence of the severity and long continuance of the winter.

Saturday, May 20th. Saw the first Buffaloes today, at a great distance passing the crown of a hill. Saw several wolves, and 3 deer, passed Jacque River.[50] Killed several specimens of *Pipilo arcticus*,[51] and have probably been among them for several days, they resemble so closely the Common Towhee Bunting that we may not have noticed them. There is a difference in the note which it is difficult to describe.

Sunday, May 21st. Stopped at the mouth of the *L'eau qui court* or Running River,[52] here we found a Fort (Fort Mitchell) which had been abandoned on account of the high waters and our folks went to work pulling down the stockades for fuel for the boat and carried off some furniture which was left in the houses.[53] Sprague shot here a *Say's Flycatcher*.[54] In the afternoon

---

48 This bird was discovered and named for Bell on this trip. See *The Birds of America,* VII (1844), 333–34.

49 On this day Harris began a long and interesting letter to Dr. Spencer, which he closed on June 1, at Fort Pierre. It is quoted in the introduction.

50 Also known as the James, Yankton, or Dakota River.

51 The Arctic Towhee. See *Ornithological Biography,* V, 49–51 (Plate 394).

52 The Niobara.

53 "It was no less than the Fort put up some years ago by Monsieur [Narcisse] Le Clerc." (Audubon, *Journals,* I, 504.) Built in 1833 and named for D. D. Mitchell, it had been abandoned in 1837 (Chittenden, *The American Fur Trade* [1935], II, 927).

54 *Ornithological Biography,* IV, 428–29 (Plate 359).

we were stopped on an island, (Poncah) said to be full of game and we took our guns to get some fresh meat. Bell shot a fine young deer with small shot. Saw three Elk and some 6 or 8 deer. There were Buffalo tracks on the Island. Sprague saw the Arkansas Flycatcher to-day.[55]

Monday, May 22nd. We have made but about 35 miles to-day. Have seen about 200 Buffaloes to-day, and at least 100 were in view at one time. Saw ten Antelopes together this afternoon. The Arkansas Flycatcher has been seen again today and Sprague shot one which lodged in the forks of a tree and could not be procured. We have seen a Meadowlark to-day which must prove a new one, its note is so entirely different from ours.[56] This morning a party of Indians on the East Bank near which we were passing beckoned us to stop, the Captain was not on deck and no notice was taken of their signal, as soon as the Boat had passed they ran ahead, secreted themselves behind trees and fired at us, at first we thought it was only a signal to stop, but the next shot passed within a few inches of the head of one of the men in the bow of the boat and fell in the water a few feet ahead. Five shots were fired and four struck the boat, one passed through the pantaloons of one of the trappers as he was sleeping below and lodged in a trunk. It was surprising that no one was hit, there could not have been less than 50 persons on deck at the time. The Captain supposed them to have been a war party of the Santee's a tribe living on the Mississippi River which frequently wanders over to this.[57] Stopped for the night at Cedar Island, covered with Red Cedar, which is to supply us with fuel for the morrow. The Captain put out a party of Hunters as soon as we landed, they are to walk some miles ahead and encamp and at early dawn start after Meat, and bring it to the shore where we can stop for them. Squires went with them.

Tuesday, May 23rd. Left the Island at early dawn, and had

[55] *Ornithological Biography,* IV, 422–25, (Plate 359).
[56] The Western Meadow Lark, known also as the Missouri Meadow Lark. See *The Birds of America,* VII (1844), 339–41 (Plate 489).
[57] See Audubon, *Journals,* I, 507.

scarcely gone 3 miles before we saw some of our hunters, and unfortunately for us and for them there was not enough water for us to land where they were, and it was about 2 miles farther before we came to shore, consequently they were obliged to leave most of their meat. They killed 4 Buffalo and had to leave nearly all for the wolves, a tongue and about 40 lbs. of meat were all they brought on board. Poor Squires had a rough time of it. They carried no blankets and the night was cold. In the morning Squires went to slack his thirst and found it to be strong Magnesia water, and they could find no other. I shot a common Rabbit today the first I have seen in a long time. After dinner we found ourselves pocketed, and the wind blowing hard we were soon fast aground[58] and had to send to an Island about 3 miles ahead for strong poles to shove us off by use of the windlass. They broke two sets procured at two different trips and we have to remain for the night and send for more in the morning. Thermometer at 92.

Wednesday, May 24th. This morning when the Barge started for the new poles, Bell and I went ashore in her.[59] We killed Redshafted Woodpecker,[60] Say's Flycatcher, Arkansas F., Lark Finch and several of the new Meadow Larks, for new I will insist it is, notwithstanding that we cannot from the books establish any specific difference, yet it is utterly impossible that the same bird in different parts of the world can have notes so totally different. But as we cannot set down these notes on paper, and

[58] In the middle of the river (Audubon, *Journals*, I, 509).

[59] It was a day filled with trouble for Sire. His log offers a good picture of the difficulties of navigation on the Upper Missouri: "We find the boat in the morning pretty much in the same situation. We set at work immediately and are just about to get afloat again when one of the spars breaks, and we are obliged to send 2 miles to look for another on an island where they are very scarce. It is 10:30 A. M. and the yawl has not yet returned. We met La Charité, who is descending the river in a skin canoe with goods for the Poncas and brings me a letter from Mr. H. Picotte. The yawl returns at last and we succeed in extricating ourselves, but we go aground again, again get off, and after having sounded again find only one passage and that a doubtful one. We lurch and break one of our rudders, but 10 minutes afterward we are afloat. We put ashore to mend the rudder, and meanwhile I have some wood cut from drift. At 6 P. M. we resume our journey."

[60] *Ornithological Biography*, V, 174–76 (Plate 416).

the world will not take our words for it if we do, we must be content to refrain from publishing this good species unless we can on our return find a something about the bird more than we can now discover to establish a specific difference: *Mais nous verrons*. We saw here for the first time the Lazuli finch.[61] I happened to see a herd of 12 to 14 Buffalo on the tops of the Hills about two miles off. I called Bell and we drew out shot and replaced them with Balls and commenced a most toilsome ascent in the heat of the day. The wind was in our favour to approach them, but unfortunately when we got within 150 yds of them, under cover of a small hill, the eddy of the wind enabled them to scent us and off they started, and we gained nothing by our very severe walk except a little experience in Buffalo hunting. We saw a great number [of] dead Buffalo calves on our tramp, and from the fact of our seeing no living ones it is evident that they were killed by the snow of the 5th. We saw far out in the Prairie a beautiful specimen of Townsend's Hare, within shot but we had nothing but Ball in our guns and it escaped us, running more gracefully than I have ever seen a animal of the genus. It stands erect on its legs while running and bounds away like a little Deer or Antelope, scarcely seeming to touch the Ground. I found a toad which differs from ours and may be new. We got on board about 3 o'clock and the boat under way ab[ou]t 4. Landed for the night on a low island which was covered with dead Buffalo calves, creating a most unpleasant atmosphere to breathe for the night. Allum in a crystalized state was found at our landing place this morning, and some of the ravines which are now dry are covered with an efflorescence which we suppose to be magnesia. Sulphur is said to be found here in abundance. The place is on the west bank and nearly opposite Bijou's Hills,[62] and about 30 miles below White River & 180 from Ft. Pierre.

While aground last evening, two boats landed on the shore near us and we sent our barge for the men. We found that they

[61] *Ornithological Biography*, V, 64–66 (Plates 398, 424).

[62] Named for Louis Bissonet *dit* Bijou (John C. Luttig, *Journal of a Fur Trading Expedition on the Upper Missouri 1812–1813*, ed. by Stella M. Drumm [St. Louis, Missouri Historical Society, 1920], 148–49).

were from Fort Pierre with Furs, there [*sic*] boats were in the form of scows and covered with Buffalo hides. They were 8 days from the Fort.[63] We passed today a bluff which was said to have been burning for two years, but it is now extinguished, it has the appearance of containing much sulphur. The fire appeared to be external as only smoke appeared.[64]

Thursday, May 25th. We have had a dull cold rainy day and have not been ashore with our guns and scarcely out of the cabin. Thermometer 50 to 53. The day before yesterday at 92. Met three Mackinaw Boats laden with furs belonging to the opposition company.[65] Expected to reach Great Cedar Island to-night but were obliged to stop short where there is no wood, but any quantity of dead Buffalo calves. The men found 2 specimens of the young Wood Rat, *Neotoma floridana,* in a hollow tree.[66]

Friday, May 26th. We put 3 men ashore at Laurel River about 60 miles by land & 150 by water from Ft. Pierre to make their way to that post with Dispatches from Capt. Sire.[67] We proceeded very slowly encountering numerous obstructions, until we reached the Great Bend, where all of our party (with the exception of Squires who is employed in taking the course of the river) went on shore about 5 o'clock P.M. to walk across the Isthmus and encamp for the night on the other side and await

[63] Sire and Audubon mentioned only one boat. Audubon referred to one man as "Mr. Charity," Sire called him "La Charité." Harris must have been mistaken in saying they were carrying furs, for Sire wrote that they were taking trade goods from Fort Pierre to the Poncas. Audubon reported them nine days from that fort.

[64] Although neither Harris nor Audubon mentions it in his journal, Audubon, in *The Birds of America* (VII [1844], 338–39), said that Bell this day shot the *Emberiza LeConteii* (LeConte's Sparrow) which appears in Plate 488. On this day, too, Audubon began a letter to Gideon Smith which has been quoted in the introduction.

[65] "These belonged to the (so-called) Opposition Company of C. Bolton, Fox, Livingstone & Co., of New York, and therefore we passed them without stopping; but . . . we had to stop also; and then some of the men came on board, to see and talk to their old acquaintances among our extraordinary and motley crew of trappers and *engagés*." (Audubon, *Journals*, I, 511.) For Fox, Livingston and Company—also known as the Union Fur Company—see Chittenden, *The American Fur Trade*, I, 367–71.

[66] *Quadrupeds*, I, 32–37 (Plate 4).

[67] In his letter of May 19 to Dr. Spencer, Harris gave the name of the river as Bazil, and the distances as 70 miles by land and 160 miles by watèr.

the arrival of the Boat tomorrow or whenever she may happen
to arrive. We took 3 good Hunters with us to carry our luggage,
act as guides, &c. &c. The distance is between two and three
miles across and 26 miles around.[68] We started on a beautiful
and very extensive level prairie lying just above the highest
freshets, and reaching about half way across, the rest was steep
and rugged hills of several hundred feet in height. On the Prairie
we found a village of Prairie Dogs, the first we have seen.[69] We
diverged a little from our path but did not succeed in shooting
any not having time to wait for them to come out of their holes
to reconnoiter after their first alarm. We found the ascent of the
hills extremely fatiguing from the peculiar nature of the soil, it
is a stiff clay mixed with shale which appears to have under-gone
the action of fire (the shale) and so moist and greasy that it was
with difficulty we kept our feet. The Geological character of this
country must receive more of our attention in descending, there
are said to be exceedingly interesting fossil remains of fishes and
shells on the tops of these hills. About this bend the strata of
Limestone which we have carried from Council Bluffs appear
to lose themselves under the bed of the River and at the turn of
the bend there is a chain of rocks across the river. The upper
structure of Yellow stone (which appears to be tinged with iron)
now only showing itself in fragments thickly strewed on the
banks superimposed by Black Shale which is forced to the summit (whereas lower down it only formed a portion of the summit). Started 4 Black-tailed Deer in crossing the hills, Bell shot
but did not stop any of them. We struck our camp on the River
shore under 6 Cotton Wood Trees growing in a clump, and after
making a good fire, Michaux and one of the Hunters started
after Deer, having still an hour or more of daylight. We had
hardly any time to refresh ourselves with a little bread and
cheese, before they brought in a fine yearling Buck of this new
animal to us. It was not long before some of the choice morceaux
were roasting before the fire impaled upon sharp sticks stuck in

[68] Audubon said, "quite four miles across" (*Journals*, I, 515).
[69] *Quadrupeds*, II, 319–26 (Plate 99).

the ground. We all agreed it was the best Venison we ever tasted, and none failed to do ample justice to the repast. Our beds were soon blown up and wrapped in our blankets with our guns by our sides, we were soon fast asleep.

Saturday, May 27th. A light rain in the night only made us hug our blankets the closer, and by the peep of day we were all stirring. We did not wait to break our fast but started off with our guns while the venison was cooking. I was out about an hour but met with nothing. Bell and the two hunters were gone 4 hours and walked several miles after Buffalo. They discharged their guns into an Old Bull at about 30 paces but he would not stop. We made no addition to our larder and by the time we had eaten again of the deer most heartily and redoubled our praises of its superior quality, it came on to rain quite hard, and we went to work to build a regular Camp of cedar boughs, fearing the boat might meet with obstructions and leave us out another night or two, particularly as our hunters having seen her from the hill-tops (whence the whole course of the river around the bend is visible) not more than two miles ahead of where we had left her at 5 P.M. yesterday. The Prarie Dog (*Arctomys Ludovicianus*) and the Black-tailed or Mule Deer (from the great size of its ears) were the only animals we saw there that were new to us on this trip, and we got no birds that we had not procured before. At 3 o'clock we left our camp and carried our effects down the river a few hundred yards as we heard the boat approaching, and we knew she would stop there to cut wood. As soon as the wood was on board we started but had not gone more than a mile and a half before we met with difficulties from the sand bars and had to send our Yawl out to sound, while performing this duty the report spread through the boat that they had been fired upon by Indians, we ran out to see but soon found that the Indians had only fired to induce them to stop. When they had found a channel we soon came up to the Indians, they were on horse back, 4 of them, fine looking well dressed fellows, they alighted and fired off their guns ahead

74

of the boat. Captain Sire who understands the Sioux language told them he would not stop there, but if they would follow us on we would soon stop for the night, when they could come on board. They mounted their horses, sitting on a Buffalo skin and we soon had them on board; their horses are the best we have yet seen among the Indians. They are of the Yanctonai tribe, a part of the Sioux nation. One of them, who is a chief, showed a treaty made with General Clark.[70] They proved great beggars and after we had given them some powder they wanted lead, as they said powder was of no use to them without balls. They staid aboard until about 12 o'clock.[71]

Sunday, May 28th. Transferred my Journal to a larger Folio.[72] I intend keeping a list of Birds & Quadrupeds in this and other etceteras.

We have had a beautiful day and few difficulties in the navigation of the river until about one mile above Fort George were obliged to stop for want of water and it is feared that tomorrow we shall be obliged to take our part of the cargo of the boat in order to cross the bar. Fort George[73] is the new establishment of the Opposition Company, it is about 30 miles from Fort Pierre. We stopped there a few moments to take in Major Hamilton[74] formerly Indian agent of this section, he is going to Fort Pierre. After we landed Mr Audubon and the Captain went down to the Fort, and as we shall not get off very early tomorrow I intend

[70] Possibly the one made July 19, 1815, at Portage des Sioux, near St. Louis.

[71] Sire merely noted: "Met 4 Yanctons who came on board." Audubon described them as "fine-looking fellows; the captain introduced Harris and me to the chief, and we shook hands all round." (*Journals*, I, 518.)

[72] And well he might—when one considers what he crowded into the pages of the pocket diary in the later part of May. These two manuscript books have been described in the preface. Notes in the small diary have been placed in their proper chronological place in the narrative.

[73] About twenty-one miles below Fort Pierre. It was built in 1842 by John A. N. Ebbits and F. Cutting for Fox, Livingston and Company (Chittenden, *American Fur Trade*, II, 929). This opposition company was bought out by P. Chouteau, Jr., and Company in 1845.

[74] Joseph V. Hamilton. At this moment, noted Audubon, he was "acting Indian agent here until the return of Major Crisp [Drips]. . . . I knew his father thirty-five years ago." (*Journals*, I, 519.)

to pay them a visit in the morning. There has been nothing of much interest today except the increase in the number of Buffalo seen, we may now say literally that we have seen thousands, in the course of a day. This morning a Common Wolf crossed the River within 30 to 40 yards of the boat, several rifles and two loads of buck shot were discharged at him but he kept on apparently unhurt. We saw 3 Buffalo swimming the river ahead of the boat but they landed before we could get a shot at them. Mr. Audubon and Squires walked down to the Fort. They found there a young Englishman of the name of Illingworth[75] who is at present superintendant of the establishment, also an assistant of the name of Taylor. One of the young Cuttings of New York, whose elder brother Robert I traveled with in Europe in 1830, was also there, he belongs to the concern, and arrived a short time since from the establishment at the mouth of the Yellowstone in a skiff, entirely alone, and he intends in a few days to continue his journey to St. Louis.[76] A few days since he was chasing Buffalo on horseback—a cow turned upon him and his horse in his fright reared up and fell upon him and sprained his ancle badly so that he is now unable to walk. It was the opinion of those who were with him that he would undoubtedly have been killed if he had not been so much hurt by the fall as to prevent his springing instantly to his feet.—Shot an Arkansas Flycatcher near the boat.

Monday, May 29th. The river was sounded this morning by the Pilots, and the conclusion is not to unload the boat but remain as we are to-day in hopes that the River will cut a channel by to-morrow. It is a curious fact that in a certain stage of the water in this River, while it is falling, there is less water in its channel than when it is lower. The reason is that water has a greater surface to flow over and discharge itself without cutting

[75] James O. Illingworth, according to letters of his in the Drips Papers, Missouri Historical Society.

[76] Some letters written by F. Cutting in 1844 are to be found in the Drips Papers, Missouri Historical Society. Audubon added: "Mr. Cutting . . . told me he had known Victor [Audubon] in Cuba." (*Journals*, I, 520.)

deep channels, but when the sand bars begin to peep above
the water and approach the surface, if I may so express myself, they form partial dams to the current, causing it to flow
more freely in the deeper parts and carry out the sand to be
deposited somewhere else. We soon shall see how this theory
works, or if it will work fast enough to answer the purposes.
Mr. Audubon and Major Hamilton walked down to the Fort
this morning and I followed in about an hour. Very fortunately I took my cane gun with me and shot with it two fine
male birds of the Black-headed Grosbeak[77]—*Coccoborus me-
lanocephalus,* a bird which has not heretofore been found this
side of the table lands of the Rocky Mountains. I shot two
Arkansas Flycatchers, a few Lark finches were killed today. In
the afternoon Mr. Audubon, Bell, Squires and myself walked
across the Praries two or three miles to a Prarie Dog Village
which Bell had found in the morning. We found it exceedingly
difficult to get shots at them, we were obliged to lie down and
wait a long time before they would come to the edge of their
holes, all that we shot succeeded in getting so far into their holes
that we could not procure them.[78] Bell saw a Burrowing Owl[79]
—We looked for Rattlesnakes among the lodges but could [not]
find any. I saw among the Burrows a Prarie Squirrel or Marmot
which I took for *tridicemlineatus.* It is the first animal of the
kind we have ever seen and I fear we shall find them still more
rare when the grass grows. Mr. Illingworth has sent out a hunter
to procure a Buffalo calf for Mr. Audubon. He had to go about
10 [16?] miles before he could begin to hunt so that there is
little chance of seeing him to-night. I must here correct an error
which we have all fallen into, and which goes to show how difficult it is for persons passing through a country to get correct information on all subjects they enquire about—Until we arrived
here everyone told us that the Buffalo calves were all dropped

[77] *Ornithological Biography,* IV, 519–21 (Plate 373).

[78] "Harris saw one that, after coming out of its hole, gave a long and somewhat
whistling note, which he thinks was one of invitation to its neighbors, as several came
out in a few minutes." (Audubon, *Journals,* I, 522–23.)

[79] *Ornithological Biography,* V, 264–69 (Plate 432).

before the snow of the 5th of May, and that there could be none in the country. Here we have positive information that there are calves to be found, and that the cows have not yet all dropped their calves. Bell saw a Magpie this morning.

[*Entry in Diary*] Killed two Black-headed Grosbeaks this morning   Males   Wrote to Dr Spencer to-day from Fort George by Mr Cutting who will go down the river in the skiff in 2 or 3 days   Bell saw the Evening Grosbeak?, a Magpie, and a Burrowing Owl—Spent the afternoon in a Prarie Dog Village but did not procure any

Tuesday, May 30th. The Buffalo hunters returned last night too late to bring their calf to the Boat, it was brought in this morning with the heads of two others. Mr. Illingworth went out himself with a hunter, they had nine miles to ride before they could commence hunting and it was late in the afternoon before they started, they killed notwithstanding, a Bull and a cow and three calves. Bell skinned out the calf and put the hide in pickle. Sprague commenced at once to make a drawing of the head of the size of life. Soon after breakfast when the pilots had sounded once more for a channel, steam was raised and the Capt. determined to make an attempt to force a passage although there were two bars to cross where there was not enough water by a foot to float the boat. By forcing the head of the boat on the bar and continuing to work the engine, we succeeded in forcing a channel through both of them by 4 O'Clock in the afternoon and we were once more on our way to the Fort. Before we started Mr. Picot,[80] Mr. Chardon[81] with several attendants joined us from the Fort in the Yawl of the Trapper. These gentlemen do not give any credit to the story of a Blackfoot chief having been killed by

[80] Honoré Picotte entered the Upper Missouri Outfit in 1830 after earlier connections with the Columbia Fur Company and the French Fur Company. Rudolph F. Kurz in his *Journal* (ed. by J. N. B. Hewitt [Washington, D. C., Bureau of American Ethnology, Bulletin 115, 1937], 235), said that in 1851 Picotte was in charge of the Lower Missouri Outfit which included Forts Pierre, Lookout, Vermilion, Clark, and Berthold.

[81] Francis A. Chardon, born in Philadelphia, was in the Upper Missouri country by 1829. For him consult Abel, *Chardon's Journal.*

one of their clerks, as they have received an express from their establishment at the mouth of the Yellowstone and not a word is said of the affair. We had about 25 miles to the Fort and were obliged to stop for the night when we were within 7 or 8 miles of our port. Nothing of interest today in the way of Natural History.

[*Entry in Diary*[82]] On the 10th and 12 inst also 26th will be found some remarks on the strata which are exposed to view in passing up the river. I will here endeavour to sum up all that I have been able to observe a[s] far as this place, Fort Pierre near the mouth of the Teton River. The Bed of stratified secondary limestone which appears at a very considerable height, say 250 feet, in the Bluffs on the Mississippi from their commencement above the mouth of the Ohio, appears to the eye to be perfectly horizontal and from the long distance which we carried it up the Mo. I have no doubt it is so. It appears to be composed of three varieties of rock, at least they are strongly marked by colour, the upper part of the bed is Bluish, the middle yellow and the lower a dark slate colour. As you ascend the river one after another of these divisions disappears below the water, no doubt from the rise in the bed of the river as you go towards its source. On reaching Bellevue the upper stratum of Limestone was even with the surface of the water and at Fort Croghan (The military Post since the abandonment of Council Bluffs) no rocks are to be seen. The debris here is gravel and water worn pebbles from a primitive formation, I observed no boulders. On Passing the old site of Council Bluffs about 30 miles above Bellevue, the Captain informed me that there was a chain of

---

[82] Harris made this long entry in the small diary, obviously in fulfillment of his obligations to the Academy of Natural Sciences. Since he himself had already incorporated similar observations in his regular daily entries, there seems good reason to bring this passage into the main body of his narrative. In the latter pages of the small diary, without regard to printed date lines, Harris had written a continuous account of his observations about this time: these notations have been entered here under the dates May 30, June 2, 6, and 8, in accordance with the internal dates which Harris used. Similar passages in September and October have likewise been brought into the main narrative. The paper Harris read to the Academy in 1845 appears in the appendix.

rocks across the River, which is no doubt the continuation of the St. Louis range of Limestone which disappeared at Bellevue. At Wood's Bluff [blank in MS] miles above Council Bluffs and ten or twelve Below Blackbirds Grave the Bluffs again put on the appearance of stratified rocks the upper bed of which is the yellow the Middle white and lower Slate colour and in their lamina like Shale, the Stone appears to be very soft and as we ascended the river some distance before we could positively determine whether it was rock or indurated clay. As we advanced it became harder retaining however nearly all the same colours the upper becoming a deeper yellow, evidently in many places strongly tinged with Iron, the middle has a yellower tinge and the lower becomes almost black. This formation continues nearly horizontal, until a few miles below the Great Bend of the Missouri the upper Bed sinks below the level of the water. This second great range of Limestone is slightly undulating in many places, but as far as we can judge it is on the whole nearly horizontal. At the Great Bend a second chain of Rocks crosses the River. For several days before reaching the Bend I observed overlying the regularly stratified rocks frequent outcroppings of what I take to be marl or soft limestone in their laminae intermixed with a blackish shale which has a glazed and burnt appearance, and the hills about the Bend contain a great deal of this substance the nature of which I am unable to determine, it appears to discompose and from a soil extremely retentive of water and so adhesive and slippery that it is exceedingly difficult to climb the hills of which it is composed, these hills are subject to continual landslides. The Hunters say that this soil continues wet throughout the longest drought of summer. This formation contains allum, magnesia and sulphur? and one or two of the knolls on the Bank of the River below the Bend, we were assured by Captain Sire and the Pilot was in a state of ignition for two years, during which time smoke constantly issued but no flame. Great quantities of fossil remains are said to be found in it, among which are some very perfect fishes. Occasional croppings out of this formation continue to within a few miles of this place—looking round from our present situation we can see none of the spots bare of vegetation by which its presence has heretofore been indicated. For 50 miles below the debris covering these formations and composing the soil of the upper Prairies is evidently of the same character as that of Fort Croghan but containing an immense number of larger boulders all of which that I have examined are of granite, but all that I can say at present about the formations on this river must be taken with great allowance for want of opportunities of close investigation. On our return I shall collect specimens by which those who are better qualified than myself will be able to come to some definite conclusion about the geological character of this great Valley.—Since leaving Fort Pierre the hills appear to be composed almost entirely of substance which I supposed to be marl or thin limestone. I have now every reason to believe it to be soft shale or clay, it is still mixed with the hard black shale which has undergone the action of fire. It displays a regular stratification and has evidently been much disturbed as the dip varies continually. A thin stratum, sometimes merely a point of a white substance, shows itself frequently in these hills, our Captain says it is magnesia and that it is sometimes used as medicine. At the Bend we found fragments of Shells in this formation. At Fort Pierre where the river has overflowed the bottoms and left a deposit, its upper surface is actually stony for about half an inch in depth and breaks with a crackling noise under your feet as you walk. I think it is harder than the substance called rottenstone, and quite as hard as the clay shale of which I spoke last. It does not effervesce with acids. This is the more remarkable as the water could not have left this deposit longer ago than 3 weeks and there have been several heavy rains within that time. I have no doubt it consists of the finest particles of the shale formation which have remained suspended in the water. Probably the picturesque clay hills of which travellers speak above this are of the same formation and perhaps rather shale than clay. After leaving Fort Pierre I observed a brownish stratified rock much broken, peeping out at about 20 to 40 feet above the river, but it is seen in but few places and is not in any more than 12 or 14 feet in thickness. There appears to [*sic*] large gaps or hollows in the shale formation (as I must call it by way of distinction) which are filled by the Boulder drift which probably covers the prairie at some distance from the river.

Wednesday, May 31st. It was not until 4 P. M. that we worked our way up to the Fort.[83] The water was so low and the sand bars so numerous. After all our complaints we are the most fortunate voyagers who ever ascended the Missouri River, we have arrived safely at this place with fewer difficulties than were ever before met with, and have made the passage in a much shorter time, and notwithstanding our very late start from St. Louis we are actually here [blank in MS] days earlier than the boats have ever reached here before. Mr Audubon went down to the fort (we were obliged to land a mile above the Fort for want of water) and the Capt went to work discharging the cargo. Here we shall leave about half our cargo and about equal proportion of our Trappers. This will cause the boat to draw less water and make better speed. The Capt still thinks it will not take more than 12 days to reach the Yellow Stone.

[83] According to Sire, they arrived at 3 P. M. The next day, writing to Lucy, Audubon declared: "Neither Harris, Squires or Myself have Shaved since we left St. Louis, and I have not once pulled off my breeches when I have tumbled down at night to Sleep." (Quoted by Arthur, *Audubon, an Intimate Life,* 456.)

JUNE
[1843]

Thursday, June 1st. I took a stroll up to the Fort this morning, it is an enclosure of strong pickets planted close together to the depth of 4½ feet and 22 feet high above the ground. The enclosure is 235 feet square, occupying therefore more than an acre of ground, within are all their buildings—dwellings, warehouses, stabling for their horses and cattle of which they have a large number. There are two bastions to the Fort. It is the manner that all the trading establishments are constructed, and they are sufficiently strong for protection against any attacks that can be made by the Indians.[1] Sprague made some outlines of Buffalo calves which they have among their cattle, with the *camera lucida.* I had my cane gun with me a[nd] had the good fortune to shoot another Black-headed Grosbeak, on my return to the Boat. Capt. Sire having discharged his cargo as well as the trappers who were to stop at this place we got under way at 12 O'Clock and crossed the river to where the Trapper lay to put on board of her our Mate Mᵣ Durac and our black Pilot Desirée who has undertaken to Pilot her down without an assistant, a pretty serious undertaking as he will be obliged to stick at the wheel the whole time the boat is running or from daylight to

[1] For a description of Fort Pierre the year after it was built see Maximilian, *Travels in the Interior of North America* (vol. XXII, Thwaites [ed.], *Early Western Travels*), 317–18. John Palliser (*Solitary Rambles and Adventures of a Hunter on the Prairies* [London, Murray, 1853], 103–104) described the fort four years after Harris's visit.

83

dark. Mr. Chardon goes up with us, and several trappers from Fort Pierre, among the rest a half breed named Alexis Bombarde[2] who is a capital hunter and will supply us with meat on the passage. Mr. Picot gave him directions to procure any animals that Mr. Audubon might wish to procure, this man we hope will be a valuable acquisition to us. We completed our arrangements with the Trapper and got under way at 2 P.M. we had to stop for wood about 15 miles from the Fort where I shot two Arkansaw Flycatchers. Soon after we left the wooding place Mr. Chardon came to the Capt. and informed him that an Indian was concealed on board whom he (Chardon) had flogged at one of the upper stations, and that he had not doubt his object was to kill him, the Capt. told him he should be put ashore, the boat was run to the shore on the Fort Pierre side, the Indian's pack was thrown on the bank, and with a push Chardon sent the Indian after it up to his waist in water. This affair will never be forgotten by the Indian, and Chardon is enough of an indian to bear it in mind also, so that it will probably sooner or later result in the death of one or the other of the parties.[3] We stopped for the night about 25 miles from the fort, the best run probably that we have made since we have been on the river, for the time. There are here some houses of a trading post which was established last year by the company but abandoned in consequence of an attack by the Indians, in which one of the latter was killed and one wounded, one of the whites was shot through the thigh, believing himself maimed for life and no longer able to procure a living, he crawled to the river bank and threw himself in.[4]

[*Entry in Diary*] Wrote a long letter of 2 sheets closely written to Dr Spencer to go by the Trapper.[5]

[2] His name was LaBombarde. "He is a first-rate hunter, and powerfully built; he wears his hair long about his head and shoulders, as I was wont to do; but being a half-breed, his does not curl as mine did." (Audubon, *Journals,* I, 529.) John Durack, mentioned above, was mate of the *Nimrod* (the Fur Company's Missouri River steamboat) in 1844. In 1850, as captain of the *El Paso,* he established a record for steam navigation of the Missouri.

[3] Cf. Audubon, *Journals,* I, 528.

[4] Sire identified this site as "old Fort George" but did not mention the incident of the suicide of the white man. Audubon did not refer to this stopping place.

[5] This was the letter begun on May 19 and closed on June 1. The sheets were indeed closely written.

Friday, June 2nd. We have made a fine run today, started at
3 A. M. and stopped at 8 P. M. The river still continues to rise, consequently the obstructions are few. It is evident the Buffalo travel
and shift their ground a great deal, we found them in very great
numbers below Fort Pierre, and when we reached here, Mr.
Chardon who had described the river a few days before told us
that when we got about 50 miles above the fort we would see
one hundred Buffaloes, where we saw one below it, we have however come over one hundred miles and have not seen 50 Buffaloes.
One of the persons[6] whom we took in at Fort P. shot a Buffalo
from the deck of the Boat this afternoon, he fired into a gang
of 12 or 14 who were lying down when the boat came upon
them and wounded a young Bull so that he left the herd, the
Boat was stopped about a quarter of a mile above where there
was some driftwood, and men dispatched after the wounded animal. They found him standing in a bunch of Bushes, and fired
into him again and killed him, he was soon butchered and
brought on board leaving nothing but the skin and the head.
Some of our hunters gave chase to the herd who had retired
slowly up the hill, but they could not overtake them. We have
seen more wolves today than usual, twelve or fourteen have been
counted, one crossed the bow of the boat to Day, in swimming
the river and was run over by the wheel and shot at by 3 or 4
persons and escaped. We passed the Shienne [Cheyenne] River
to-day on the west side.

[*Entry in Diary*] The formation continues the same today,
what I took to be rock yesterday was an outcropping of the hard
shale, of a reddish colour, it begins to show itself more frequently.
The boulders appear to increase in quantity and in size. I observe to day in the soft shale fissures at right angles to the strata
containing a transparent crystallized mineral which I suppose
to be gypsum. I also procured a specimen of the white substance

---

[6] Apparently this was Charles Primeau (Audubon, *Journals,* II, 6). At this time
he was a clerk of the American Fur Company; later (in 1850) he was a partner in
Harvey, Primeau and Company, the new Opposition Company.

supposed to be magnesia, it covers the sides of the hills of soft shale in small patches quite white, and is evidently deposited by the rain springs which are now dried up and have left an efflorescence of this substance on the shale, sticks on every thing which it has passed over, it may be collected in considerable quantities tolerably pure.

Saturday, June 3rd. Alexis a half-breed hunter who was put on board at Fort Pierre and placed entirely under Mr. Audubon's direction went ashore last night about eleven o'clock and walked several miles ahead in order to get a few hours hunting before the boat could overtake him. He came on board at 10 o'clock having procured only 3 Prarie Dogs.[7] The shot we had furnished him with proved too large for these animals, and they were unfit for drawing or skinning. Mr. Audubon took very particular measurements of two of them, male and female. We stopped to cut wood a short time before dinner on a sand bar and a Wolf was reported on the bar. Bell, the Carpenter and I started after it with our guns. It was at the upper end of the bar and when we were within 120 yards it ran across the bar and dropped below the bank, as though he intended to take the water across the narrowest channel to the Main land. On reaching the spot we could find no wolf. Bell ran across the bar, not more than 20 yards and when he reached the Bank, Mr. Wolf was 20 yards out in the river swimming for his life, which was not long spared him. Bell fired a load of Buckshot into his head, and killed him instantly. He floated down and was picked up by the boats yawl. The rascal had the cunning to make a feint of taking the water on one side and ran around the point of the bar, under shelter of the bank and jump into the water on the other side. Mr. Audubon preserved the head and feet, of the latter Sprague made figures of the natural size, showing the front and back of both and fore and hind feet. Forty measurements were taken before the body was thrown overboard. He measured from the

[7] The next day Audubon wrote: "I forgot to say that along with the three Prairie Marmots, he brought also four Spoon-billed Ducks, which we ate at dinner to-day, and found delicious." (*Journals,* II, 4.)

tip of the nose to the root of the tail 41½ inches. Tail vertebra 15 in. Height at Shoulder 27½ in. of hind parts 26⅝. We saw two magpies today and a Goose with one Gosling.

Sunday, June 4th. We passed the old Riccaree Village where Gen¹ Ashley was beaten by the Indians with the weapons which he sold them and lost 18 of his men.[8] It proved a great advantage to him in pecuniary point of view as he was driven to another point of the country where he procured a large quantity of Beaver Skins for a mere trifle. Stopped for wood at an old trading post and tore down the house which was built of Ash logs and made us most excellent fire wood. Saw but one wolf today and very few Buffaloes. Bell shot a sparrow closely resembling Henslow's Bunting about which we are very doubtful. Stopped for the night at another abandoned trading post of the company.[9]

Monday, June 5th. This morning saw five Buffalo on the margin of the River under a very steep bluff. Seeing little prospect of their escaping we got our guns. The leading Buffalo was some distance ahead of the others and succeeded in finding foothold to ascend the Bank, the others missed his track and the boat hurried them on to a spot where they could neither ascend nor walk along the margin and they were obliged to take to the water and swim directly across the bow of the boat. We now felt sure of some Buffalo Stakes, and we posted ourselves in the bow. Some six or eight balls and two loads of Buck Shot were fired at them within fifteen paces of them, but alas none were stopped. The fault was no doubt in waiting until they had crossed the bow of the boat, as we had nothing to shoot at but their heads, and the back of the head is so completely shielded by the great mass of bone connecting the horns that it would

---

[8] The attack occurred on June 2, 1823; Ashley reported twelve men killed and eleven wounded (of whom two died); consult Donald McKay Frost, "Notes on General Ashley, the Overland Trail and South Pass," *Proceedings of the American Antiquarian Society,* October, 1944.

[9] Sire wrote in the *Log:* "Stopped again at La Chapelle Point where we take in the remains of the Primeau houses. Passed *La Bourbeuse,* Fort Manuel, and camped at Primeau's Fort a little below Beaver River."

require a nice shot to kill them in that position. Had we fired when the side of the head was presented, in the region of the ear one or two of them must have been killed, especially with the Buckshot. We watched them across the river at about two-thirds the distance one of them dropped away from the rest and grounded on a sand bar, where after resting a few minutes he swam again towards the shore where he doubtlessly perished and perhaps the whole of them as the bank was too steep for them to climb.[10] Our progress has not been good today in consequence of having taken wood at one of the Company's houses (which are now becoming frequent) which had been cut for the boat and had been over-flowed and completely watersoaked, they were obliged to put rosin into the furnace to make it burn.[11]

Tuesday, June 6th. Last night the Capt. ordered the engineer to call the hands at 12 o'clock to get up steam that we might take a very early start so as to reach Fort Clark at the Mandan village to-night, the prospect seemed very fair until about 8 o'clock we were bothered by sand bars and lost three hours and thereby lost the chance. While detained here we saw a flock of 25 Canada Geese & another of 18 passing to the North, this is the more remarkable as we have seen them in pairs for a long time and within a few days have several times seen the old geese accompanied by goslings. We passed the "Square Hills"[12] this afternoon—a short time before dinner we met 4 Mackinaw boats belonging to our company going down the River. We stopped and gave them 4 men in place of four they had taken at Fort Clark in consequence a like number having deserted and gone back to Fort Union.[13] Mr. Kipp[14] late superintendent at the Fort

10 Audubon reported an incident on June 5 which Harris omitted: "We passed this afternoon a very curious conical mound of earth, about which Harris and I had some curiosity, by which I lost two pounds of snuff, as he was right and I was wrong." (*Journals*, II, 7.)

11 Cf. Sire, *Log*: ". . . Bouis' wintering house, where we fill the boat with worthless wood, which makes me curse all the rest of the day."

12 ". . . which, of course, are by no means square, but simply more level than the generality of those we have passed for upwards of three weeks" (Audubon, *Journals*, II, 9).

in the Blackfoot country at the Falls of Missouri was with these boats and returned with us to Fort Union. These boats carry with them a man of the name of Johns who was recently badly shot by the Blackfeet Indians. They confirm the report that one of their Clerks having shot a Blackfoot Chief. They say that the traders are obliged to confine themselves to the fort, and that only five of the Blackfeet are admitted at a time to trade. This state of affairs will prevent our visiting that interesting region. It has been raining nearly all day and we have done nothing in the way of shooting. To-morrow soon after breakfast we hope to reach the Village, and after so severe a storm we trust we shall have fine weather to pass the most interesting portion of the River containing the famous clay Bluffs which have excited so much notice from travellers. This morning there was a heavy white frost at 6 A. M., the thermometer was at 41. Wrote to Dr Spencer by the barges.

[*Entry in Diary*] Wrote a short letter to Dr Spencer by 4 Mackinaw Boats we met to day.—

[*Entry in Diary*] About 40 miles below the Mandan Fort the shale & clay formation first noticed below the great Bend disappears below the bed of the river, the Stratum which overlies it I believe to be the brownish stone seen soon after leaving Fort Pierre, I have had no opportunity whatever of examining this Rock and cannot speak of its character. On passing the mouth of Cannon Ball river yesterday we noticed a remarkable formation of this stratum of round masses of the rock in the divisions of the strata many of them apparently perfectly spherical and from 18 inches to 30 inches in diameter, some are as perfect as cast balls, and others appear to be flattened or composed of two

---

[13] "Mr. Kipp had a peculiar looking crew who appeared not much better than a set of bandits among the Pyrenees or the Alps; yet they seem to be the very best sort of men for trappers and boatmen. We exchanged four of our men for four of his, as the latter are wanted at the Yellowstone." (Audubon, *Journals*, II, 9.) The mackinaws were continuing to St. Louis in charge of Bruyière (Sire, *Log*).

[14] James Kipp, a Canadian. Much about him can be found in the journals of Maximilian, Chardon, Culbertson, and Kurz.

sections of a sphere, from a smaller arc up to a hemisphere, joined together with mathematical nicety, and surrounded by a belt or zone at the junction, which zone corresponds with the line of division of two strata. I had observed traces of this peculiarity in this bed of rock the day before, and this evening say 30 miles below the Mandans I noticed it again. Cannon ball river takes its name from the presence of these balls. They are said to contain crystals and are hollow in the center. Square Hills about 30 miles below the Mandans are several hundred feet high and appe[a]r to have stratified rock on their summits of the same colour as the last named formation. It is not until we pass the Mandans that the remarkable clay hills spoken of by Catlin and others are met with.

Wednesday, June 7th. Arrived at the Mandan Village this morning at 7.[15] The village is now occupied by the Ricarees old enemies of the Mandans, the latter having been obliged to succumb since their fearful reduction by the Small Pox, they have retired two or three miles further up the river, and are now considered as incorporated in the nation of the conquerors. The day has proved most unfortunate for our visit, a cold northeast wind and rain pouring down nearly the whole day. Notwithstanding, as this is our only day here, we determined to see all we could and walked up to the Fort and procured us an Indian Guide who took us to the Medicine Lodge and into his own lodge where we partook of the hospitality of the inmates by taking their mush.[16] We certainly paid our visit under very unfavorable cir-

[15] That is, Fort Clark. Audubon thought it "a poor miniature representation of Fort Pierre" (*Journals,* II, 13–14).

[16] The Medicine Lodge was about twenty-three yards in diameter. "Looking around, I saw a number of calabashes, eight or ten Otter skulls, two very large Buffalo skulls with the horns on, evidently of great age, and some sticks and other magical instruments with which none but a 'Great Medicine Man' is acquainted." In the lodge of the guide a man "made signs for me to sit down; and after Harris and I had done so, he rose, squatted himself near us, and, getting out a large spoon made of boiled Buffalo horn, handed it to a young girl, who brought a great rounded wooden bowl filled with pemmican, mixed with corn and some other stuff. I ate a mouthful or so of it, and found it quite palatable; and Harris and the rest then ate of it also." (Audubon, *Journals,* II, 12–13.)

cumstances, not at all calculated to draw from us so bright a picture as our illustrious predecessor, Catlin, has given to this place.[17] We all came to the conclusion that it was one of the dirtiest places we had ever seen human beings congregate in. The lodges are pretty much as he described them in a circular form &c and all covered with earth, and they are built so close together that there is barely room for two persons to pass between them and pick their way among the filth. In spite of the cold and storm these kindly sons of the praries were shoeless, breechless and shirtless, the universal Buffalo robe being their only covering, and that generally thrown gracefully into their lap when they are seated. To do them justice however they are a fine noble looking race of men, above the average in height and stout, with clean sinewy limbs but without the muscular development of the white man. Compared with our little Canadian Trappers below they are very giants and yet such is the superiority of civilized over savage culture that the Trappers will traverse the country of the most hostile tribes and generally succeed in triumphing over mere force and numbers. Our boat was crowded all day with Indians and we had to keep our staterooms locked and a sharp lookout besides to prevent thieving, for such is the character of nearly all these tribes. That this faculty should have been acquired through their intercourse with the whites I can hardly credit, but I will not venture yet to form an opinion on the subject until I have seen more of them. The only event of interest which has occurred was the calling together of the head men of the village on board the boat to the number of 134 to partake of a cup of coffee and some buiscuit and have a speech translated to them from our worthy Captain and another from Chardon recounting to them the great advantage that must accrue to them from continuing to trade with *our company* and having as little to do as possible with the opposition

[17] George Catlin, *Illustrations of the Manners, Customs, and Conditions of the North American Indians* (7th ed., 2 vols., London, 1848), I, 81–88. Such comparisons were not entirely fair, for Catlin was describing the Mandans while they were a powerful and prosperous tribe; Audubon and Harris were visiting Arikaras who occupied an old Mandan village.

&c. &c. after which a quantity of tobacco was distributed among them after which the council broke up with apparent satisfaction on both sides. The evidence of the great mortality among the poor Mandans is seen in the numerous small mounds on the prairies around the village, where the bodies were thrown on the surface and a small mound raised over them, these mounds are still bare of vegetation. The mortality was too great for them to give them the usual burial rites of their people by elevating the bodies on a scaffold as described by Catlin.[18] I regret very much that we shall not have an opportunity at this time to see the small remnants of the Mandans, a people who have excited so much attention from their differences in colour, habits and customs from all the other tribes on the continent, and about whom so much has been written. We are assured that some families of them were nearly white and that many of them had light hair. The village is on a fine bluff of the Prarie of 50 or 60 feet above the river, and with the Fort near it forms a picturesque scene and under more favorable circumstances would have called forth some of our enthusiasm which has been terrifically chilled by this dismal weather. It has cleared off this evening and the boat will be under way at 3 o'clock in the morning. We are told that it has been raining here for eight days.

Thursday, June 8th. The weather proved very fine this morning with the wind from the north. About 12 miles from the Mandans we stopped near the village of the Minatarees or Grosventres and were detained about an hour with the ceremony of presenting tobacco and making speeches as of yesterday. Nothing else of interest has occurred today with the exception of one of the men having caught a young hare (L. Townsendi) It was grown to nearly the size of a rabbit, and was so strongly marked as not to be mistaken. This settles a question which arose between Mr. Audubon & Dr. Bachman as to another hare which Townsend brought and which they did not describe as new fearing it might be the young of the species. Townsend will

[18] *North American Indians,* I, 89–90.

therefore have the credit of having added another new species to our Fauna. The hills today are beginning to put on those remarkable forms which Catlin and other travellers ascribe to them in this portion of the river.[19] There is not however much variety in the colours of the Clays of which they are formed. There is a stratum near their base which contains three seams of a substance which appears to be an imperfect coal. We have made an excellent run today, nearly sixty miles and if we continue at this rate our anticipations of making the shortest trip will be fully realized.

[*Entry in Diary*] The stratum containing the round stones has dipped below the water, the hills now (above the Mandans) are almost entirely clay stratified, with a stratum some 20 feet from the water containing in places 3 seams of what appears to be an imperfect coal, they are about 2 feet apart, the lower one say 3 to 4 feet thick, the middle one 2 ft. and the upper 8 or nine inches, this line of stratum alternates with this substance and a brick red clay or perhaps the pumice described by Catlin, but we have had no opportunity whatever of inspecting it. The surface of the upper hills when exposed to view is covered with boulders and we can see that the boulder formation varies in thickness in different places.

Friday, June 9th. A white frost this morning was followed by a beautiful day, saw a good deal of game today—the bottom lands are now much better covered with timber than they have been for some hundreds of miles, and we are told that the balance of the route is pretty well timbered. Saw a good many elk to-day, they are fond of timbered bottoms. Passed the Little Missouri River—having started with a good supply of wood it was late when we stopped. Bell and I shot some Emberiza Pallida & Bay-winged Buntings.[20] While we stopped a Buffalo Cow swam the River and landed 2 or 3 hundred yards above the boat. Mr. Kipps hunter shot it in the head at a few paces under the steep bank

---

[19] *North American Indians*, I, 69–78.
[20] *Ornithological Biography*, I, 473–75 (Plate 94).

which the animal could not ascend, and fearing it might float away he sprang into the water and got astride the cow until a rope was thrown to him from the shore, which he made fast and then swam along side of it to the boat where it was soon hoisted on the forward deck and cut up in very short time. This cow appeared to be about 7 years old and measured 8 feet from the tip of the nose to the root of the tail 4 ft 9½ inches at the shoulder and 4 ft 2 in at the Rump. Mr. Audubon saved the head to be outlined size of life, and intends to preserve it in pickle. The butchering of the cow on the deck was a novel and interesting scene, the dispatch was quite equal to hog killing in Cincinnati. A couple of Indians we took on board at Fort Clark (Mandans) watched the operation with an intent not a whit less than that of novices—as soon as the cow was opened they seized upon the stomach which is usually called the Manifold, emptied the contents, dipped it in warm blood of the animal, and no Lazaroni of Naples could have done better justice to his Maccaroni nor in quicker time. I could not be induced to taste it although assured by old hunters that it was really delicious. The udder was served in the same way by the Indians. Our Yawl was damaged in coming to this place. It was taken on board and we crossed the river to a sand beach where there was plenty of drift wood, and while the men were engaged in cutting it Bell & I went out with our Guns. I started an Elk and followed him and soon saw him again at about 200 yards. I had ball in my gun—succeeded in getting within about 120 yards of him and as he showed indications of starting I fired but did not hit him, in this way I followed him until I got four shots 2 standing at long shots and 2 running, none of which told. This has taught me that with the large animals in this country there is no need of being in a hurry about shooting, by a little art in still hunting you may easily approach them as they never, like our wild deer in Jersey, go off at a full run for miles, but always stop and look about them and ascertain the nature of the danger which threatens them, when it is not difficult to approach them by hiding (when you are in the woods) and approaching quietly under

94

cover, always being careful they do not get wind of you. After the last shot at the Elk and while following him to get another, six Buffaloes crossed the track about 200 yds ahead and I went after them, but the bell ringing and they having gained the Prairie I gave up the pursuit, on getting on board I found that Bell had been amusing himself with firing at this gang of Buffaloes, which then consisted of 7 and a calf, he fired 5 times, once with small shot at the calf which he wounded, and he also wounded badly a young bull, but the Bell ringing he had to leave them, they were no doubt killed as the gang passed me minus these two. One of the Negro fire-tenders shot two Townsend Hares with his rifle—one was so badly shot that he left it on the ground, the other he brought to Mr. Audubon. It was measured and weighed.—Weight 6½ lbs. Old Male.

	Inches
Length from nose to root of tail	21½
" " " " end " "	26½
" " " " anterior canthus of eye	2¼
" " " " opening of ear	4¾
" " fore to hind claw stretched	37
Height of ears	5½
Between anterior of eyes	1⅞
Length of eye	¾
Across the head	4⅝
Over " "	5¼
Length of forefoot to end of claws	3
Heel to end of claws	5⅝

Saturday, June 10th. We stopped last night in a fine looking bottom for game and Bell & I left orders to be called at daylight. We were up at half past 3, and soon found an Elk which we followed for some distance but could not get a shot at it. Bell went on the Prarie and shot a Sharp-tailed Grous,[21] the first we have seen. When we returned on board we found that we had

[21] *Ornithological Biography*, IV, 569–71 (Plate 382).

been within 300 yds of some Buffalo which were feeding in the bottom ahead of us but hidden by a point of the Bluff, and that two hunters had started after them, who were to go ahead and be picked up by the boat. We had not gone more than a mile when one of them came to the Bank and told us they had killed two Buffaloes. The boat came to, the trappers were dispatched after the meat, in a very short time we saw a portion of them returning with the meat of one on their backs, and the rest of them, 35 in number, dragging the carcass of the other by a long rope. We were soon under way and the meat was soon butchered and in the larder. I saw a gang of Elks as we passed along consisting of at least 30. We now appear to have really got into a game country. We passed through the Great Bend to-day (Great Bend the 2d) and here we found the Clay Hills very picturesque and beautiful, but not yet answering the description given by Catlin as regards colouring and we are beginning to fancy there has been some stretching of the imagination. We shall be able to judge better when we have seen some more of them. Soon after passing the Bend a party of Assineboin Indians 2 or 3 men and a half a dozen squaws[22] and children hailed the boat and their head man came on board, and the Captain presented him with some tobacco and he went off in a huff because he could not also get some powder and lead. On the opposite side of the next bend we saw another small party of Indians approaching the shore. The Cap[t] however refused to stop for them all [so?] that we were under the necessity of offending two parties of Indians in one day.[23] We saw in the Great Bend 5 Bighorns[24] at one time and 3 at another and again 3 more.

Sunday, June 11th. We continue to make fine running today, the small rise that has taken place in the river has been sufficient to carry the boat over all the sand bars. It is very probable we

---

22 Ten Indians altogether, said Audubon (*Journals*, II, 25); four lodges, according to Sire (*Log*).

23 The same Indians (Sire, *Log*).

24 *Quadrupeds*, II, 163–72 (Plate 73). Audubon first mentioned them in his entry for the next day.

Camp on the Missouri

from a drawing by Isaac Sprague

View on the Missouri River, above Great Bend

from a water-color drawing by Isaac Sprague

American Bison or Buffalo

from Audubon and Bachman,
Quadrupeds of North America, Vol. II, Plate LVII

shall reach the Yellowstone to-morrow night. This morning a Buffalo was seen under the Bluff which was too steep for him to climb. Guns were soon ready, just before the boat reached him he turned into a ravine. We were surprised to find on approaching it that he was waiting for us within point blank shot, a round of three or four guns were fired first without sensible effect and he turned to run up the ravine, when another round brought him to and he tumbled headlong into the ravine, and we lost sight of him—having plenty of meat on board the Capt would not stop for him and we left him for the wolves and Ravens.

Monday, June 12th. We have seen today great numbers of Elk and the Common Deer, we also saw a pack or 12 or 14 Sharptailed Grous. Can it be they have not paired at this late season? We have not yet seen a Grizly Bear. The Capt says he has never been on a trip up the river without seeing 3 or 4 of these animals. On passing some hills about 3 miles below the Mouth of the Yellow Stone we had the satisfaction of seeing a large band of about 23 Bighorns bounding over the steepest part of the hills, it was a beautiful sight and we are anxious to try our skill in procuring some of these rare animals, although everyone tells us that it will be difficult undertaking. We reached the Fort about 7 o'clock P.M. having performed the trip in some 17 hours less than 7 weeks and arrived here earlier in the season by one day than has ever been done before and made a quicker passage than any other boat by about 15 days.

Tuesday, June 13th. The Captain has been very busy in discharging and taking on cargo, and we have been equally busy in closing our letters[25] as the Captain assures us he will start for

[25] Audubon dated the following short letter to Gideon B. Smith from "Fort Union, three miles above the mouth of the Yellow Stone river, lat. 47° 20′ north June 13, 1843" (*Niles National Register*, LXIV [July 29, 1843], 347). "We have arrived safe, all well, yesterday afternoon at this place, which is unlike anything I ever saw before. I cannot write you a long letter, on account of the confusion and excitement at this moment among us. We are in the very midst of the game country. We saw yesterday no less than 22 mountain rams together, scampering over the high clay hills close to our boat. We have made the quickest trip ever performed by steam to this place, and that without touching a single snag, or having scarcely an accident worthy of remark. We intend leaving this on our way downward, on the 15th or 20th

St. Louis tomorrow morning, as the river is falling and he has a natural antipathy to sand bars and snags. Mr. Culbertson[26] is the superintendant at this station, he has been on board and offered us his services and the command of all the means of the establishment to further the accomplishments of our views. We paid a visit to the Fort which is constructed on a plan similar to the others, excepting that the logs which, in others, are planted in the ground are here framed, on a stone foundation, so as to form a gallery from which a beseiged party may fire over the ramparts at the enemy. The building and appointments throughout are of a description superior to any Fort we have seen on the river.[27] We remained on board the boat today and intend to sleep on board tonight—we have taken nearly all our baggage to the Fort where we have a room about 12 by 14 for our party of 6, for old Mr. Provost,[28] the captain of the Trappers up to this place is now one of our party, and will take Command of our barge and pilot us down the river. We have heard the Blackheaded Grosbeak singing beautifully today in the bushes near the boat. Wrote Mrs Patterson.

Wednesday, June 14th. We got our beds and few etceteras on shore this morning and at seven o'clock the Omega got under

---

of August, and proceed slowly to afford us all opportunities possible to collect whatever we can, as well specimens as knowledge of things that we could not study on our way up."

26 Alexander Culbertson (1809–78), after Kenneth McKenzie probably the most important fur trader on the Upper Missouri. In 1840 he succeeded McKenzie in command of Fort Union and in 1848 was in charge of all the Upper Missouri and Yellowstone River posts. The best brief account of him is that of Anne McDonnell, "Fort Benton and Fort Sarpy Journals," *Historical Society of Montana Contributions,* X (1940), 240–42. See also, among others: Maximilian, *Travels in North America;* Abel, *Chardon's Journal;* Audubon, *Journals;* Kurz, *Journal;* Chittenden and A. T. Richardson, *Life, Letters and Travels of Father De Smet* (4 vols., New York, 1905); and Hazard Stephens, *Life of General I. I. Stevens.*

27 For an elaborate description of this fort, written on July 30, 1843, at the request of Audubon (?), see *Journals,* II, 180–88.

28 This is the famous Etienne Provost, one of the claimants for the discovery of the South Pass. By this time he has been more than thirty years in the Upper Missouri country. P. Chouteau Jr. & Co. Ledger GG, 348, shows that Etienne Proveau was paid (for Audubon) $214 at the rate of $50 per month for his services from June 13 to October 19.

weigh—as the Captain told us he was going to take in wood a couple of miles below we concluded to walk down to the wood-yard and make our congée to our worthy Captain, we soon found our task was not so easy as we had calculated upon, the distance was not far short of three miles and through a bottom covered with a thick growth of young timber and a heavy under-growth and a good part of the way without paths, in fact we did not reach the boat until a few moments before the Captain had got his wood on board, and we bade him adieu and wished him a speedy passage home, and we took our leave of the Omega in a heavy shower of rain.[29] In returning with those belonging to the Fort we found a Cart road and got along without diffi-culty. The rest of the morning was occupied in putting our "fixings to rights" so that we could camp on the floor of our narrow quarters. As the day of departure of the Boat is always held as a holiday at the Fort, we could do nothing more in the way of business. In the afternoon it was proposed that Mr. Cul-bertson and some of his most expert hunters should show us how wolves were run down on horseback. There was no difficulty in finding the game as they were always to be seen prowling about within a mile of the Fort. It was not long before Mr. Wolf made his appearance—the horses were sent for (to the Prarie) and were soon ready for the chase. Mr Culbertson got the start and started his beautiful Blackfoot Pied mare at full speed, when within a half mile of the wolf, who turned and galloped off leisurely until Mr C. was within two or three hundred yards of him when he started off at the top of his speed, at this moment Mr C. fired his gun to show us his dexterity in reloading while his horse was at full speed. The interest in the chase now became highly exciting but unfortunately the beast took for the rising ground and both wolf and pursuer were lost sight of over a small hill. In a very short time we saw Mr C. returning at full speed and we soon perceived he was holding the wolf on the

[29] The *Omega* reached St. Louis in time for breakfast on June 29 (Sire, *Log*). The next day the *Missouri Republican* listed cargo as 800 packs of buffalo robes, 30 packs of beaver, and about 25 packs of tongues.

horse in front of the saddle. As he came nearer the Fort he practiced a maneuvre which is common among the Indians and hunters which we had not seen before, that of guiding the horse while at full speed by the inclination of the body, the reins being thrown upon the neck, as they necessarily were during the chase for the convenience of loading and firing—it was well done and had a fine effect as he leaned over to one side the mare performed a gentle curve in that direction when he would suddenly shift his body to the other side and the well-trained animal swayed over in the required direction, thus making for the last half mile in a serpentine track. This beautiful exhibition was performed in almost as short a time as I have taken to relate it, the distance rode was about 3 miles and we all regretted that we had not thought of taking the time. The wolf was shot through the lungs and shoulders (both of which were broken) from the horse while both were at full speed, he had two bullets in the gun and both passed through him. The performance of the mare must not be forgotten, and has given us a more favourable impression of the Indian horses than we had before entertained, instead of exhibiting signs of distress we had looked for, the noble little animal did not draw a long breath, and the motion of her nostrils was scarcely quicker than when she started— in a few minutes she was turned out on the prarie to graze with the rest of the horses. I look upon the performance of the horse as excellent when it is considered that she had never eaten a mouthful of grain in her life, but it is said that this is nothing to what she performs in a day's hunt. In the course of the afternoon chase was given to another wolf, but as he took across the hills at a very unfavourable place covered with rocks and stones the hunters did not think it worth while to continue the chase. In returning to the Fort, they gave us an exhibition of loading and firing as they do in Buffalo hunting, frequently killing five and six Buffaloes with a common single barreled flint gun without drawing a rein on their horse. They generally put five or six bullets in their mouth, and when they fire they pour a charge of powder into the left hand from the powder

horn which hangs over the right shoulder, throw it into the
barrel, which is hastily struck on the saddle to shake down the
powder so as to pass into the pan to prime it, then throw in a
bullet wet with saliva of the mouth which causes it to adhere
to the powder and prevents it falling out when the muzzle is
depressed to fire. In this manner these gentlemen fired from
12 to 14 times each in riding about a mile, but without ball.
It will be readily seen that a percussion gun cannot be fired
with the same facility on account of the inconvenience of putting
on the caps. We retired early but had not been long in bed
before we were called to attend a ball, we would willingly have
been excused but as our host was one of the musicians and took
a lively interest in the fun, and moreover it was in the apartment
adjoining our room precluding the possibility of sleeping, we
all got up to see the fun and admire the Indian ladies of the
Fort as they stepped it off to Mr. Culbertson's violin, Mr. Den-
ny's[30] clarionet, and Chardon's drum. It was kept up until one
o'clock of the morning when we most willingly returned to our
beds.[31] Mr. Chouteau[32] and Mr. Murray[33] arrived this afternoon

[30] This is Edwin Thompson Denig, who was born in McConnelstown, Penn-
sylvania, in 1812. He figures frequently in the accounts of Maximilian, Chardon,
Audubon, Kurz, and De Smet. *His Indian Tribes of the Upper Missouri* (the Assiniboin) (ed. by J. N. B. Hewitt), was published in the *Forty-sixth Annual Report of
the Bureau of American Ethnology*, 375–628. John C. Ewers has published in the
Missouri Historical Society Bulletin (VI [January, 1950], 198–215) Denig's account
"Of the Arikaras."

[31] Audubon wrote: "Mr. Culbertson played the fiddle very fairly; Mr. Guèpe the
clarionet, and Mr. Chouteau the drum, as if brought up in the army of the great
Napoleon." (*Journals*, II, 35.) "Guèpe" may be an error of transcription; it does not
seem to occur elsewhere in the sources consulted. Note also that two different drum-
mers are mentioned.

[32] Audubon described him as "son of Auguste Chouteau" (*Journals*, II, 33).
However, Larpenteur mentioned in 1842 an Auguste Chouteau who had taken the
"outfit for the Crows" to Fort Van Buren (Fort Alexander) and in 1845 stated that
this same man was clerk in charge of men at Fort Union (*Forty Years a Fur Trader*,
I, 166, 222). This must be Auguste Liguest Chouteau, son of Paul Liguest Chouteau,
and nephew of Pierre Chouteau, Jr.

[33] Audubon identified him as "a Scotchman, Mr. James Murray, at whose father's
farm, on the Tweed, we all stopped on our return from the Highlands of Scotland"
(*Journals*, II, 33). In 1842 he had succeeded Larpenteur in command of Fort Alexander
on the Yellowstone (*Forty Years a Fur Trader*, II, 175). When Palliser traveled up
the Missouri with him in 1847, he was still in charge of the Crow post (*Solitary
Rambles*, 83).

with two Mackinaw boats from the Crow country, the men were left with the boats at the mouth of the Yellow Stone and they came on foot to the landing opposite the Fort and hailed for a boat which was sent for them, they report the snow being 3 feet deep when they left the station on the Yellow Stone.

Thursday, June 15th. The Crow boats arrived at noon to-day and Mr. Audubon purchased for two strings of beads a fine young Badger from a squaw who came in one of them, it is a beautiful little animal and very tame and full of play.[34] It has a singular appearance from its very flat body and long hair projecting at its sides and covering its very short legs and black feet, when taken hold of by the back of the neck and turned on its back it has the form of a large snapping turtle. Bell and I were out with our guns to-day we found nothing rare excepting a Lazuli Finch which I shot. Bell shot a common crow which is rare here. The gentlemen of the Fort seem disposed to keep up their frolic a little while longer so that we cannot get fairly under way with our work.

Friday, June 16th. Two parties of hunters[35] went over the river today to hunt Antelopes for Mr. Audubon, but returned without any, reporting those they saw too shy to be approached. Mr. Audubon and I walked out with our guns and procured a few good birds but nothing new.[36]

Saturday, June 17th. But little done today. Owen McKenzie[37] went after antelopes on horseback and took Squires with him, they returned without game and we began to fear they will be difficult to procure. The most interesting event of the day was the shooting of a Wolf by Bell, after dark from the battlements of the Fort.

34 "It snarled and snapped, and sometimes grunted not unlike a small pig, but did not bite." (Audubon, *Journals*, II, 35.)

35 One of these hunters was the famous Black Harris (Audubon, *Journals*, II, 35–36).

36 "Harris has a new batch of patients, and enjoys the work of physician." (Audubon, *Journals*, II, 37.)

37 Half-blood son of Kenneth McKenzie. He was murdered in 1863. Much about him can be found in Audubon, Palliser, Larpenteur, Culbertson, and Kurz.

Sunday, June 18th. Provost started very early this morning to visit a lake on the other side of the river, some 6 or 7 miles down to ascertain if there were any signs of Beavers or Otters about it— Alexis, Mr Chardon's hunter, went with him to look for antelopes, about 1 o'clock the latter returned and reported his having killed two of these animals and that Provost had killed a Deer. A mule was harnessed to the cart and Mr. Audubon and I went with him to bring home the game. He took us in the cart through a blind road in the woods grown up with underbrush and obstructed by fallen timber, over which we had a rough ride for about 2 miles when we emerged upon a bottom prairie covered with Artemesia or Herbe Sante [Sainte] as it is called by the voyageurs, on the edge of this prarie in the woods we found one of the antelopes and the meat and skin of Provost's Deer. Alexis had put his jacket over the head of the antelope to keep off the Wolves and we found all safe. A few hundred yards out in the Prarie we found the other Kabri[38] as they are here called with some other article of clothing attached to it, with like good effect. Our meat loaded we started for home by way of the prarie, a longer road but better and safer for a loaded cart, the fine mule drew us three and the game with perfect ease and went on a trot where the road was hard and level. We saw three antelope on the way, but as they evidently saw us it was useless to attempt to pursue them, in fact they soon put themselves out of reach of pursuit, galloping off in beautiful style. We crossed the woods again to reach the Ferry, but as we entered it by the road which is constantly used by the hunting parties that go out from the Fort, we found it in excellent condition. As we rode along through the woods I saw a Deer peeping at us over some bushes at a distance of about 35 yards. The cart was stopped and I showed its head which alone was to be seen, to Alexis, who gave us the reins and dismounted, he leveled his rifle, producing of course from a half-breed Frenchman a volley of lowly uttered *sacrés,* the piece was reprimed and a good long

[38] More commonly, *cabri.* See *Quadrupeds,* II, 193–205 (Plate 77). See also Harris's entry for July 21.

aim taken before the trigger was pulled, when the head of the deer disappeared and all was still. He aimed at the head and shot it through the neck and by the time we had dragged it to the cart it was dead. It was a very large female of the Common Deer as we supposed and was evidently suckling a fawn. Our mule still went on bravely with the addition to our load. We got home just as dinner was over, and as soon as we had procured some refreshment we took the measurements of our Antelopes, and cut off the head of the oldest and finest for Sprague to make a drawing of. They are unfortunately in very bad pelage having partly shed their winter coats and what remains is so loose that we fear it will fall off in the pickle into which the skins are to be put. On examining the old winter hair I discovered in several places small patches of *fine wool* attached to it and almost ready to fall off, so that it is evident that fact has heretofore been overlooked by naturalists that this animal has in winter a very fine wool covering its body beneath its long and very coarse hair. It is impossible to say in what quantity this wooly covering exists, but Mr Audubon will make arrangements to have first rate skins sent to him next spring which will settle the matter if it is faithfully attended to. In the evening two more *Common Deer* were brought in by some hunters who went out in the afternoon on this side of the river. While examining the books to compare these animals with the descriptions the idea struck me that the tail of these Deer was much longer than that of our Common deer and that the animal was decidedly larger. I mentioned it to Mr. Audubon and he requested me to go into the Ice house and cut off the tails of the two Deer last killed and bring them to be measured. I did so, and we found the measurements to exceed even those given for the *Long-tailed Deer* of the Rocky Mountains. As these two deer were unfortunately ruined by this operation I will say nothing more about them until we procure more specimens accurately. This morning three Mackinaw boats[39] started for St. Louis and I wrote by them to Dr. Spencer. In the evening Bell and I went

[39] Murray's boats.

to watch for wolves on the Ramparts. Bell fired at one and wounded him badly and he went off. In about half an hour another made his appearance and we agreed to fire together at a signal and we brought him low.[40]

Monday, June 19th. This morning proved cold and rainy and we did not go out, but it cleared off partially in the afternoon and Bell and I went out. Bell shot a Yellow-winged Woodpecker with a red stripe on the cheek (instead of a black one as is common in this species). This is no doubt a new species to our Fauna, but I am inclined to think that I have somewhere seen a specimen of this bird and that it will not prove entirely new.[41] As we returned home Bell and I fired together and shot a small bird which proves to be an entirely new *Anthus* or Titlark.[42] After trying some time to procure more of them without success we returned to the Fort thinking we had had Glory enough for one day and after supper went to work to measure our new birds. Bell also found the nest and eggs of the Lark bunting, which we hope will be an acquisition for our friend, Dr. Trudeau.[43] We have not been on the ramparts to shoot wolves tonight as it is still cold and rainy, but the storekeeper[44] promises to call us very early in the morning before the gates are opened, when he assures us there will be several Wolves close to the Fort picking up garbage and that we cannot fail getting a shot or two.

Tuesday, June 20th. It was raining again this morning and there being no wolves we were not called. It rained most of the morning; hunters went out to shoot for Mr. Audubon but procured nothing. In the afternoon Bell and I walked out to the hills back of the Fort and shot one of the New Meadow Larks, 2 or 3

[40] A white wolf, according to Audubon (*Journals*, II, 40). See *Quadrupeds*, II, 156–62 (Plate 72).

[41] This is the Missouri Red-Moustached Woodpecker described in *The Birds of America*, VII (1844), 348–49 and Plate 494.

[42] The Missouri Titlark, which Audubon named for Sprague the next day. See *The Birds of America*, VII (1844), 334–36 (Plate 486).

[43] Dr. James DeBerty Trudeau.

[44] Charles Larpenteur (Audubon, *Journals*, II, 41). One of his duties was to open the gates at sunrise.

Chestnut-collared Lark finches and some Rusty Grackles[45] which Bell and Mr. Audubon think are new, the principal differences being in the size and in the bill, it appears to be a somewhat larger bird with a stouter bill. I tried fishing this morning, but had no success. Catfish are the only fish taken here, they are small compared to the catfish taken in the lower part of the river and in the Mississipi to its mouth, but while the large catfish is so indifferent that it is only eaten by the negroes, the fish of this portion of the river and of the Yellow Stone are really delicious. They are much larger than those taken in the Delaware and Schuylkill. Sprague pointed out to me to-day a passage in Lewis & Clark's Journal[46] with which we were unacquainted before but which goes far to confirm us in the opinion of the whole of our party that the Meadow Lark of this country is a new one, although we are not prepared without thorough examination and comparison to vouch for any of the differences mentioned by them with the exception of the notes of the bird about which there can be no question. It surprises me that Mr. Nuttal[47] could have passed through this country without noticing this bird as he is so remarkably accurate in describing the notes of birds, indeed, he is almost the only man who has written the language of the birds. I shot a Wolf from the Ramparts[48] about 11 o'clock but did not call anyone to open the gates.

Wednesday, June 21st. Bell went over the river this morning with Owen McKenzie to hunt Antelopes and Deer but they were not successful, in returning Bell shot in the woods a small Hare (with a rifle) but so badly it was not fit to skin, he brought the head and legs, and it is undoubtedly a new Hare, less in size than the Common Rabbit with short ears and legs and a slender

[45] Brewer's Blackbird. See *The Birds of America*, VII (1844), 345–46 (Plate 492).
[46] See note 51 for June 21.
[47] For Thomas Nuttall consult Francis W. Pennell, "Travels and Scientific Collections of Thomas Nuttall," *Bartonia*, No. 18 (1936), 1–51. Harris refers to the trip with Townsend in 1834–36.
[48] The pickets of the fort were fifteen feet high; on the inside about five feet below the top a balcony or walk was built which ran all around the inside of the fort: "It is a favorite place from which to shoot Wolves after nightfall and for standing guard in time of danger." (Denig as quoted by Audubon, *Journals*, II, 184.)

head, its feet and claws are completely hidden in a strong covering of hair, it still has part of its winter pelage which is remarkably long and thick and much the same colour as the Rabbit.[49]
Mr. Audubon and I walked out in the morning for a short time
before dinner, got nothing but the Eggs of Sparrow Hawk which
were in the deserted hole of a Woodpecker about 10 feet from
the ground. Mr. A. being the heaviest man offered me his shoulders and by standing upon them I was able to introduce my
arm in the hole and take out the eggs. In returning I discovered
that a remarkable note of a bird which we have heard for some
days and which has given us a great deal of useless walking, by
appearing to proceed from a certain spot, and as soon as we
reached it it sounded in another direction, was the note of our
little new Titlark, and that it sings while flying in the air in
the manner of the European Skylark and of our Shore Lark,
(which we witnessed at Edwardsville and Bunker Hill in Ill.)
Bell returned with a confirmation of this discovery which he
was informed of by Owen McKenzie, and he afterwards saw
the bird singing in the air. The wolf which I shot last night
proved to be a very old female nearly white, and not worth
skinning. Sprague was out this afternoon and had the good fortune to procure a very fine specimen of the Arctic Bluebird,[50]
another instance of the very wide range of the birds found in the
Oregon Territory, a vast number of which no doubt range to
the Mississippi instead of the Rocky Mountains as heretofore supposed. After tea Mr Audubon, Bell and I went out to look for
the new Hare in a piece of bottom land which had been cleared
near the Fort and which has grown up with rose bushes, willows
and Buffaloe berries so as to make it impossible to drive them
out of it, we walked along some wood roads which pass through
it until it was too dark to see to shoot but none of them came
out to feed, although we were told by every one about the fort
that they abound in that spot. We hope soon to procure some
good specimens. I neglected last night to give the extract from

[49] The *Lepus artemisia* of the *Quadrupeds*, II, 272–73 (Plate 88).
[50] *Ornithological Biography*, V, 38–41 (Plate 393).

Lewis and Clark's Journal about the Meadow Lark and will insert it here. It was on the 22d. of June while they were making the portage around the Great Falls of Missouri. They say "There is also a species of Lark, much resembling the bird called the Old-field Lark, with a yellow breast and a black spot on the croup, though it differs from the latter in having its tail formed of feathers of an unequal length and pointed; the beak is some-what longer and more curved, and the *note differs consider-ably*."[51] Mr. Chardon gave us yesterday a highly interesting but apalling description of the ravages of the Small-pox in 1837 among the Mandans and Ricarees, he was at that time in com-mand of Fort Clark.[52] He says it was brought up by the steam-boat Assineboin[53] belonging to the Company, and that the In-dians were informed of it and warned not to have any inter-course with the boat, but that a chief came on board and sat a long time along side of one of the men who had just recovered from the disease, and when he went away stole the man's blanket. When Mr C. ascertained the fact he sent around the village to try to recover the blanket, offering a new one in its place, but the thief being a chief he considered it too great a stigma on his character to be exposed in such an act and as might be expected he was the first victim and in a very short time it began to spread in the village. The men of the nation at this time were principally away in the praries on a hunting or war party. Mr C. sent a run-ner urging them to remain where they were if they valued their lives, but they insisted in spite of all remonstrances in coming home to their crop of corn. The disorder now began to spread at a frightful rate and a suspicion arose among the Mandans

[51] Sprague may have had with him either the Paul Allen edition of the *History of the Expedition under the Command of Captains Lewis and Clark* (2 vols., Phila-delphia, 1814) or the 1842 abridgment edited by Archibald M'Vickars; if the first, the reference is to I, 279; if the second, to I, 236. My guess that it was the Allen edition is supported by a further reference to the work on June 22. In *The Birds of America*, VII (1844), 339, where this bird is described by Audubon, M'Vickar's edition is acknowledged, but this notation presumably was written in New York.

[52] Cf. Audubon, *Journals*, II, 42–47. Chardon too caught the smallpox; only twenty-seven Mandans, he said, lived through the epidemic.

[53] He should have said *St. Peters*. The *Assiniboin* had burned on the Upper Missouri two years earlier.

that it had been introduced by the traders with the intention of killing them off, particularly as the Ricarees who were living with them, mixed up in the same lodges were not yet attacked. Some of the young men attempted to take Mʳ C.'s life and the whites were obliged to shut themselves up in the fort. One day Mʳ C. and several others ventured to sit out at the entrance of the Fort when a young Mandan advanced and shot the man who was sitting next to Mr. Chardon, dead on the spot. The Indian ran towards the graves of his people and was pursued and overtaken by the whites, he begged them not to kill him until he reached the grave where all his relatives had gone before him, he was spared until he walked to a mound which he mounted and was immediately dispatched. Mʳ C. related a singular story of a Dove pursued by a Hawk which flew in at his windows one day when he was seated with several chiefs of the Mandans and Ricarees, the whole party in a melancholy mood brooding over the calamitous situation, the Dove sat still on the table for a minute or more and flew away. One of the Chiefs asked Mʳ C. what the bird had said to him. Knowing the superstition of the Indians he instantly conceived the idea of making capital out of the circumstance. He told them it informed him that he had been sent by his great Father down the river who saw his situation and knew that there was some bad young men among the Mandans who sought his life and were using all their art to persuade the people that he was acting treacherously with the Mandans and was in league with the Ricarees to kill off the Mandans, and to assure the latter it was all a lie, and offering his protection against all his enemies. The chiefs all got up and shook hands with him, and expressed themselves satisfied with his good intentions towards them all. He related several instances of self destruction by the Indians after they were attacked by the loathsome disorder, and of some who killed themselves without being attacked, particularly one poor fellow who had lost his only child a beautiful boy on whom he doted, as soon as the child was buried he told his squaw that he had always been a good husband to her, that he had not like most of his people took a wife for a short time and then when tired of her cast her off, that he had always been faithful to her and never took another wife, that now they had lost the joy of their life, the bad medicine of the whites was destroying all their people, they had no longer anything worth living for, and begged her to let him shoot her and then he would destroy himself. She consented at once, he took up his gun and shot her and then drawing a knife he gashed himself across the vitals and was soon dead by her side —Another story of two young men who were sitting in the Fort entirely untouched by the disorder, talking of the horrors of their situation and the dreadful death they were certain of meeting. At length they came to the conclusion to destroy themselves and commenced a violent dispute as to the best mode of accomplishing the end, one recommended a mode sometimes practiced among them of placing an arrow at the bottom of the throat and forcing it down with both hands into the lungs, the other insisted that the knife was the best weapon for the purpose, the dispute ran quite high between them at last the one that had recommended the knife told the other to try his method and he would see how he liked it, the words were hardly spoken before the arrow was forced into his head and he was a corpse, the other instantly drew his knife and gashed himself to death. It was some weeks before the Ricarees were attacked and the Mandans were nearly all dead before the men in the Fort caught the disorder, not one escaped an attack, though most of them had been vaccinated, but only 3 or 4 died. His account of the horrors were truly thrilling and such as only could have been given by a witness.

Thursday, June 22. This morning Mr Chardon and Mr Harvey[54] started for the Blackfoot station with a keel boat and about 35 men,[55] they were saluted by discharge of cannon when they

[54] Alexander Harvey (1807–54), who in 1846 became one of the founders of Harvey, Primeau and Company. For him consult McDonnell, "Fort Benton and Fort Sarpy Journals," 302–305; and Chittenden, *The American Fur Trade,* II, 683–87.

[55] According to Audubon, "thirty men . . . Chardon, thirteen squaws, and a number of children, all more or less half-breeds" (*Journals,* II, 50). He gave the name of the boat as the *Bee.*

left us. Bell and I were out all morning. B. procured the female of the Yellow-winged Woodpecker with a red stripe on the cheek which he had shot on Monday, it appears so exactly like our common golden-wing that it would pass for one in any collection, and the measurements are about the same, still if we succeed in finding more similar specimens of the male we must set it down as a new species. Since we met with the Red-shafted Woodpecker we have frequently seen yellow-winged bird[s] which we would not shoot supposing it to be the common ones, it is very probable they were of this kind. Bell shot three females of the Arctic Bluebird and I shot a Lazuli Finch. In the afternoon Mr. Audubon went into the woods with McKenzie to hunt for hares but did not find any, they started an animal in the bushes which they did not see but McKenzie supposed it to be a Grizly bear, he followed it and returned in an hour or two and said that he had seen its tracks but could not find it. I went on the prarie to look for the New Larks, saw several singing in the air but could not find any on the ground to shoot. I watched their mode of flight very closely for half an hour, at times with my pocket glass. They ascend to a considerable height, performing gyrations in the air somewhat after the manner of the English Skylark. The flight is undulating for 8 or 10 seconds closing their wings to their bodies like the woodpeckers, then they stop and hover in the same spot, while they utter their singular wire-like notes which may be heard at a great distance, beating their wings all the while with a rapid motion, their song last[s] 5 or 6 seconds when off they start again on their wave-like flight for a few seconds, and then again salute their quiet mates who are listening to them with delight from their nests somewhere on the prarie below. I have watched them for more than half an hour and they have generally tired me out. Venture,[56] the hunter from the fort, shot a deer this afternoon not far from the fort and a cart was sent out to bring it in. We took the measurements of it at once and Bell skinned it and put it in pickle. The measurements are as follows:—

[56] This is Bonaventure LeBrun (Audubon, *Journals*, II, 51, 56).

Measurements of Doe of Long-tailed Deer shot to-day

	Inches	Doe shot 26th.
From nose to end of Scull	12¾	12¼
" " " anterior canthus of eye	7¼	
" " " root of ear	13	
" " " end of ear	19¼	18½
" " " root of tail	59	57½
" " " end of hair on tail	75½	
" " " point of shoulder	24	25
Length of ear from opening	6¼	6
" " tail vertebra	11	11½
Length of hair beyond end of tail	5½	4½
Bredth of ear	3	2¾
" between the eyes at posterior canthus	5	
Around the head behind the eyes	17¼	17
" " Nose at angle of mouth	9	9
Height at shoulder	37	35
" " rump	40	38
Girth behind shoulders	36	34

We cut off the tails of two Bucks of this Deer a few days before we thought it possible that they could be Long-tailed Deer of Lewis and Clark they both measure 17 inches in length including the hair which in one of them was 3 in. beyond the end of the bone and in the other 5 inches, owing perhaps to one having lost more of its winter coat than the other—making the vertebra of one 14 in. long and the other only 12. It would be a great satisfaction to us to know how the Deer of Lewis and Clark was measured. On looking into their Journal I find that they remark on the 6th day after leaving this place that the Deer they saw were principally of the Long-tailed kind.[57] Now six days journey above this, the boat dragged by men against the current cannot be a very great distance, probably not a

[57] This reference is in the Paul Allen (1814) edition, I, 205; it is not in the abridged M'Vickars version. The entry was for July 3, 1805.

hundred miles. Still it is doubtful whether they do not use the term long-tailed to distinguish it from the Black-tailed Deer, whose tail is shorter. It is still a matter of doubt whether it differs from our common Deer east of the mountains which is known to vary in size, being larger at the North and smaller in the South. It will require to experiment in different parts of the country before this interesting question can be settled. The Deer of this country is undoubtedly much larger than that of the Middle States. But then the Deer of Maine is very much larger also but it appears to differ from this Deer by having the leg bone very stout while this deer has a remarkably slender delicate leg.

Friday, June 23rd. Mr Audubon and I had old Peter put to the Carryal this afternoon and rode down to Fort Mortimer[58] and found that they had been obliged to move their pickets around to the rear in consequence of a rise in the river in the Yellowstone washing away the bank on which their Fort is built, the back buildings of the Fort as it was before the rise now are the Front ones, they appear to be in rather a destitute situation. A Mr Collins[59] quite a young man from Kentucky appears to be in command, one of them is named Wallace[60] and says he is from Philadelphia, that he left there in 1824, that his Father kept a hardware store at the corner of 9th and Market sts. We staid about half an hour and were treated very politely. In riding down Mr. Audubon shot one of the New Larks and in returning we each shot another. On our return we found Bell with a Say's Flycatcher, a fine male Arctic Bluebird and a male Lazuli Finch. Squires went across the river with Venture and McKenzie to procure Buffalo meat.

Saturday, June 24th. Bell went out with Provost before breakfast to try and shoot a Doe in the point of the woods above the

[58] Built by Fox, Livingston and Company in 1842.

[59] Audubon gave his first name as John and said he was from Hopkinsville, Kentucky (*Journals,* II, 53, 57).

[60] "We saw a large athletic man who had crossed the mountains twice to the Pacific; he is a Philadelphian, named Wallis, who had been a cook at Fort Union four years, but who had finally deserted, lived for a time with the Crows, and then joined the Opposition." (Audubon, *Journals,* II, 53–54.)

Fort by imitating the cry of the Fawn on an instrument made by Provost yesterday, he did not succeed. After breakfast I took a horse and rode up the river four or five miles, and succeeded in procuring one Sharp-tailed Grous which I shot on the wing from the horse. I took Provost's call with me and tried it in a small island of timber about a mile beyond the point, at the first call a Doe came within 30 feet of me, she stopped behind a bunch of trees and in endeavoring to change my position to get a shot I stepped upon a log and my foot slipped and before I could recover myself to shoot she had seen me and was out of sight in the bushes. I followed her and got sight of her once more but could not get a shot. I returned through the point of timber and tried the call several times, but could not bring any more to me. In the afternoon Bell and Mr. Audubon rode down to the Fort again and on their way killed more of the new Larks. Sprague was out and killed another, and what is of more consequence discovered its nest with 5 eggs, it is built of grass and placed in a hole in the ground so that the top of the nest is even with the surface, the eggs are thickly spotted of a chocolate colour. Mr. Audubon remarked that it had very rarely happened to him to discover a new bird and to ascertain all its habits and to procure its nest and eggs in the course of a few days as has been the case with this bird.

Sunday, June 25th. The Buffalo Hunters did not return until about 3 o'clock this afternoon. Buffalo have become so exceedingly scarce that they had to ride nearly 50 miles before they found any, they killed 3 Bulls and Two Antelopes and a hare for Mr. A. The carts did not get back and land their meat in the Fort until 10 o'clock. They saw two bears near a lake where the ground was too muddy to run them. Saw a good many Antelopes but only two hares, several magpies were seen.

Monday, June 26th. The principal events of the day are as follows. Provost was out this morning and killed a fine Doe of the Long-tailed Deer (?), it was not quite as large as the one shot on Thursday. I have put along side of the measurements of that

Deer to save writing, see last page [June 22nd] —Bell & I walked out with our guns and procured 3 Lazuli Finches, and a Prarie Finch shot by Bell, the Female was with it but not procured, these are the only birds of this species we have yet seen. On our return we found a strange Fish had been caught by one of the Trappers, it had run into shoal water and he took it out with his hands. It is a sturgeon of a description quite new to us, it has a long pointed snout very small eyes and very large mouth and the vertebral scales form a very slight and almost even ridge without any of those strong protuberances of the sturgeon of the Delaware. Mr Audubon believes that it is not the sturgeon of the Mississippi and the Ohio.

Tuesday, June 27th. Bell rode out with Owen McKenzie this morning after breakfast to scour the country on this side the river in search of Buffalo. In consequence of their scarcity on the other side and the great distance the hunters are obliged to ride before they can be found, it has become a matter of some conse-quence to find them somewhat near the Fort. They rode about 30 miles out and got on an eminence where they could com-mand a view of the country for many miles around but no signs of Buffalo were to be seen. They chased a Deer and were evi-dently gaining on him when he took them down a steep bank into the swampy bottom lands of Muddy Creek where they could not follow him. Bell's remark on the appearance and mode of running [of] this Deer nearly satisfied us that it is the long-tailed Deer of Lewis & Clark and in connection with the other observations we have been able to make are conclusive to my mind at least that it is distinct from the *C. virginianus* or Com-mon Deer of the East. He says that when pushed to its utmost speed it does not run with an even stride like a horse or the common Deer but takes two or three short irregular and peculiar jumps throwing its long tail first on one side and then on the other, and then takes an enormous leap which he estimates at 25 feet—That peculiar shuffling motion was noticed by Lewis & Clark and goes far of itself with those who are acquainted with the habits of the common Deer to establish a difference. We think that by accurate measurements here and comparison with the undoubted virginianus we shall be enabled to settle the question. They ran and killed a Wolf—saw a Swift Fox in the muddy bottom and had no opportunity of running him. Saw several Antelopes and many signs of Grizly Bears[61] where they had been digging roots—Saw a good number of Magpies, chestnut-collared Lark finches and some other rare birds, but none that we had not seen before. They returned soon after 5 P.M. Mr Audubon & I went out this morning to search for *Racine Noir* or Black root, the antidote of the Indians against the bite of the Rattlesnake. It is kept dried and used by placing a ligature above the wound and applying the root well chewed to the wound, it is said to be excessively acrid and to act by its caustic powers on the flesh. If this be the fact the lunar caustic would be more speedily effective and might be carried by all parties in danger from those deadly reptiles. We have been disappointed in not finding this country to abound with Rattlesnakes as we were told it did. We have not seen one since we have been here, and Mr Culbertson who has been here some years says he has never seen but two. In the afternoon I walked out again with Mr A. to hunt for the small hare which all tell us abounds in the bushes near the Fort. Still we cannot find them. When tired of searching for them I went out in the Prarie to look for some large bones of the Boss or hump of the Buffalo which I had seen a few days ago. I did not succeed in finding the same skeleton but procured two, which measured each 19 inches in length. They are the processes of the spine of the Bull which extend to this enormous length above the point of the shoulder, inclining a little backwards, there appears to be about 12 of them gradually diminishing in length down to the middle of the back, whence the processes to the tail are about the size of those of an ordinary ox of the same size. Mr A. intends to procure two skeletons of the entire animal when we can procure good specimens. I enclosed the labours of the day by shooting a Wolf from the battlements.

Wednesday, June 28th. The wolf I shot last night proved to be a fine Grey Male and Sprague made a fine outline of it with the Camera lucida. Bell told me that when running the Wolf yesterday he attempted to check his horse and came very near having his leg bitten by him (the horse). He is an American horse and has done nothing for the last 7 years, he is now 14 years old, but hunts Buffalo and other animals and is the swiftest horse belonging to the establishment, and McKenzie says that it is his invariable practice if checked while in pursuit of an animal to bite at the leg of the rider. Last night the scow belonging to the Fort got adrift or was set adrift by some evil disposed person and was nowhere to be seen this morning. Two men were immediately dispatched on horseback about 12 miles down the river with instructions to follow the bank in returning. They came back without any tidings of the boat. The general belief is that she was set adrift by the fellow Wallace belonging to Fort Mortimer. It appears that this man had an Indian woman who ran away from him and took refuge in the fort where she now is, and that Wallace without making any demand of her threatened retaliation by shooting the horses or cattle, and has frequently been seen lurking about the Fort. This is a serious loss, particularly at this time as they are very busy in building and fitting out the Mackinaw boat for Mr. Kipp to ascend the Yellowstone to the Crow establishment and he was to get off this week, they have also a skiff building for our use, and the men have to cross the river two or three times a day to work out the timber in the woods, where men are also engaged in burning charcoal for the Blacksmith's use. The skiff belonging to the Fort was taken by Mr Chardon when he went to the Blackfeet— Fortunately the Mackinaw was so nearly finished that she was launched about 8 o'clock this evening and was despatched immediately across the river to releive the charcoal burners who have been all day without provisions. McKenzie who went down the river stopped at Fort Mortimer on his return to inquire if

61 It was not until August 22 that Harris and Audubon saw grizzly bears. *Quadrupeds*, III, 141–52 (Plate 131).

they had seen the boat or if any of their men had deserted and stolen her. They knew nothing about her, and Wallace remarked that he supposed he was suspected. One of their men told McKenzie that he had shot a Bighorn for Mr Audubon and wished him to send down for it. A Horse was put to the carryall and Bell & Squires went down for it. It proved to be a female, it was skinned, leaving the head and legs entire, so that it answered very well. It was in winter pelage for the most part and is coated almost precisely like the Antelope with a thick covering of very coarse and tender hair, breaking as though it were rotten, with a fine wool underneath. I supposed that this tender state of the long hair of these animals was owing to its being dead and about to fall from the body, but Mr A. informs me that he has skins of both of them in New York in perfect winter pelage with the hair precisely similar. Venture has been out since Monday to procure animals for Mr. A. he returned this afternoon with a Doe of the same Deer which we have heretofore found here & a yearling Buck Elk,[62] both skinned. He shot also a Prairie Wolf,[63] which we have not yet seen, he skinned it out and hung the skin on a tree until his return today when he found it so spoilt and fly blown that he did not think it worth bringing. The Doe was remarkable for having the rudiment of one horn on her forehead, in the velvet, but appearing to be entirely detached from the bone, she is in silk and doubtless had a fawn. The Hunters here say they have occasionly found them with two small horns, but never before saw one with only one. Nothing remarkable to-day in the ways of birds—a good many wild pigeons have been seen about the woods today. The hunters at the lower Fort killed Buffalo yesterday near the mouth of the Yellowstone on the lower side, and to-morrow McKenzie will go to look for them on this side of that river. When Buffalo are found Bell and I are to make our maiden effort at running them, we are to be furnished with the two best Buffalo horses belonging to the Fort, and Mr. Audubon and Mr. Culbertson will fol-

[62] *Quadrupeds*, II, 83–94 (Plate 62).
[63] *Quadrupeds*, II, 150–55 (Plate 71).

low as spectators drawn in the Carryall by old Peter. We are
to take an extra cart to bring home any animals which may be
procured for our use.

Thursday, June 29th. Took Brag this morning and hunted well
the small Wormwood Prairie a mile above the Fort for Sharp-
tailed Grous but could not find any. I killed a Woodpecker of
an intermediate colour between the Yellow-shafted and the Red-
shafted, it was a female. This determined us to examine very
closely before we decided that the Yellow-shafted birds killed
by Bell on the 19th were distinct from the Red, to ascertain all
we could about them. Mr A. & Bell went in the afternoon to
the tree where they had their nest and cut it down. The young
which were in a putrid state had the same colours as the parent
birds. At the same time they cut down a tree where he had killed
a pair of Red-shafts and the young were found distinctly marked
with red. This looks very much like their being of different
species, as it is not probable it is age that makes the difference
when we find young birds not yet able to fly distinctively, indeed
almost as strongly marked with Red as the old ones. It is however a very interesting question and we intend pursuing it further. In the afternoon Provost went out with his rifle and killed
a Doe by imitating the cry of a Fawn, and when they went with
a cart to bring it back, he and I took our guns and went with
the cart, immediately on entering the Wormwood Prarie I saw
a Grous sitting on a stump and shot it by approaching it under
cover of another stump. After the Deer was put in the cart Provost & I walked on trying his call at several places in the woods
adjoining the Praries, but without success—We then crossed the
Prarie to a small piece of timber on the other side adjoining the
Bluff where I had called one to me on the 25th. We placed ourselves at the leeward point of the timber, a few sounds on the
call brought the Deer at full speed to within 10 feet of the spot
where we were hid behind the bushes, she saw us and attempted
to turn to regain the woods when she passed us about 25 yards.
I then fired at her, but perceiving that though staggered by the

shot she did not fall, I fired my second barrel, she reeled again but went on towards the bluff, at a slower canter, she soon began to slacken her pace, then came to a walk and at last laid down— when we came to the spot she was quite dead. I had put 8 shot into her, it was the last which was the most effective, the first having struck her hind parts. I sent Provost to the Fort about 2½ miles for the cart while I remained to shoot birds in the woods. Before leaving he took off his coat and hung it on a pole to keep off the wolves and Ravens, who always approach at the sound of a Gun to look out for their share of the plunder. While he was absent I shot a Woodpecker which we believe to be Harris's Woodpecker, but it is so much like the Canada Woodpecker that we cannot decide without comparing specimens.

Friday, June 30th. We were out again with our Guns this morning, nothing of importance was procured except another Woodpecker shot by Sprague, a female, which is intermediate between the one shot by me yesterday and the full-coloured Red-shaft—Thus we have 4 varieties in the colour of the underside of the wings and the tails of these birds which are otherwise alike in markings, which would induce us to believe them to be of the same species, had we not ascertained that one of them at least mates with its own colour and produces young of the same colour. The question is becoming more interesting and more difficult. The afternoon has proved very rainy and cold and nothing has been done. Provost went down to the other Fort this morning and learned that their long looked for express from Fort George arrived last night with letters from Mr. Cutting recommending us strongly to their attention. They bring news of a battle between the Sioux and Gros ventres, in which the former were defeated, the latter lost three of their tribe and a white man who resided with them as Blacksmith. The Sioux had 8 killed.[64]

[64] Was this, rather, the attack made by the Sioux upon the Pawnees on June 27, in which LaShapel, the American interpreter, was killed? See the St. Louis *New Era*, July 13, 1843. This attack had taken place at Willow Creek, 150 miles up the Platte. The blacksmith survived, but his wife was killed.

JULY
[1843]

Saturday, July 1st. The storm cleared off in the night and the morning was fine and cool, but the ground was [so] wet from the great quantity of rain which fell that Mr Culbertson advised our going out on horseback, and as Bell was still stiff from his long ride on Tuesday we took a couple of old horses and walked them out about 3 miles. In crossing the ravine called Garden river we saw a Wolf in the road in the middle of the ravine. We tried to push our horses on to overtake him, but we soon found they had no run in them—having a load of Buck Shot in one barrel I gave Bell the reins of my horse and ran behind a bushy tree until I got within shot of him, Mr Wolf standing all the while looking at Bell and the horses. I fired and he scrambled a few paces up the hill and laid down, we walked up to him and finding him not quite dead Bell fired a pistol ball into his head and another into his side which put him out of his misery. We proceeded toward the head of the ravine, and found the nest of the Arkansas Flycatcher with 3 fresh eggs. I shot an Arctic Bluebird and a female Sharp-tailed Grous. In the afternoon Sprague and I walked out in search of the tree where he shot his female Woodpecker yesterday with the light coloured Red Shafts, on approaching it we heard the poor young ones clamouring for food, one of them had left the nest and was on the ground unable to fly. I secured it and found it was a male of about the same colour as the mother, but what was most re-markable there were strong rudiments of a *black stripe* on the cheek like the male of our Golden Wing. We had no means of cutting down the tree or we would have secured the two which remained in the nest. Before we returned Sprague shot a male adult bird with precisely the same markings as our common Yellow winged bird, and without the means of comparison would say that it could not be distinguished from that bird. He also shot a *light coloured* Red shafted bird just fledged with a *black stripe* on the cheek. I also shot a similar bird just fledged, and a newly-fledged Yellow Shafted male bird with the *red stripe* on the cheek the same as the adult bird shot by Bell on the 19th. Here we are all in a heap with these Golden wings & Red shafts—We have the *Red-shafted Bird* with *Red cheeks,* and *Newly-fledged birds* with *red shafts* and *black cheeks, Yellow-winged birds* with *Red cheeks* and with *black cheeks,* both adults. I would give a great deal to have Dr. Bachman here with a dozen specimens of Golden-wings from our side of the moun-tains, wouldn't we make a night of it?[1]

Sunday, July 2nd. Mr Audubon sent a man to cut down the tree where Sprague shot the female *light-coloured Red Shaft* on Friday. Three more young were found in it(?), one appeared to have been dead some time and was a *Yellow Shafted* bird, supposed to be a female as it had neither the red or black stripe on the cheek, one was a Male bird with a *black stripe* on the cheek, shafts coloured like the adult fem. The other was a fe-male without any stripe, shafts same colour. I must here mention that there is a possibility that the bird with the yellow shafts was from another nest, as there was another hole about 4 feet

---

[1] Audubon reports this day's activities in greater detail and adds: "After all this Mr. Culbertson proposed to run a sham Buffalo hunt again. He, Harris, and Squires started on good horses, went about a mile, and returned full tilt, firing and cracking. Squires fired four times and missed once. Harris did not shoot at all; but Mr. Cul-bertson fired eleven times, starting at the onset with an empty gun, snapped three times, and reached the fort with his gun loaded. A more wonderful rider I never saw." Audubon also tells us that "This evening Mr. Culbertson presented me with a splendid dress, as well as one to Harris and one to Bell." (*Journals,* II, 71.)

below, but which on examination showed no signs of having a
nest in it, nor is it probable that two birds so querulous as these
would have built so close together. Every new fact in regard
to these birds seems to throw us into further difficulty. Can it
be possible that the Red-shafted Woodpecker puts on all these
varieties of colour down to an exact counterpart of our Golden-
wing, or is there another Species which we may call the Pale-
coloured Red-shaft which puts on these varieties. Or are there 4
species here. The true *Red-Shaft* (of which no fact has come to
our knowledge to prove that it ever varies) *The light coloured
Red Shaft with a black stripe on the cheek of the Male. The
Golden-wing with a red stripe on the cheek of the Male. The
Golden-wing with a black stripe on the cheek of the Male,* which
may or may not be distinct from our common Golden Wing.
It will be observed from these notes that we have of these four
varieties adult males of three of them with the cheek marks as
stated above, we have the young of all of them with perfect
cheek marks, except the true Red Shaft, and we further find
that the young birds have the *cheek mark from the nest* and that
there is a correspondence with the adults except in this one instance where there is a shadow of a doubt about the bird which
differed from the rest having been from the same nest. We must
wait further developments before we can pretend to decide this
curious question. Provost having been down to Fort Mortimer
brought us word that Mr Collins who is in charge there was
very sick and Mr Culbertson and Mr Audubon rode down to
see if any assistance could be rendered, they brought back word
that he had a high fever and he would be glad if I would come
down and bring some medicine and prescribe for him as he had
not a particle of medicine of any kind in the Fort, not even a
dose of salts. I took a lancet, some calomel and some salts and
also an emetic. I found him with a pulse of about 90, lying in
a small skin lodge on which the sun beat with no little power,
their fort having again been encroached upon by the river   they
were obliged to abandon it the night before. He said his bowels
had not been moved for four or five days, complained of pain

in the head, but none in the back or limbs, under these circumstances I did not consider it necessary to bleed him but left him an emetic, and ordered ten grains of calomel at night to be followed by a dose of salts in the morning, and promised to see him again to-morrow.[2]

Monday, July 3rd. This morning, our new skiff being finished, we crossed the river to hunt Deer with a call, we divided into 3 parties, Mr Audubon & Provost—Squires and McKenzie, and Bell & I and took different routes. Provost and Mr Audubon were the only ones who saw Deer. Mr. A. had three shots at long distance but did not kill any. We returned to dinner. This weather proved excessively hot and we laid by in the middle of the day. Mr Audubon has engaged a famous hunter[3] belonging to the other Fort to procure Bighorns for him at ten dollars per head to be paid for in such articles as they might need at the prices of the country, sugar $1 per pound, tobacco the same, &c, &c. (of the prices of the necessaries here I will give you a list as soon as I can procure it). This afternoon they came up for a cart to bring up a female Big-horn and a female Mule or Black-tailed Deer, I took the opportunity to ride down in the cart to see my patient and found him somewhat better. The emetic had done well but the calomel and salts had not operated so freely as I could have wished and he sent a man up with me for more medicine. I sent him some cathartic pills and some more salts and a Dover's powder to be taken to-night. The Big-horn was a fine old female but in bad pelage not having entirely shed the winter coat, she weighed 140 lbs. The Deer was rather better shed and weighed 132 lbs. Said to be small and probably a young of last year, she had had a fawn this season. The heads

---

[2] "Harris had an accident that was near being of a serious nature; as he was getting into the wagon, thinking that a man had hold of the reins, which was not the case, his foot was caught between the axle-tree and the wagon, he was thrown down on his arm and side, and hurt to some extent; fortunately he escaped without serious injury." (Audubon, *Journals,* II, 72.)

[3] Apparently Boucherville, who is mentioned by Audubon in his entries for July 6 and 13 and elsewhere in the journals.

were taken off both of them to be outlined and the skins taken off to be put in pickle.

Tuesday, July 4th.[4] Bell and I walked out this morning to hunt Deer and took a ravine which puts into the Wormwood Prarie about a mile and a half above the Fort, we soon found a track of large Deer and commenced beating all the little clumps of bushes where a Deer would be likely to lie. We had not gone far before I drove out a fine Buck and Bell fired and wounded him. We followed the course he took and Bell soon saw his horns in a bunch of wormwood, he stepped back a few paces to beckon to me and while doing so the Deer jumped up and ran towards the deep ravine. Bell ran and headed him as much as possible and fired both barrels at him but apparently without effect, we again followed and at the distance of about a quarter of a mile I started him in a point of bushes, and although I was very near him when he got up I could not see him for a small bush that was in the way, and the wind blowing fresh I did not hear him, when I reached the point I saw him going off at about 60 or 70 yards and discharged both barrels, but unfortunately I was too much in a hurry in firing my first and undershot him, and he went off again apparently untouched, at both the first and second startings after Bell's first shot we found blood where he laid down and as he did not run more than a quarter of a mile each time we knew that he was badly wounded, the blood moreover was frothy and evidently came from the mouth. We followed him into the next branch of the ravine where we hunted for more than two hours when we bent our steps toward the Fort and got our dinners. In mentioning the facts to Mr. Culbertson, he advised us to get our horses immediately and take Owen McKenzie with us, which he believed would find the deer if he was not already eaten by the Wolves. We were soon under way, and after a little delay in chasing a fox who very easily distanced

---

[4] "Although we had some fireworks going on last evening, after I had laid myself down for the night, the anniversary of the Independence of the United States has been almost the quietest I have ever spent." (Audubon, *Journals*, II, 74.)

our horses, and a little more in finding the spot where we lost the Deer, we commenced our search anew. We observed that Owen passed over the ground apparently very carelessly, without searching the bushes as faithfully as we had done before, but in a short time he became separated from us and we heard the report of his gun, which we knew was either the Deer, or a signal that he had found it. We soon galloped to the spot where we had the mortification to find what the Wolves had left us of the Deer, which was only the head and spinal bones. In the space of about 4 hours they had eaten everything but the parts mentioned the legs and about one third of the skin, there was only one wolf remaining at the repast, although it must have taken several to have demolished in so short a time so large an animal. He was still in velvet, but his horns nearly grown and very large, his summer coat appeared to be complete and of a beautiful red colour. We took a few measurements as well as we could.

From the nose to the opening of the ear				12¾ inches.
"	"	"	"	end of ear	19
"	"	"	"	root of tail	62

We saw on one of the hills to-day some fine specimens of petrified wood, fragments of trunks very much compressed, the pieces were not more than 3 or 4 feet long, compressed to about 14 inches the longest diameter and six the shorter. They are composed of a fine sandstone.

Wednesday, July 5th. This proved a very rainy disagreeable day with the wind to the northwest of East, nothing was done in the way of shooting.[5] Squires and Provost went out in the afternoon of yesterday about two miles up the river and had the skiff carried up on a cart so that they might hunt today in a point of woods which is said to abound with Elk and Deer and occasionally a Grisly Bear. They crossed over and hunted without success

[5] Sometime on this day Provost told Audubon much about the beaver: *Journals,* II, 76; *Quadrupeds,* I, 347–59 (Plate 46).

until dark and were obliged to camp without any supper, it rained
hard all night and in the morning they went out and saw plenty
of game, but the rain so wetted their guns that they would not
go off and they were obliged to take the skiff and drop down
towards the Fort where they arrived at about half past 11 A.M.
without having eaten since they started soon after dinner yesterday. In the afternoon it held up a little and I took Mʳ Audubon
in the carryall down to Fort Mortimer to see my patient Mʳ
Collins, and had the satisfaction to find him much better notwithstanding he had passed a very uncomfortable night in consequence of the rain beating into their shanty of a fort which
they have put up in a hurry since the demolition of the old one,
by the Freshet of the Yellowstone. They appear to be in a very
destitute situation, in want of the common necessities of life,
and dependant entirely upon their hunters for their means of
supporting life.[6] They are in daily expectation of the arrival of
their steamboat from St. Louis, whose arrival however is very
doubtful in the present low stage of the water. The success of
this opposition to the old Fur company appears to be very doubtful, as they have not only to contend against very strong oppo-
nents but also against the ruinously low prices of fur at this time.

Thursday, July 6th. Bell and I started this morning with Owen
McKenzie, after breakfast, on horseback to hunt Deer &c in a
point of timber 4 or 5 miles above the Fort which has not been
hunted in a long time. On the way we gave chase to a Wolf but
the rascal took to the hills and our horses could not mount them
so fast as he did and he gave us the slip. We crossed a bluff
which juts down upon the river, it is about 200 feet in height
and affords a beautiful prospect for miles up and down the river[7]
and to a great distance over the praries on the opposite side, while
towards the praries on this side the view is limited by the higher
clay bluffs which form an arc of a circle on either hand of 2 or 3

6 "We found the men there mostly engaged in playing cards and backgammon."
(Audubon, *Journals,* II, 76.)
7 This may be the "Pilot Knob" that Audubon referred to on July 1 (*Journals,*
II, 70).

127

miles in extent and are very picturesque from their rugged forms, cut out from the high prarie by the torrents of past ages, leaving many isolated hills some of a domelike form and others with square tops and entirely bare of vegetation, showing the various strata of different coloured clays, some of these strata near the top of the red brick colour described by Catlin but not exhibiting any signs of ignition that we could discover, indeed some portions of these strata were hardened into clay shale of the same colour. There are occasional narrow veins of sandstone corresponding with the clay strata and others of clay shale apparently, which always corresponds in colour with the clay and are scarcely to be distinguished from it. In one part of these hills we saw several pieces of sandstone jutting out from the clay banks in a horizontal direction and nearly perpendicular to their face, of a form which struck us as very remarkable.—One projected from 8 to 10 feet and was very similar in form to the compressed trees we saw yesterday, the oval form was quite as regular, but instead of the laminae being concentric like wood they were in the direction of the longest diameter of the oval end of the slab, in fact it was regularly stratified sandstone, by some, to me unaccountable process worn into its present regular form, how far it extended into the bank we had no means of ascertaining. It appeared to be in situ. The other pieces which lay around were not quite so regular in form, the sides not being perfectly parallel, but grew thicker at one end. Bell had seen similar stones to these on his ride in search of Buffalo on the [blank in MS]. On reaching the timber in the bottom adjoining the bluffs, we dismounted and tied our horses at the edge of the woods so that they could feed on the grass, and started on foot on our hunt, we saw many signs of Deer and Elk but could not succeed in raising any. We were too late in the day to find them feeding, in consequence our hunt not having been made up until after we arose in the morning. On our return we saw a Red Fox in the Wormwood prarie above the Fort, and as he was some distance from the woods we gave chase to him, at first we gained on him and then he took the lead very handsomely, but on

Fort Union

from a pencil drawing by R. F. Kurz, 1851

View on the Upper Missouri
(clay bluffs 1,800 miles above St. Louis)

from a painting by George Catlin

nearing the woods, Owen having the fastest horse, put the whip into him and gained very fast on him, showing very plainly that a good horse will outrun the foxes of this country, he fired his rifle but of course without effect. Not satisfied with our mornings hunt Bell & I took the skiff after we had dined and crossed the river. Sprague went with us to take a sketch of the Fort. In passing along a road in the woods a Deer crossed it making a stop in the middle, we both fired, but in too great a hurry and missed our venison. We followed the course the Deer took and when nearly at the end of the timber, I used Bell's call to imitate the cry of a fawn, and a fine doe came bounding through the bushes at about 35 paces from us, we discharged 3 barrels at her as she crossed an opening, Bell 2 & I one, and she disappeared in the bushes but at so slow a pace that we had no doubt she was mortally wounded. We reloaded and took her track and found her quite dead about 50 yards in the thicket and what is very remarkable we could find but one shot that struck her and that in the middle of the thigh, and on taking out the entrails there were no marks of their having been wounded. When she was skinned at night, that whole side up to the shoulder was filled under the skin of the meat with clotted blood, and there was an appearance in the ribs of the shot having struck her, we intend examining the skin more closely in the morning. We cut a pole and made an attempt to carry her but I found it rather heavier than I liked to carry for a mile and a quarter and I went back to the landing place where a couple of men were making charcoal to get them to carry it for us, unfortunately they were just drawing out a pit, and they could not both leave it, so that poor Bell was obliged to take one end of the pole and march off to the skiff with it which he did very cheerfully. The tail vertebra of this Doe measured $10\frac{1}{2}$ inches, she was not a large one. On reaching the Fort we found a war party of Assineboin Indians just arrived, the greater part of them had their faces painted black, they were miserably clad and looked more like infernal than human beings. In the evening they were singing their war song in the Indian lodge at the gate, and most of the squaws belonging to the Fort being of the same nation were singing and dancing to the same tune and followed by all the children, making a most hideous uproar, to the great alarm of poor Brag who stuck very close to my heels.[8] There is news of the lost scow having been seen on a sand bar about 10 miles down the river. Owen is to start in the morning in search of it.

Friday, July 7th. Owen rode this morning down the river to the spot where the hunters from the other Fort had reported having seen the scow boat, without having found any traces of it, he saw a couple of Buffalo Bulls swimming the river, they reached the bank on this side, but it was so steep that they could not ascend it and they put back again. After dinner Mr. Audubon, Bell & I walked four miles on our yesterday's route, through a broiling sun, to hunt for the little hare which has puzzled us so much to procure, one of which was shot by Bell on the 21st of June with a rifle.—The signs were abundant but although Brag beat the bushes well nothing could be raised and we returned with empty bags, with the exception of a Raven shot by Mr. A. We examined again the curious slab of sandstone noticed yesterday. I find that the laminae do not lie parallel with the longest diameter of the elliptic end of all these stones, but inclines at different angles in many of them. Another fact which escaped our notice in our hasty examination of yesterday, is that they are not embedded in clay but in a very soft sand stone of the same colour as the whitish clay of which the greater part of the hills appears to be formed, but I have no doubt that in many

8 "Whilst we were sitting at the back gate of the fort, we saw a parcel of Indians coming towards the place, yelling and singing what Mr. Culbertson told me was the song of the scalp dance; we saw through the telescope that they were fourteen in number, with their faces painted black, and that it was a detachment of a war party. . . . Mr. Culbertson sent Mr. Denig to ask them to come in by the front gate of the fort, and put them in the Indian house, a sort of camp for the fellows. They all looked miserably poor, filthy beyond description, and their black faces and foully smelling Buffalo robes made them appear to me like so many devils. The leader, who was well known to be a famous rascal, and was painted red, was a tall, well-formed man. . . . The chief, to show his pride and delight at having killed his enemy, has borrowed a drum; and the company have nearly ever since been yelling, singing, and beating that beastly tambour." (Audubon, *Journals,* II, 77–78.)

places where we see a thin stratum of sandstone, it is always accompanied by this imperfect rock of sandstone of considerable thickness. This soft sandstone contains nodules which I take to be iron pyrites.[9] Squires and Provost started this afternoon to renew their hunt in the point[10] over the river of which they were disappointed by the storm of Tuesday night and Wednesday morning. We passed near them in returning and heard Provost making use of his call and soon after we heard the report of his rifle (Squires gun).

Saturday, July 8th. Squires and Provost returned this morning with the skin of a Doe shot by the former, his maiden shot at Deer, it was brought to them by Provost's call. In the afternoon Bell & I walked through the point of woods above the Fort in search of Deer, but did not see any. The weather today and yesterday has been very hot. In the evening I shot a Wolf from the Fort. It proved a fine one and the head is to be drawn by Squires and the skin pickled.[11]

Sunday, July 9th. The weather not so hot to-day. Provost made a visit to Fort Mortimer to-day and brought word that Mr. Collins was quite unwell. In the afternoon Mr. Audubon and I rode down to see him. He appears to suffer more for the want of good wholesome nourishment than from any other cause. He sent a man back with us and we sent him some Rice and a couple of bottles of Claret Wine and a few doses of Quinine. They are at present entirely without food, they depend entirely upon hunting and their hunters have been out two or three days. They are anxiously expecting their steamboat with supplies and talk of sending their skiff down the river to meet it.[12]

[9] Audubon had a better opinion of Harris as a geologist than Harris had: "of [that] valuable science he knows a good deal" (*Journals*, II, 82).

[10] "We saw a patch of woods called in these regions a 'Point.'" (Audubon, *Journals*, II, 80.) See the discussion of *pointe* in McDermott, *Glossary of Mississippi Valley French*, 123.

[11] Provost reported this day that a porcupine was being kept for Audubon at the Opposition fort: "so Harris drove me over, at the usual breakneck pace, and I bought the animal" (Audubon, *Journals*, II, 82).

[12] Audubon does not mention this visit to Fort Mortimer on the ninth.

Monday, July 10th. Provost, Squires & Owen started after breakfast this morning with horses and a cart and Mule to hunt Antelopes. They expect to return tomorrow. Bell has been quite unwell to-day, he is very costive and has an evident determination of blood of the head. I cannot persuade him to be bled and with difficulty induced him to take some Lee's pills last night, they have proved of little effect, he has taken a dose of salts this morning. In the afternoon I took a horse and rode up the river to the spot visited on Friday to renew the search for the little Hare which is evidently in considerable numbers. And yet so timid are these little animals that we can discover no signs of them at a distance of more than two or three yards from the thick bushes where they take shelter during the day, and where they are perfectly secure from their enemies. About half an hour before sunset I placed myself on the bank of a deep ravine opposite some bushes on the other side, where the signs were numerous and fresh. I remained with the utmost patience until 9 of the clock when no longer being able to see I gave it up for a bad job. Before leaving I approached the bushes quietly and could hear the little rascals moving about in them. There is nothing in the country which has puzzled us so much to procure as this little rabbit, said by everyone to be abundant. If we go into the bushes, principally rose bushes, they are so thick that we cannot see them when they start, and if we lie in wait for them in the morning and evening they wont come out to be shot, and there is no dog to be had who will follow their tracks. Mr. Audubon has offered a reward for them and a young Indian has been out nearly every day for the last two weeks without being able to procure one. I forgot to mention yesterday that Mr A. procured from a man at the other fort a porcupine,[13] supposed to be a young of last year. There appears to be little doubt that it is a species entirely different from those of our northern states and Canada.

Thursday, July 13th. Bell & I have both been sick for the last

[13] *Quadrupeds,* I, 277–86 (Plate 36).

two days. I bled Bell the day before yesterday. We both feel
pretty well recovered to-day, but did not go out until towards
evening when we crossed the river to look for the little Hare,
but were again unsuccessful. Bell shot a Wolf that was lying
under the bank of the River, just as we were landing. He had
no doubt swam across and was too weak to scramble up the
bank or to swim a little farther up the stream where he could
have made a good landing. Mr Audubon, Mr Culbertson &
Squires took a ride in the carryall to the prairie where they
usually cut their hay, about 10 miles down the river, they saw
within a mile of the Fort 17 Wolves together, among them
two Prarie Wolves. They shot a bird which is no doubt from
Mr Audubon's description a New Lark, but they could not
find it in the bushes. As they intend to go in search of it again
tomorrow I will not add anything more until we find whether
it is procured or not. They saw a number of Grous. They also
killed a Bob-o-link[14] which is believed to be the common one
although the white on the back is pure white without any
mixture of yellow.

Yesterday Mr Culbertson had an *Indian Puppy* killed for a
Dog Feast which he had promised us for some time. It was
killed and immediately held over a hot fire until the hair was
crisp. It was then scraped off with a knife, the entrails taken
out and the head cut off, and the rest thrown at once into a
pot over the fire and boiled until done, and then served up in
Indian Style in a large dish without bread, salt or any other fixings. The Old Hands appeared to enjoy it, particularly M^r C's
Squaw,[15] Mr Audubon declared it was equal to young Pig and
ate quite heartily of it.[16] I might have tasted it had it been a real
Indian Feast, but as I did not feel very well I let it pass this time

[14] *Ornithological Biography*, I, 283–87 (Plate 54).

[15] This was Natawista, whom Culbertson married legally at Peoria in 1859. At
the time Audubon and Harris knew her she was about eighteen or twenty years old.
For an appreciative account of her see McDonnell, "Fort Benton and Fort Sarpy
Journals," 243–46.

[16] Cf. Audubon, *Journals*, II, 85.

rather than risk a rebellion from that important member of the body corporate, the Stomach.

Friday, July 14th. Mr Audubon, Squires & I went this morning to search for the Lark they saw yesterday. We found the mate of the one he shot and two young ones, it proved to be the Shore Lark, which breeds here in considerable numbers. In returning I shot a Sharp-tailed Grous. Mr Culbertson presented me this afternoon with a beautiful Blackfoot Shirt made of the skin of the Kabri or Antelope. This shirt belonged to a cheif called by the French *Le Soulier de femme* or *Woman's Moccassin,* it is beautifully worked with dyed porcupine quills and ornamented with the scalp locks of his enemies slain in battle. This is the same cheif who killed a Mr Vandenburg[h] of the Company's serv-ice, some ten or eleven years ago. Towards evening we had an exhibition of riding on the Prarie. Mr Culbertson, with *Squires & Owen,* dressed as Blackfeet chiefs and M^r C's and another squaw dressed, the first in Blackfoot, and the other in Assineboin costume astride their horses, started and performed some fine evolutions at full speed, the Squaws quite as much at their ease on the horses as the men. Mr Culbertson took my Cane Gun to give a trial in case they should see a Wolf. They started one in the Ravine of Garden River. Mr C. on his Blackfoot Mare was soon along side of him and shot him in beautiful stile with the little Gun, which carries what they call the *trade ball* (the only ball that is used in the country to fit all sizes of guns) most beautifully. A little later the horses were saddled again and another for me and the three gentlemen & I started on a regular Wolf hunt. We were hardly outside the Fort gate before the cry of Wolf was raised and off we started at full speed. I had the cane gun, which was unloaded and for the first time I attempted to load while the horse was running. I soon found that a com-mon powder horn is better for the purpose than a patent flask. I got the load in after a fashion, I was up in good time and was preparing to shoot when Mr Culbertson fired and shot the Wolf and the next leap my horse jumped over him. The Wolf was not quite dead and I discharged my little piece at him, and found that nearly all the powder I had put into my hand while running, to throw into the barrel had blown away, and merely sufficient to carry the ball out of the gun was left. This Wolf was on the level prarie and made but a short run for his life. We hardly reseated in our saddles before a second Wolf was seen on the hills and off we started at full speed. This fellow made a better run, as the ground was more in his favour, the first shot from Owen crippled him and Mr Culbertson and I had a race for the next shot. I fired first and the Wolf fell and as Mr C. approached he gave him another which finished him. This Wolf ran about a mile. We proceeded about a mile further before we saw another which was at a long distance, and he started at a rapid pace. We were now quite among the hills and Mr Wolf proving faster than the others succeeded in making his escape among the ravines after giving us a handsome chace of about a mile over a very rough country. Soon after we had lost sight of him and while still on the search, a young Townsend's Hare started from under my horses feet and stopped within a short distance. I stopped my horse and shot him with the ball I had intended for the Wolf. It was now growing near dark and we bent our steps toward the Fort.

Saturday, July 15th. Mr Audubon, Mr Culbertson, Bell & I in the carryall with two horses in tandem, Squires and Owen & Provost on horseback and three men with a mule to the cart on which was placed our skiff and a tent and our baggage, started this morning after breakfast on an expedition to the Yellowstone which we have been talking about for some time, to look for Elk, Bighorns and Beaver. We were provided with nothing in the way of eatables but about a dozen hard buiscuits, such as are used by sailors. Our intention was to hunt a while on the north side of the Yellow Stone, then take the skiff and drop down to a good place among the hills on the other side for Bighorns, and then to a spot at the mouth of the Charboneau River, where there is said to be a Beaver Lodge & Dam. We crossed the

Missouri at the Fort in a scow which we left well fastened to the Bank to be ready on our return to ferry ourselves back with. We followed the level prairie on the banks, of the Missouri to the Junction of the Yellow Stone, then kept on a similar prarie up the river to a distance of about 20 miles from the Fort. We reached this spot early in the afternoon encamping on the open prarie directly on the bank of the river. While the rest were pitching the tent and arranging the camp Bell, Owen & I went out on an adjoining point of timber to look for game. The tracks of Elk were very numerous, paths were beaten in all directions so that there was no difficulty in getting along, although the undergrowth of Rose bushes and the Small Red-barked Cornus, which is smoked by the Indians on the Lower Missouri, was exceedingly heavy. We walked for some time and not finding the game on foot so near the middle of the day, we sat down to await their feeding time. As the evening approached the Mosquitoes became so abundant that after trying to combat them for some time we were obliged to beat a retreat even at the risk of going supperless to bed without having eaten since breakfast. On our return we found that Mr Audubon had caught four small catfish, and with a cup of coffee and a small piece of soaked biscuit we managed to make a light meal. The day had been excessively hot, but with a good breeze, which failed at night, and we all spread our beds outside the tent, and we were soon comfortably sleeping beneath our Mosquito nets. About 12 o'clock we were aroused by the approach of a thunder gust and by the time we could tear up our *fixings* and bundle ourselves and things into the tent it came on to rain very hard with a strong wind and incessant thunder and lightning. I got a situation near the entrance of the tent and soon found that the rain was beating in and the wind was tearing the tent cloth, and there was danger of its getting under and carrying off the whole tent into the river and I was obliged to hold on to the two corners with my feet and hands while the rain continued to pour down in torrents for about half an hour, during which time I got soaked to the knees, and my coat wet through from being obliged to sit

136

against the weather side of the tent. As soon as the rain ceased
and the wind abated I pulled off my moccasins and stockings
and wrapped myself in my blanket spent the night as comfortably as the mosquitoes would permit.

Sunday, July 16th. We were stirring at an early hour and spread
our beds and blankets to dry while a cup of coffee was making
of which we partook without a particle of anything to eat.
Provost and Bell went out with their guns but returned without
game. Mr Audubon too was entirely without bait, and we began
anxiously to look out for a Wolf that he might be run down
and used for bait, various discussions going on at the same time
about the quality of Wolf flesh, some averring most stoutly that
a good fat Wolf was better eating than *Dog meat.* It was not
long before a Wolf was seen and Owen was started off on one
of the hunting horses, he soon found he had an ugly customer,
for we have discovered that there is a very great difference in
the running of wolves. It was not until he had chased him several
miles and fired 7 or 8 shots at him that he could claim the Wolf
as his own—as soon as we found he had killed him an old
horse was sent to bring home the game. While we were watching the chace Mr Culbertson discovered a Buffalo at a distance
of three or four miles. The Blackfoot was soon saddled and he
started off in pursuit. He stopped on his way for Owen to join
him as he returned from the Wolf hunt and the two went on
slowly to where he had lost sight of the Buffalo at the foot of
the hills. They proceeded slowly to give Owen's horse time to
blow after the hard chace she had had, and we continued to
watch them with great anxiety. It was nearly an hour before I
saw Mr C. in chace of the Buffalo which passed into a ravine
from which I could see that they did not emerge until I saw Mr
C. standing on the edge of it. I then felt sure that the Bull was
killed, although the distance was so great that we did not hear
the report of any guns nor see the flash. We immediately ordered the cart to go for the meat and Bell and I had a horse put
to the carryall and drove to the spot. We met Mr C. returning

who told us that it was a remarkably fine Bull, and that he
thought we should not be able to procure a better specimen for
skinning. On reaching the spot we found a fine large Bull of
very good colour having shed all his winter coat but the summer
hair having only commenced growing over the hinder parts and
the mane and long hair of the legs and throat much shorter
than the others that we had killed on the river. The head too
was somewhat damaged by the operation of taking out the
tongue which Mr C. had carried to the camp. (I forgot to mention that Squires started with us on *old Peter* to see the Bull but
when he met Mr Culbertson and the tongue—this deponent
sayeth not. I retail this joke upon Squires as Mr A. informs me
it was at Mr C.'s request that he turned back as the horse was
wanted.) Under the circumstances we determined to carry back
the skin of the Bull, and had taken his measurements and commenced operations when a messenger arrived from Mr Audubon with orders to bring the skin. At this stage of the proceedings Owen discovered another bull making his way slowly
across the Prarie directly toward us. I was the only one of the
party who had balls for his gun and I would gladly have claimed
the privilege of running him but fearing that I might make out
badly on my first trial with my large Gun which is altogether
too heavy to run with (weighting eleven pounds) and supposing the meat could be carried to the Fort where it was much
wanted. I handed my gun and balls to Owen and Bell and I
placed ourselves on eminence to view the chace. Owen approached the Bull who had continued to advance and was now
about a quarter of a mile distant. The Bull either did not see
him or did not heed him and they advanced directly toward
each other until they were about 70 or 80 yards when the Buffalo started at a good run, and Owen's mare, which had already
had two hard runs this morning had great difficulty in preserv-
ing her distance. Owen soon perceived this and applying the
whip pretty freely he was soon within shooting distance and
fired a shot which sensibly checked the progress of the animal
and enabled him quickly to be alongside of him when he dis-

charged the second barrel into his lungs, passing through the shoulder blade, which brought him to a stand precisely in the position represented in Catlin's work of the wounded Bull.[17] And it gives me pleasure to bear testimony to the faithfulness of that representation, particularly in this country where poor Catlin finds no quarter, and if we are able to believe all we hear of him there is not a word of truth nor a faithful illustration in the whole of his book. But to return to the Bull—Bell & I started now at the top of our speed and as soon as we were within speaking distance called to Owen not to shoot again. The Bull did not appear to be much exhausted, but he was so stiffened by the shot in the shoulder that he could not turn quickly, taking advantage of which we approached him, as we came near he would work himself slowly around to face us and then make a pitch at us—We then stepped to one side and commenced discharging our six-barrelled pistols at him with little more effect than increasing his fury at every shot. His appearance was now one to inspire terror, had we not felt satisfied of our ability to avoid him. I came however very near being overtaken by him through imprudence. I placed myself directly in front of him and as he advanced I fired at his head and then ran directly ahead of him, not supposing he was able to overtake me, but casting my head over my shoulder I saw Mr Bull within three feet of me, prepared to give me a taste of his horns. The next moment I was off the track and the poor beast was unable to turn quickly enough to avenge the insult. Bell now took the gun from Owen and shot him directly behind the shoulder blade, he stood tottering for a few moments with an increased gush of blood from the mouth and nostrils, fell easily on his knees and rolled over on his side and was soon dead. He was a very old animal in poor case and even if he had been fat, with one cart we could not have taken all the meat to the Fort.[18] When I discovered this

[17] Apparently a reference to Catlin, *North American Indians*, I, 25 and Plate 10.

[18] Phillips B. Street, in "The Edward Harris Collection of Birds," 179–80, has called attention to the curious similarity of Harris's and Audubon's accounts of the buffalo hunt on July 16. His conjecture that some error was made in transcribing Audubon's journal appears sound, for Harris relates the same story about himself in

I was very sorry that I had not run him myself, feeling satisfied
as I now do that I could have killed him easily, running him
alone without the excitement of competition which may take
place when we have our long promised Buffalo hunt. We left the
Buffalo for the Wolves and birds of prey and returned to the skinning of the first which had much the best skin of the two. The arrival of the cart with two men and the messenger sent by M^r
Audubon relieved me from the necessity of assisting in the
operation of skinning, and I mounted Old Peter who had been
ridden by the messenger, and made my way as fast as possible
to see what chance there was for breaking my fast, it was nearly
one o'clock when I got there, and I made a light meal of the
remains of some catfish which had been boiled and drank some
of the broth which was very palatable. When Bell had finished
the skinning and returned to camp we consulted as to further
movements, and it was decided that Mr Culbertson, Mr A., Bell
and I should return to the Fort and leave Squires and Provost
to go down the Yellowstone in a skiff and remain as long as
they pleased or until they could procure something worth bringing home. We struck our tent and packed up our baggage and
started at half past 3 o'clock, the cart with the meat and skin
starting at the same time and Owen on Mr Culbertson's mare.
We traveled at a very good pace, stopping occasionally to see
Owen endeavour to approach an antelope of which we saw
several, as we also did in going out. One of the animals Owen
fired at and missed, another in its company appearing less shy
Owen endeavoured to approach but he took good care to keep
just out of gun shot, but when Owen gave up the chace and
galloped off on his horse, the Antelope galloped after him and
followed him for some distance, which Owen perceiving he rode
behind a little eminence and dismounted, concealing himself to
await its approach leaving his horse without hitching. We
watched them until we saw that Owen's ruse did not succeed

his letter to Dr. Spencer begun on December 1, 1843, at New Orleans. In that letter
he says that Audubon was away fishing when this happened (see introduction). We
know, too, that during this trip Audubon was regularly avoiding the more strenuous
forms of hunting.

and then went on leaving him still pursueing the animal on foot
to endeavour to get a shot. After riding between three and four
miles we were surprised to see his horse following us. We hitched
him to a tree and proceeded to the river opposite the Fort. Supposing Owen would not be there very soon to help us ferry ourselves over Mr Audubon, Bell and I stopped about a mile back
in the woods to eat service berries which are now ripe and in
great abundance. We found them very grateful after the poor
fare we had had on the Prarie and we ate heartily of them. When
we reached the scow we found that Owen had taken a short cut
through the woods and got there before us. We decided not to
wait for the cart, and left our waggon and all the baggage but
the guns and ferried ourselves over, arriving in good time for
supper. We saw nothing new on this trip. Bell shot a sharp-
tailed Grous. Saw a Sand-hill Crane, two Golden Eagles, Rice
birds, Curlews and Bartram's Sandpiper.[19] Some of the men saw
some wild geese on the Bank of the river near our encampment
when they first arrived, they took to the water and swam down
the river, neither old nor young being able to fly at this season.
Two men arrived at the Fort to-day from Fort Pierre, with letters
but we have heard no news that they have brought.[20] They were
23 days on their way and saw no Indians.

The measurements of the bull that was skinned are as
follows:

	Inches
From nose to root of tail	111½
Tail vertebra	17
Hair at end of tail	13
Extreme length	141½
Length of head	25½
Heighth at shoulder	65¼
or 16 hands 1¼ in. high	

[19] Golden Eagles: see *Ornithological Biography,* I, 58–65 (Plate 11), and II,
464–69 (Plate 181); Curlews, III, 240–45 (Plate 231); Bartram's Sandpiper, IV,
24–30 (Plate 303).

[20] Audubon noted that "one is a cook as well as a hunter, the other named
Wolff, a German, and a tinsmith by trade, though now a trapper" (*Journals,* II, 96).

Height at rump	58½
From top of shoulder to point of brisket or greatest breadth of neck	31½
Knee to bottom of forefoot	15½
″ ″ ″ ″ hindfoot	22
Nose to anterior canthus of eye	13¼
″ ″ root of ear	14
From anterior canthus of eye to root of horn	5½
Between eyes in a straight line	12⅝
Length of ear	5½
Between horns in a straight line at root	11
″ tips of do	18
Length of eye	1¾
Breadth of do.	1¼
Breadth of nose	7
Heighth of flesh part of do.	3¾
Between the nostrils	2⅜
Length of do.	2½

Weight of skin with the head and leg bones attached and uncleaned 290 lbs.

Monday, July 17th. As we lost our usual day of rest yesterday we made up for the loss today, and I recollect nothing worth writing. By the by poor Bell did not come in for his share of rest for he had to go to work with the assistance of a coloured man who came up from Fort Pierre, and who is to hunt for us for the balance of time that we remain here, to clean and prepare the skin of the Bull and salt it down. The bones of the head were taken out entire and skin and bones of the legs just filled entirely a Pork Barrel.

Tuesday, July 18th. This morning Mr Audubon, Mr Culbertson and I took a ride to the Hay field about a mile and a half above the Fort where several of the men[21] have pitched their tent and

[21] Audubon found "among them one called Bernard Adams, of Charleston, S. C., who knew the Bachmans quite well, and who had read the whole of the 'Biographies of Birds'" (*Journals*, II, 97).

commenced the Hay harvest to supply to [the?] large stock of horses and cattle for the winter. It is a beautiful bottom prarie covered with a sort of blue-stemmed grass said to be of the best quality which the country produces for winter fodder. They expect to cut several hundred loads and are obliged to begin before the grass is quite ripe as we should prefer it in the Jersies and the cutting is not finished until it is much older than we should like it. There are some two or three hundred acres which are fit for mowing, and they are so fortunate to have this meadow fit for mowing this year, supposed to have been improved by the unusual rise of the river this year having completely flooded it. They usually cut their hay ten or twelve miles down the river. The saving of labor can be largely appreciated by a Jersey Farmer. We found everything going on well, took a drink of river water out of their cask, and turned our horses towards a ravine where I found a few days ago some fine specimens of the small yucca of this country in flower. We soon found them and pulled up one of the roots to carry home for Sprague to draw. I had also seen before in a branch of this ravine a reed or small cane growing in a wet place which was different from anything we had seen before on the river, but unfortunately I was unable to find the spot again. While hunting for the reeds, a large owl started from some old cedar trees and it struck us as being of a very light colour, it appeared to be about the size of the barred owl as it flew. Mr Audubon alighted from his horse and followed it for some time but lost it without being able to get a shot. While following it he heard the note of a bird which was new to him which he soon procured and found to be the Rock Wren or Rocky Mountain Anteater of Say.[22] In the meantime I continued the search of the Reeds and while doing so shot two Say's Flycatchers and missed a Shrike, which I believed to be the loggerhead Shrike.[23] At this moment I also heard the new note of the Wren when Mr Audubon called to me from the bottom of the Ravine and I left it with the intention of returning after dinner.

[22] *Ornithological Biography*, IV, 443–45 (Plate 360).
[23] *Ornithological Biography*, I, 300–302 (Plate 57).

We returned to the Fort and about 3 o'clock started again on three horses with Bell in the place of Mr Culbertson. And we were so fortunate as to procure three more of the Wrens and the Owl all of which were shot by Bell. The Owl we found to be the great Virginian long-eared owl[24] instead of the barred and in a remarkably light coloured plumage, very similar to the one which was found by Richardson in the Fur Countries and described by him as a new bird, but which had to be striken from the list, as it differed in no respect from the Virginianus except in colour. The measurements correspond within half an inch in length and one in the extent of the measurements of the male given by Mr Audubon, being that much smaller than his bird.

Measurements of the Whitish variety of the Great Horned Owl

Bill to tail	22½
" " end of claws	23¾
" " pinion	5½
Wing	14¾
Alar extent	55
Tarsus	2¼

proved on skinning to be a Young Female that had not bred, possibly of this season.

We observed that the habits of the Rock Wren correspond with those heretofore recorded of it, with the exception that it runs into holes in the clay banks and lives entirely among them instead of among the rocks. Mr Audubon shot another bird this morning in the entrance to a hole, Mr Culbertson dug out the hole entirely as he supposed without finding the bird but on our return in the afternoon, we continued the search for the bird and discovered another passage in the hole which had escaped his notice and which ran upwards and came out at the surface of the ground in a bunch of Wormwood, and by which the bird, probably being only wing broken had escaped. We now discovered that a heavy shower was approaching and put off for the Fort, without stopping for my Reeds which I had found in the

[24] *Ornithological Biography*, I, 313–18 (Plate 61).

meantime. Mr Audubon was mounted on Old Peter and it was quite necessary that he should *keep a grinding* as he sometimes expresses himself if he wished to reach the Fort with a dry jacket. Bell and I galloped off to the Haymaker's tent to get a drink of water and soon overtook Old Peter and kept a short distance ahead of him to encourage the old critter to mend his pace. We succeeded in reaching the Fort before it rained hard. The shower proved a heavy one and there appears now to be a prospect of a good deal of rain falling in the night.

Wednesday, July 19*th.* It rained most of the night and the Prarie was wet this morning and we were not out with our Guns in fact the ground within walking distance of the Fort is pretty well used up for new or rare birds or quadrupeds and the walking distance is very much circumscribed by the excessive heat of the weather. In the afternoon we were busy in making preparations for our long expected Buffalo hunt which is to come off to-morrow somewhere on the Prarie lying between the Yellowstone and the Missouri, where all the meat is killed for the use of the Fort. It has now been several weeks since the hunters have been out, the last time they were gone three days and travelled forty miles before they found Buffalo, so that our success is very doubtful.

Thursday, July 20*th.* We breakfasted early this morning and by 8 o'clock had crossed our horses, baggage, and carts and set out from the opposite side of the river, with two horses before the carryall in which Mr Aud, Mr Culbertson, Mr Bell & I rode followed by two carts with 2 mules each carrying the baggage and provisions, Squires riding in one of them, with a driver in each and one man to attend to our four hunting horses.[25] We mounted the hills by a middle road between the rivers and proceeded at a slow pace through a broiling sun. We stopped several times to endeavor to approach Antelopes of which we saw

25 For this buffalo hunt, see Audubon, *Journals*, II, 102–107; *Quadrupeds*, II, 32–55 (Plates 56 and 57). See also Harris's letter to Spencer, December 1, 1843, quoted in the introduction.

a number as we passed along, and although they were not very shy we could not get within killing distance of any of them. About 12 o'clock we reached the valley of Fox River which runs into the Yellowstone, it is a small stream in wet weather, but has no running water at this time. We were just about crossing it when Mr Culbertson looked back and saw 4 Buffalo Bulls, quietly grazing at the distance of about a mile and which had previously been hid from our view by a rise in the Prarie. We quickly saddled our hunters and arranged our dress and accoutrements for the chace and started with the whole of our equipage in a direct line for the herd covered by a small eminence behind which we left the carriages with Mr Audubon so that he could ascend the mound and have a fine view of the chace while we filed off to the right, keeping out of sight behind the hill so as to come upon them in such a way as to force them to run in the fine level valley of Fox River, thereby ensuring a fine run and at the same time give Mr. Audubon a good view of the chace. Our approach was a good one and as there was a bull apiece for us we agreed to stick to the bull of our choice without interfering with that of our neighbor. As soon as they commenced to run Mr C. gave the word for us to start which we all did at full run, the bulls soon separated, two were followed by Mr C. & Bell and Squires and I took those which went to the right. Knowing that Squires had the fastest horse I waited for him to choose, he fired into his bull and I crossed his track after the other, just as I was passing him his horse had come up with the Bull who turned him, and instead of turning off gradually to the right as he (the horse) should have done (the hunters always ride to the right of the Buffalo) he stopped suddenly and wheeled to the left behind the Bull, this movement being unexpected to Squires he lost his seat and fell to the ground, the bull proceeding without attacking either horse or rider, I checked my horse long enough to ascertain that Squires was not disabled (for he was on his feet in a moment and in pursuit of his horse) and pushed on after my game, which I soon overtook and fired striking him in the middle of the thigh, a few strides more brought me directly opposite him and I shot him in the lungs just behind the shoulder. I rode along side of him reloading my gun, which I had just accomplished when I saw blood gushing in a stream from his mouth and nostrils in such a way that I knew he must soon fall, I therefore turned away and galloped after Squire's horse which I caught and brought back to him. On looking around I saw that my Bull was down. Squires soon mounted and as his Bull had stopped a short distance to look after his companions, he and I started in pursuit, determined if possible to avenge the mishap of poor Squires. We had not proceeded far before Squires discovered that the muzzle of his gun had become stopped with earth in his fall. I exchanged with him, one of my barrels being loaded and on we pushed, on approaching him Squires fired and struck him behind so as not sensibly to arrest his progress, we pushed on again at a rapid pace, but through some difficulty in loading he did not get another shot and from the effects of his fall he felt so much overcome as to be unable to proceed any further and turned back and I took the gun to make another effort to secure the long winded monster who had now led us a long chace. The Bull soon came to a steep clay bank which he stumbled down for about 15 feet, I was fortunately far enough off to check the speed of my horse and walk him down it. This prolonged my chace but at last I came up with him. As I raised myself in my stirrups, leaning a little towards the Bull, and was on the point of pulling the trigger the Bull made a rush at my horse, I was so eager in the pursuit as to have forgotten all the cautions which had been given me on this head and as my horse wheeled off to the right I lost my balance and came to the ground between him and the Bull, I was on my feet in an instant, and as the Bull paused to consider whether he should put his threat into execution I levelled and snapped both barrels at him, broadside to me, at the distance of about 20 feet and the Bull pursued his way. On examining my Gun I found that in falling, the heads of the cocks which cover the caps had become filled with earth, which prevented the caps from exploding. I caught my horse but found myself so completely out of breath with my long chace and my fall that I gave up the chace and slowly wended my way back to the spot where I left my Bull and which I found to be between three and four miles, happy to find that I was not much bruised and had escaped the horns of a vicious old Buffalo Bull, and purchased besides another good lesson in running Buffalo. When I got back I found that Mr Culbertson & Bell had each killed their Bulls and I was happy to find that Mr Audubon had had a splendid view of the whole chase. When the Bulls first separated, the two which were selected by Mr C. and Bell ran close together and crowded each other, turning round to the left at the same time in such a way that it was with difficulty either of them could get a fair shot, until Bell fired at one in the hinder parts which separated them and each followed his own. Mr Culbertson's Bull was the first that fell, mine next and then Bell's at the distance of about a mile and a half. It was determined to cut up Mr Culbertson's Bull and mine which were both remarkably fat and send the meat at once in one of the carts back to the Fort. We each cut off the tails of our bulls as trophies and as soon as they were butchered and a cart despatched we proceeded to a small river a couple of miles beyond Fox River to pitch our tent with the intention of proceeding on the morrow. When within a half a mile of the new camping ground we caught sight of a small herd of Buffalo just beyond it. A consultation was held as to running them tonight or taking our chance of finding them or others in the morning. We were all willing to defer it until morning except Squires who felt anxious to redeem the opportunity he had lost in the first chase by his fall, and we all consented to run. We started cautiously as before and wound around the hills until we came in open view at about 600 yards distance when we formed into single file under the lead of Mr. C. and walked our horses to within a couple of hundred yards of them when off they started. On counting them we found that there were eight of them, all Bulls. Mr C. took a Bull which separated from the herd at once and went around some hills to the right. We each chose a Bull and discharged our guns into them, but as we had been more cautious this time not to ap-

proach too near their horns our shots though well aimed were
not so effective and the Bulls kept up with the herd which took
towards the valley at a rattling pace, we followed for about two
miles during which time I got two more shots at my Bull and
finally he turned around and made a rush at me which I was
prepared for and easily avoided, he now began to fail and after
running away from the herd about a hundred yards he came to
a stand in a ravine, and stood with the blood gushing from his
mouth and nostrils, at the same time showing a strong disposition for battle. I levelled at him once more and my gun snapped.
I now saw that he was failing fast and I did not attempt to fire
again—he fell in a few minutes—in the meantime Bell had his
Bull down about 150 yards behind me and had rode up to see the
death of mine. Squires continued on in chace of the herd but
did not kill his Bull feeling too sore from his bruises of the morning, which were not slight, to follow any further. We now regretted having destroyed these noble beasts for no earthly reason but to gratify a sanguinary disposition which appears to be
inherent in our natures. We had no means of carrying home the
meat and after cutting out the tongues we wended our way
back to camp, completely disgusted with ourselves and with the
conduct of all white men who come to this country. In this way
year after year thousands of these animals are slaughtered for
mere sport and the carcasses left for the wolves. The skins are
worth nothing at this season. The horse I rode is one of the best
belonging to the fort for the chase of the Buffalo, he is said to be
an Indian horse from the Blackfoot country of a roan colour
about 14½ hands high, remarkably stout built with strong short
limbs, can run fast enough to overtake the fleetest Buffalo and
has good wind and great powers of endurance. In approaching
the herd he needs no guiding, you throw the reins on his neck
and he runs to within 15 or 20 feet on the right side as soon as
you fire he shies off gently to the right to avoid a rush from the
animal, if you have not killed you load your gun at once while
he continues to run along the side of the animal with the reins
on his neck. This is rather difficult for a beginner but I succeeded

once very well, the other charge I was obliged to stop him, this makes the chace too long and is one of the great faults of a young beginner, indeed it is the main thing in Buffalo hunting to load your gun quickly while the horse continues at full speed. There is but little difficulty in hitting so large a mark and the faster your horse runs at the moment at taking aim, the more steady will your aim be. We did not get back to camp until after dark and at one time felt somewhat apprehensive that we should not find it, but on calling we were answered by a loud shout from the camp and we were soon among our friends recounting our exploits over a good cup of coffee, some hard buiscuit and the boss or hump of one of the Bulls killed in the morning. Mr C. had wounded his bull and brought him to a stand but at such a distance that he did not go after him, as he was mounted on a young mare of three years old who was fatigued with the morning run.

Friday, July 21st. We passed a good night under the Mosquito nets outside of the tent and were up at the break of the day and after taking a cup of coffee we started off on foot to hunt for Cabri or Antelopes, but did not succeed in getting any although Mr Audubon decoyed one within 60 or 70 yards by lying on his back and kicking his heels in the air.[26] On our return to camp about eleven o'clock we packed up and started for home. On our way we visited the carcasses of the 3 Buffaloes slain in the morning of yesterday for the purpose of carrying off the horns, we saw but one wolf at the remains and as he walked away he was so completely filled that he looked more like a hog than a wolf. On our way home we saw two more Bulls, but we were already satisfied with our sport and did not molest them. We reached home about half past four in the afternoon and found

---

26 That is to say, Harris, Bell, and LaFleur, a mulatto hunter, went off after antelopes. It was sometime later in the morning that Audubon joined Harris and played decoy: "In about twenty minutes he [the antelope] had come two or three hundred yards . . . when about sixty yards off I could see his eyes, and being loaded with buck-shot pulled the trigger without rising from my awkward position. Off he went; Harris fired, but he only ran the faster for some hundred yards, when he turned, looked at us again, and was off." (*Journals*, II, 106.)

that the man[27] who was sent with the meat yesterday was lost on the prarie and was obliged to lie out all night and did not reach the Fort until 10 o'clock this morning with his meat nearly spoilt. We found at the Fort a small party of Assineboin Indians who had arrived in the morning. Just about as the gates were being closed in the evening another party of 12 or 15 arrived, singing their war songs as the[y] marched towards the Fort, we had just finished supper as the[y] approached and were on the ramparts watching them, when the bell sounded for the second supper, which brought them instantly to a halt, and one of them fell flat on the ground. Two or three head men were admitted inside and the rest were obliged to take up their lodgings inside the double gates of the Fort in front.

Saturday, July 22nd. About one o'clock this morning[28] I was called up to attend one of the Indians who arrived last night, the messenger said he had been bleeding at the nose for a long time and would soon bleed to death if relief were not soon afforded. I told him to get some ice immediately. I found the report but too true he was still bleeding freely and his pulse quite low and frequent. I applied the ice to the back of his neck, the top of his head and between his legs, bathing his head well with ice water, placing him in a sitting position with his head inclining a little backwards, this checked the bleeding in some measure, but I could not stop it until I could get some alum burnt and powdered and stopped his nostrils with pledgets of cotton covered with the burnt alum which stopped the bleeding at once. I learned from the Indians who were with him that bleeding at the nose was very common among them and that they frequently fell victims to it. This is not at all surprising, as their heads are almost always uncovered. This party of Indians are from one of the Northern branches of the Assineboin Tribe and were on their way to make war on the Grosventres, as they called it, or

27 Pike, a clerk at the fort (Audubon, *Journals,* II, 104).

28 Audubon recorded this incident as of the twenty-third. When they returned to the fort on the twenty-eighth after a three-day absence, Audubon noted that this "poor wretched Indian . . . died yesterday morning" (*Journal,* II, 121).

in other words to steal horses from them: All the other bands of the Assineboins have recently made peace with the Grosventres but this tribe had not heard of it and were not to be baffled in their design and determined to proceed. We did not go out to-day as the weather was excessively hot, the thermometer at 90 in the shade[29] and we were all feeling the effects of our hard riding of Thursday.

Sunday, July 23rd. The Buffalo meat that was thought fit to use was put upon the ice, but by this morning it was entirely spoiled and was thrown away, and Mr Culbertson had determined to cross the Missouri again to-morrow to endeavour to procure some for his men who are hard at work securing their hay. But this afternoon a Bull showed himself on the edge of the hill about a mile back from the Fort and immediately three others placed themselves alongside of him. The temptation was too strong for Bell and I and we determined to join Mr Culbertson in the chase, although we knew the ground was very bad to ride over. We were soon ready and the Bulls keeping their position suffered us to make a long circuit to leeward. We reached the top of the hill about two hundred yards from them just as they had determined to march back the way they came, the sight of us set them off at a full run and we followed as fast as we could, they took at once into a deep ravine and gained on us considerably, but rising to the top of a hill which was tolerably level we each got a shot and wounded our Bull, Bells separated from the rest and he left us, Mr C. and I followed the other three who took across the ravines to the East through the worst ground they could find. Mr Culbertson however kept close to them and soon had one down. I followed as well as I could but lost ground and it was not until Mr C. had killed his second Bull and had fired a shot into mine that I overtook them. At this moment Mr C. lost the flint out of his gun, which gave me an opportunity which I might otherwise have lost of killing the Bull which I had lodged two bullets into at the commencement of the chase.

[29] Audubon's record showed the temperature as "99°–102°" (*Journals*, II, 108).

The whole chase did not probably occupy 20 minutes and we secured a fine parcel of meat for the use of the Fort. It has been a year since any Buffaloes have been seen so near the Fort and we begin to hope that the number of Bulls we have seen within a few days indicates the approach of the larger herds and the vicinity of cows, as this is the height of the rutting season. A good run after cows will satisfy us of our ability to manage this kind of hunting. The cows are much swifter than the bulls, but there is not so much danger in approaching them as they seldom turn upon the horse and are more easily killed. The only danger is in the faster riding. All the Bulls that we have killed are uncommonly fat for the season, in consequence of the frequent rains of this summer having kept the grass in fine order, whereas it is usually completely burnt up by this time.

Monday, July 24th. Soon after breakfast Mr A., Bell & I went out with Mr Culbertson to the scene of yesterday's slaughter to take the measurements and weight of the largest Bull which was purposely left untouched last night as we knew the wolves had become very scarce of late in consequence of there being no Buffalo in the country. The conjecture was right—the Bull was untouched by Wolf or Buzzard and we proceeded to take his measurements and to weigh him, he proved to be a very large one and quite fat for a Bull at this season—He was cut up in a rough way in such pieces as could be weighed by the steelyards which reached only 335 lbs. For want of time we did not weigh the fore and hind quarters separately—care was taken to weigh the entrails with their contents and as much of the blood as was clotted and could be handled, so that our allowance for the loss of blood and for liquid that escaped from the paunch by an accidental cut was only 25 lbs. In this way the weight was 1777 lbs. and we all thought that an additional 3 lbs. might fairly have been added to the losses which would make his weight 1780 lbs. and there is little doubt but that he would have gained 220 lbs. of fat by the commencement of winter, which would make the weight 2000 lbs. at which they have heretofore been estimated, and which I should think a safe one for a large sized fat Bull. Saw two Bulls at a distance of several miles travelling towards the river.

Measurements of Buffalo Bull

	Inches
Length measured from nose following line of head and back to root of tail	131
Height at shoulders	67
Or 16 hands 3 inches	
Height at rump	57
Tail vertebra	15½
" hair	11

Tuesday, July 25th. Nothing of importance done to-day excepting preparations for a hunt for cows across the river.

Wednesday, July 26th. We took a very early breakfast this morning and by [blank in MS] o'clock we started from the opposite side of the River from the Fort with M^rC. Mr A. Bell & myself in the Carryall, drawn by two horses, 2 carts with 2 mules each, in one of which Squires rode and also Owen McKenzie and two of the clerks Pike & Moncrevier[30] with two drivers and 5 hunting horse led behind the carts. We started by the same road we took on our last hunt. The weather was pleasantly cool with a strong breeze blowing and no mosquitoes. We saw a number of Bulls in parties of 1, 2, & 4 before we had gone 6 miles from the fort and we began to anticipate plenty of cattle in a short time, but after this we passed the hunting ground of last trip on Fox river and that of our camping ground some miles further without seeing anything more than a straggling bull or

[30] Jean Baptiste Moncrévier had been a clerk of the company at Fort Union at least as early as 1833 (Maximilian, *Travels in North America,* XXIII, 188); he was fired in 1844 for getting drunk on a trip to the Blackfeet and for giving twenty gallons of liquor to the men (Abel, *Chardon's Journal,* 238, note 127). According to Denig the front gate of the fort was decorated with a painting of a treaty of peace between Indians and whites executed by Moncrévier (Audubon, *Journals,* II, 185). Audubon reported on August 7 that they had had "a sort of show by Moncrévier which was funny, and well performed; he has much versatility, great powers of mimicry, and is a far better actor than many who have made names for themselves in that line" (*Journals,* II, 138).

two. At length it began to grow late in the day and it became necessary for us to obtain something for supper as we had only a small supply of bread and some coffee. It was determined therefore to run the first Buffalo we should see whether Bull or Cow. At last a single Bull was seen lying down, and the preparations were made for the chase. It was determined to give Squires a chance to kill this Bull as he had been so unfortunate in the former hunt. Mr C. & Owen accompanied him to see fair play between him and the bull and I mounted my hunter and followed to see the sport without taking my gun with me. Squires made the first shot and struck the Bull and some shots were afterwards fired by Owen & Mr C. before Squires reloaded and came up to the Bull again. He approached very near to the Bull and fired, his bad luck however still followed him. The Bull turned on him and as his horse sprang to get out of the way, she jumped into a small gulley of about 18 inches depression and he lost his balance, was obliged to throw his gun away and only saved himself by clinging to the mane of the horse until they were out of danger. Poor Squires was terribly frightened, his escape was more narrow than that of the last hunt and he would inevitably have been killed or most seriously mangled had he fallen from his horse, as the bull was so close that no human interposition could have saved him. The chase continued for about half a mile further and he was not brought to the ground until he received a dozen balls, several of which were in the vital parts. Soon after Squires mishap another bull was seen at a distance of about a quarter of a mile standing looking at the chase. I now regretted not having brought my gun with me, but it was too late to return to the waggon for it, as Owen gave chase to him and killed him after a run of about ¾ of a mile. As the first Bull was very old and poor, meat for our supper was cut from the last one and we proceeded on our route. Owen was sent to the top of a high hill on one of the horses to look out for more cattle so that we might if possible fill our carts before night with meat and despatch them for the fort early in the morning. He soon made signs to us to proceed towards the N.W., and when he joined us, said that he saw a large band of cows in that direction, we proceeded across the next valley for two or three miles, but on ascending the hill we discovered that what he had taken for cattle was a clump of trees. As it was growing too late to look out for more we proceeded in the direction of the best camping ground which was some miles distant at the foot of some hills called Les Trois Mamelles or the Three Butes. We had not gone far before we met a band of 8 cattle approaching us, we immediately made preparation for the attack and while doing so they approached within 200 yards of us and stopped, the Bulls showing evident signs of displeasure at our appearance, we found them to consist of 7 Bulls and one cow only but as our Bull meat was not very palateable we determined to sup on cow meat. As it was not our intention to kill any of the Bulls the Cow was soon separated from the band and by her superior speed soon left them all behind. Owen was ahead and approached her in a manner that satisfied me of the difference between running Bulls & cows as regards danger, he rode for some time within 8 or 10 feet of her, his gun missing fire repeatedly in consequence of the high wind that was blowing. (flint guns are universal in this country) Finding that he had no chance he retired and Mr Culbertson gave her a shot. Bell then came up and discharged two barrels into her which put a stop to the chase. I rode back for the carts while the hunters were butchering the cow. While butchering this cow the Bulls returned and looked at us from the distance of two or three hundred yards, the leader making repeated advances as near as one hundred yards as though meditating an attack. Mr Culbertson says that he has frequently been alarmed by the very near approach of Bulls under similar circumstances but that he has never known them to attack. On my return a Swift Fox [blank in MS] started from a hole immediately under my horse's feet, it immediately occurred to me to try the speed of this animal which has been pronounced to be superior to that of any animal of the prarie and even of the fleetest horse. He ran up a moderate ascent which was much in his favour and yet in a quarter of a

mile I completely overran him and obliged him to double and
pass around my horse, both of my barrels snapped as soon as I
overtook him, but the chance of my hitting him would have
been small as I was loaded with a ball. This chace was made in
the presence of the whole party and Mr. Audubon in particular
had a fine view of it, so his history of this beautiful little Fox
will settle the question of its miraculous speed forever.[31] This
chase was made without whip or spur on an Indian horse, but
a good one. It is to be regretted that my gun was out of order
and that I was not loaded with small shot, as we have not yet
procured a specimen of this animal, this being the first we have
seen. The cow meat was soon in one of the carts and we proceeded to our camping ground near the three conical hills, about
200 feet in height from the level of the Prarie, they are called the
Trois Mammelles and are visible from a great distance, where
we found good water for cooking and for the use of our horses,
we had taken good care to bring a supply of Missouri water for
our own drinking, as all the water of the prairies is more or less
brackish and some of it highly impregnated with salts of magnesia or some other mineral substance. I should have mentioned that while butchering the cow a large band was seen at
a distance of 3 or 4 miles of apparently 60 to 100 cattle, and we
promised ourselves a fine chase in the morning. The day has
been delightfully pleasant and cool with a strong westerly
breeze, which continued through the night, so that we had no
use for mosquito bars. We camped near some timber and saw
the fresh track of a very large Grisly bear at the watering place.
We saw today a hawk about the size of the Red-tail with a
white head and breast, differing entirely in form from the Fish
Hawk, which we have not seen here. Killed a Titmouse black-
headed, very long tail, whole length ⅞ in. longer than atricapillus.[32]

[31] *Quadrupeds*, II, 13–17 (Plate 52); Audubon mentions here that they had had
their first sight of this animal on June 7 at Fort Clark where Chardon presented them
with one he had caught in a trap.

[32] On this day also Bell and Harris shot a Baird's Bunting, another of the "new"
birds. See *The Birds of America*, VII (1844), 359–60 (Plate 500).

Thursday, July 27th. Mr Bruin did not visit us or our horses last night and we were up at the break of day between 3 & 4 o'clock but as our horses were a good deal jaded from their running and their long drive of about 30 miles from the Fort, we sent our hunters after Antelope while Mr Culbertson and I walked to the top of one of the Mamelles from which we had a most extensive view including the whole distance, about 20 miles, between the Missouri and the Yellowstone. The horizon was bounded on nearly every side by the *Mauvais terres* or clay hills, such as are represented in Catlin's Book. These Mammelles are of a similar character but are covered with large blocks of a conglomerate of coarse white sandstone filled with water rolled pebbles of great variety, such as are found in many places on the sea shore, among which were some specimens of agate of different coloured veins. These blocks have evidently fallen from a stratum near the summit as the sub-stratum of clay has been washed away. Our hunters could not find antelopes and we got under way about [blank in MS] o'clock. We proceeded in the direction of the large band of cows we saw last night and Owen was sent ahead to find them. On the way a Townsend's Hare started before the waggon. Mr Audubon was so anxious to get it that he fired with buckshot and missed it. I loaded with No. 3 and followed it and succeeded in approaching it where it had squatted to hide away, and killed it, it proved to be an old female suckling her young. Owen made signs from a hill that he had discovered cattle, when we came up to him we found that it was not the large band, but a small one of 12 or 15 and in a direction towards the Fort, and as they were travelling fast we mounted at once and followed at a smart gallop. It took us near half an hour to overtake them and we found to our disappointment that there were 8 Bulls and 4 cows only. This gave us a cow apiece (Squires had declined running as the hurt he received in his first chase had become irritated by the run of yesterday and gave him much pain) and we determined to be satisfied with them, as we now had so much widened of our distance from the band seen last night that it might take us the whole day to find them.

We were soon among the band, Owen as usual ahead, one or two shots were made before I could select a cow and when I found one I saw she was wounded I gave up the chace, as each of the hunters was in pursuit of his cow and they were soon all killed. I felt deeply chagrined at this unhandsome treatment, after coming so far to chase a cow and after Mr Culbertson had taken so much pains to gratify us, to be thwarted in this ungentleman-ly way was exceedingly provoking. It had been announced at starting that there was a cow for each of us. It proved to be Mr Owen McKenzie who had played me this dirty trick, which he thought very smart. Had I known it in time I could easily have run in and fired both barrels into his second cow before he could have reloaded his single barreled gun after his first fire. One of the cows proved a fine large one and it was measured and skinned for Mr Audubon. This occupied more time than the butchering of the other cows. We now pushed on for a camping place for the night in the direction of the Fort as we were too far to reach home before night, taking the upper hunting road or one which passes nearest the Missouri. Passed in sight of the first Buffalo killed yesterday which was still untouched by the Wolves, an evidence of the scarcity of Buffalo, as Wolves are their constant attendants. We directed our course towards a Gap in the hills called the Coupe, which is cut down to the level of the adjoining prarie and has placed in front of each entrance a conical hill of clay of about 50 feet in height, the coupe itself being somewhere about 100 feet. Here we expected to find water and encamp, but the spring was dried up and we were obliged to proceed four miles further, where we found a small quantity of water of in-different quality. There was no wood in sight and we made a good fire of Buffalo dung and as soon as our carts arrived sup-per was prepared. Some of our hunters feeling rather hungry took some of the liver of the Buffalo and threw it on the *coals* and ate it with an appetite, merely scraping off the ashes with the back of their knives. It is a constant practice with all the hunt-ers I have seen to eat certain parts of the Buffalo raw at the time of cutting them up. These are the Manifold, merely emptied of its contents and dipped in the blood of the animal, pieces of the liver, and udder of the cow eaten in the same way, and the marrow and the brain are also eaten raw. We had another cool windy night and slept well under the tent without mosquito bars.

Friday, July 28th. All hands were stirring this morning at daybreak and while a cup of coffee was making two of the men were dispatched after the horses which had strayed out of sight from any of the immediate eminences. They were found at the distance of two miles near the head of Fox River, notwithstanding all the worst of them were hobbled. This section of the country being the neutral ground between the Blackfeet and the Crows & Grosventres is very little frequented by Indians and it is not therefore thought necessary to piquette the horses. We proceeded to the dividing ridge of the waters which flow into either river and had a fine view of the country for the whole distance to the Fort which we reached by 9 A.M. and enjoyed a good breakfast soon after. The balance of the day we made a holiday of.

Saturday, July 29th. This morning Mr. A., Bell, Moncrevier, Pike and I crossed the river at sunrise to look for rabbits feeding in the roads but as usual were unsuccessful, not being able to see any. After breakfast Bell and I went to the Mauvais terres near the hayfield to hunt for Rock Wrens. Killed 3 & a Loggerhead Shrike. (I should have mentioned that on Thursday morning at our encampment at the Trois Mameles Bell shot a Titmouse very similar in its markings to the common Northern Chickadee, but which measured ⅞ of an inch more in length, than the measurements in Mr Aud[ubon's] Syn[opsis],[33] appears to us to have a larger tail and more white on the secondaries, and its note although very similar appears softer and less hurried in the utterance.[34] I also shot a female Sharp-tailed Grous

33 John James Audubon, *A Synopsis of the Birds of North America* (Edinburgh, Black, 1839). This was a one-volume summary of the information contained in the *The Birds of America* folio plates and in the *Ornithological Biography.*

34 This is Harris's Long-Tailed Chicadee; for his description of it see the appendix.

Bull Boats on the Missouri

from a pencil drawing by R. F. Kurz, 1851

Bell's Vireo (Male)
Rattle-snake Root

from Audubon's *Birds of America*, Vol. VII (1844)

and Bell shot one of her young ones which was about the size of a turkey just hatched and resembled it very much, it could fly. I went out again in the afternoon to search for more of the brood but did not find any—On the Buffalo hunt Bell killed three finches of the kind he killed down the river on the [blank in MS] which so closely resemble Henslow's Bunting, its note is very similar to the short-billed Marsh Wren of Nuttal, it frequents the ravines of the praries where there is long grass and water.

AUGUST

[1843]

Wednesday, August 2nd. For the last few days I have been resting to recruit my strength a little. Finding myself weak and unable to endure the fatigue I could at the commencement of the expedition, and observing that I was growing thin, I was weighed and found I stood at 133 lbs—A short time before I left home I weighed 157½ lbs., a falling off of 24½ lbs. in a few months. My health is perfectly good but I feel too weak to endure any great exertion and have determined to spare myself a little during the hotest of the weather to enable me to work more in going down the river. The causes of this great falling off of flesh I believe to be the following. In ascending the river in the steamboat, as soon as they commenced cutting wood we availed ourselves of the opportunities thus afforded to go ashore to shoot, the time of remaining being uncertain and seldom more than one half to one hour we walked in a hurry and frequently we were led to a considerable distance in following a bird we wished to procure, and while in hasty pursuit the first bell would ring to call us back and we would start on a run, this has occurred 2, 3 and four times a day and each time I would return with my clothes completely saturated with perspiration, this sweating process continued until we reached Fort Union, when Bell and I were out every day until the 10th of last month when we were both knocked up by the heat having been out two or three days with the Thermometer at 90. Since that time I have felt much weaker. Another cause of my losing flesh here is the nature of the food, which has been principally animal, and that either Buffalo meat or dried Buffalo meat, badly cooked, with *Short cakes,* instead of light bread, or coarse hard buiscuit, and frequently I have been unable to partake of enough of this food to support nature. I am thankful that my health has not given away and I hope yet to be of service to the expedition. The most serious cause of regret that I feel for my present inefficient condition of the body, is the being unable to accompany Bell and Owen McKenzie who have set out this morning on horseback to go two days journey up the Yellowstone[1] in search of the Cock of the Plains,[2] which, or birds very similar were seen by Owen about two weeks ago on his return from carrying an express to M[r] Kipp on his way to Fort Alexander, the Crow station.[3] As a sportsman the shooting of this bird is the height of my ambition, and I am now compelled to abandon forever the idea of killing one. This morning a party of five or six Chippeway Indians of the Cree tribe[4] on horseback came in to trade a few robes and dressed skins, their principal object was to get whiskey, they had been to the other Fort and not being able to get it there, came to pay us a visit, after trading for blankets, ammunition &c. they left us and went back to the opposition Fort. After dinner M[r] Audubon & I took a ride in the waggon to look for a petrified tree which Bell and I had seen a week or two ago, we were unable to find it, and returned with a very imperfect specimen of petrified wood. Soon after we returned a party of Assineboins consisting of 6 or 7 men and some squaws and children and a great many dogs drawing their lodges and peltries came to the fort, the men were mounted. A very short time after their arrival one of the Chippeways came up from the other Fort and walk-

[1] For Bell's account of this journey see Harris's entry for August 8. Cf. Audubon's transcription from Bell's journal (*Journal,* II, 176–77).

[2] *Ornithological Biography,* IV, 503–507 (Plate 371).

[3] Built in 1839 on the Yellowstone opposite the mouth of the Rosebud (Chittenden, *The American Fur Trade,* II, 939). According to Kurz it was still in operation late in 1851 (*Journal,* 235).

[4] So Harris described them.

ing in among the horses of the Assineboins took one of them, a very handsome white horse which we had all been admiring and led him out, at the same time throwing down a robe to the Indian who had the horse, the Assineboin was not satisfied with this and seized the halter of the horse, an altercation ensued when the Chippeway handed the other his gun, then gave him all his powder and balls and finally his looking glass—the Assineboin appeared now to be satisfied and the other marched off with the horse by the back gate of the Fort, presently we heard the discharge of a gun and Mr. Culbertson came in and said the Assineboin had shot the Chippeway's horse, we ran out of the back gate, and saw the Chippeway dismounted from his own horse which he had rode to the Fort and endeavoring to get off with the White Horse by dragging at his halter, two or three Assineboins now commenced pursuing him and finding he could not get off with the horse he dropped the halter and ran for his life, the late owner of the white horse was among the pursuers and dropped on his knees to fire at him as he ran, but the other commenced *serpentant,* as the French traders term it, or running in a zigzag course and he did not fire, the pursuit was not continued and the poor Chippeway went away leaving behind probably all he was worth in the world. We now went out to examine the horse which was shot and found that the ball had passed through his thigh, in the fleshy part and had entered the bottom of his belly. It appeared that the horse was shot by one of the Assineboins who had an evil eye on the Chippeway on account of one of his relations having been prescribed for when sick by one of that nation and died under his hands. These kind of affrays are of constant occurrence among these *unsophisticated* children of nature. I have found that a person runs a great risk in administering medicine to these people, and yet they are always begging it of the whites when they are sick. A week or ten days ago an Indian died in the Fort to whom I had been administering the Iodide of Potash ever since I have been here, and while the medicine lasted with decided good effect, Mr Dennick [Denig] the principal clerk assisted me in attending the poor

fellow. He died and was buried during the absence of his brother, who was accosted civially by Mr Dennick on his return, but
the brute refused to speak to him, as soon as I heard of this I
armed myself and continued so until he left the Fort. This un-
grateful scoundrel had been living in the Fort since spring with
his brother and all his family and had been subsisting in the
charity of the company, having solicited permission to remain
a short time *until his brother died*—and he would have died long
ago had it not been for the attention of Mr D. and others in the
Fort, and yet it is most likely that if this scoundrel has ever an opportunity to take the life of Mr D. or myself without danger to
himself he will do it without hesitation.

Thursday, August 3rd. The Assineboins sent word to the other
Fort that the Chippeway might come and get the White horse
this morning, the one that was shot having died during the night.
He came with two of his friends well armed and mounted and
after a few words, probably in explanation of the cause of the
attack, carried him off without molestation. It is probable that
this affair would not have stopped so soon, but the Chippeways
have a long distance to travel through the Assineboin country
before reaching their own—of course they will remain quiet
until a better opportunity of revenge presents itself. To-morrow
we are to cross the river again on a hunt for Buffalo. Sprague
and I went to the hills back of the Fort to collect Geological
specimens in this afternoon.

Friday, August 4th. We had an early breakfast this morning
and by 6 o'clock started from the opposite side of the river. Our
route was the same as we have heretofore taken, midway between the two rivers. We took but one cart to bring home fresh
meat, probably because Mr Culbertson & I were the only hunters, Squires, Provost & Lafleur went yesterday up the Missouri
to hunt Bighorns and Owen & Bell were up the Yellowstone.
We began to see Bulls, singly and in small parties before we
reached Fox River, and soon after meeting a single Bull Mr C.
took the opportunity of trying a Grey horse which he brought

along for the purpose of ascertaining if it was fit to run Buffalo. He ran the Bull for about a quarter of a mile, but could not overtake him—as he carried no whip it was attributed to that circumstance, and it was determined on the next trial I should ride along side to encourage him, and in the mean time we manufactured a whip to persuade him. A Bull was soon discovered directly in our track, and when near enough we mounted our steeds, and made the approach. The horse appeared to run well enough until within a certain distance of the Bull, when no efforts of the rider could induce him to approach any nearer, after labouring some time with the whip Mr C. gave me the word to go ahead. I was soon along side of the Bull, and a ball from each barrel as I passed brought him to a stand-still at once and in a few seconds he fell and died. We took nothing but the tongue of this animal as he proved too poor and rank for eating. While engaged in cutting out his tongue there came up a severe thunder gust with hail, which gave us a good wetting, as soon as it subsided we examined our guns and proceeded. On rising the next hill we saw in the valley ahead a band of 70 to 80 Bulls and Cows quietly grazing. This was the best promise of Sport we had yet seen. We commenced making our approach at a distance of about half a mile, and while moving slowly forward several scattering Bulls got the wind of us and ran directly for the herd, fortunately the alarm did not spread, and we had a fine opportunity of hearing as we approached the bellowing of the Bulls, for the first time that I have heard it distinctly. We made a good approach and rushing into the herd the cows from their superior fleetness were soon separated from the Bulls. Mr Culbertson had directed me to keep near him and seeing him after three cows which had separated from the rest I followed. He shot one of them down and I soon overtook one of them and fired breaking her foreleg, she fell but was soon up again and ran with some speed on three legs. While preparing to shoot her again I saw a portion of the band which had gone around a small hill, coming across it directly toward me, I reloaded and awaited them and after giving chace for a few yards

I was mortified to find they were all bulls, I now returned and put another ball into the Cow as she was hobbling away quite fast. After reloading I mounted a small eminence and found that while I was waiting for the Bulls the Cows had got so far ahead that I was unwilling to give my good horse so severe a run as would have been necessary to overtake them. Mr Culbertson now soon returned having shot 3 cows, he requested me to go back and look for his first cow, while doing so I discovered a cow walking up a hill at the distance of about a mile. I soon ascertained that Mr C.'s cow was not in the neighborhood where she was shot, and pushed my horse after the straggler which had now disappeared over the hill. On reaching the top I found the cow standing on the other side, and it was not until I had given her a severe chace of a quarter of a mile down the hill where she had the advantage, that she stopped before I was near enough and showed fight. I now found that there was more danger in approaching a wounded cow than a Bull in consequence of their superior swiftness, and it was not until she had run me off the ground several times that I could manage to give her a shot which stopped her running. I then approached and finding she was not likely to die, very quickly I fired another ball into her lungs which finished her. I now returned to my own Cow which I was surprised to find still on her legs and moving about, another shot soon finished her, and we all went to work to secure the meat. The cows all proved remarkably fat and Mr. C. determined to carry them all home with the aid of the white horse who had disgraced himself as a runner and was condemned to be a pack horse for the remainder of his career. It took us until night to get all the meat loaded, and we were obliged to camp without any water for our horses, we had taken the precaution to bring enough for ourselves when we crossed the Missouri. Mr Audubon & I not being of much use in cutting up beef &c made ourselves useful in carrying Buffalo dung to the camp to make a fire, and while so employed we would laugh outright at the idea of our friends at home having a peep at us in our new employment, piling on one arm the *Prarie wood,* which we had

to embrace very closely to prevent its falling, and when the cap-
ping piece was placed on the pile, clapping our chins upon it to
secure its safe passage to the camp and marching off with another lump in our right hands. Our supper was soon ready and
this time we conformed to the custom of the Praries by eating
the livers and kidneys roasted on the *live embers,* though I took
the precaution to skin them pretty deeply. A smart shower in the
night drove Moncrevier & Pike our only assistants inside the
tent, they having preferred sleeping outside while it was fair.

Saturday, August 5th. In the morning we started on our return
and after traveling several miles found water for our horses, we
saw but two or three straggling Bulls on our way back. Antelopes were not so numerous as on our former trips and much
more shy. Wolves remarkably scarce. I rode my hunting horse as
the waggon had to be loaded with our tent, camp equipage and
baggage, while the four cows with the heads entire were packed
upon the cart and the poor condemned Buffalo hunter. In passing along the road in front of our caravan I saw a young Swift
Fox and although it might easily have been caught, yet we were
fearful there might be a hole very near into which it would run,
it was therefore determined to shoot at it, and I shot him as he
attempted to run away. I saw another of the white-headed hawks
before we reached home, which was accomplished by one
o'clock. A hearty dinner and a nap after it completely restored
me. The weather for the past few days has been very cool and
bracing and I now feel my strength much recruited. We were
not at all troubled with mosquitoes on this trip. In the evening
we heard from the other Fort that a party of their men who had
gone to the other side of the river in the scow had been attacked
by Indians and one of them wounded in the ear, while they report having killed one of the Indians. Probably in a day or two
we may get a correct version of the affair.

Sunday, August 6th. It has been difficult to ascertain who were
the Indians who attacked the men of Fort Mortimer yesterday.
Two parties of Assineboins had been crossed in the scow and

one of them were sitting on the bank at the time of the attack and the men supposing them to be the agressors fired upon them and the[y] fled to the bushes. After the affray they brought this party back again and they insist upon it that it was a war party of Yanctons, but suspicion rests very strong upon the other party of Assineboins probably the truth will never be known.

Monday, August 7th. The weather has again become very hot after a delightful spell of cool weather. Bell,[5] Provost & Lafleur started this morning to go about 15 miles up the river to hunt Bighorns, soon after they set out 6 half breeds from the other fort, came up for the same purpose bound for the same place on Mr Audubon's account. They pushed off to endeavour to join our party. In the afternoon I crossed the river to look for rabbits, as usual without success, when I got back to this side, it was not quite dark and I went to the point above the Fort where I saw one and fired at it at a long distance, but did not stop it. It is very remarkable that with all our efforts we cannot procure one of these little hares since the one Bell shot in two with a rifle. It is evidently a new hare and I fear we shall be obliged to leave the country without getting a specimen. They are remarkably timid and keep very close in the bushes, which are so thick that it is impossible to see any small animal among them, and they only make their appearance in the roads and on the edges of the bushes early in the morning and late in the evening, and on the slightest alarm they spring into the bushes again. They are besides very scarce supposed to be owing to the unusual overflow of the bottoms having destroyed great quantities of them this spring.

Tuesday, August 8th. This morning Mr Larpente[u]r[6] took Mr Audubon & I in the waggon to a hill of sandstones about 2 miles north of the Fort to search for shells and impressions of leaves which we had found in some of the fragments about the Fort,

---

[5] Bell and Owen had returned on the afternoon of the fifth (Audubon, *Journals,* II, 131).

[6] In his autobiography Larpenteur made no reference to Audubon and his friends.

but we were entirely unsuccessful. I should have mentioned that I got up at daylight this morning to hunt rabbits, in the point, but again without result. On our return from the quarry, Mr Culbertson told us that he had sent Owen across the river to run a band of Buffalo whose bellowing had been heard soon after we started. I now recollected that I had heard the noise in the morning while watching for rabbits and took it for the bellowing of the Bull of the Fort. Had it not been for this unfortunate mistake I should have had another fine run after Buffalo cows. Owen returned soon after dinner having killed two cows and would have killed three, the number he was commissioned to bring back, had not his stirrup broke. He found a band of upwards of 300 principally cows, and what is very remarkable they were at a distance of 6 miles from the Fort, the morning being very hazy, almost foggy, and very still, the little air that was stirring coming directly from them. They were on the bottom prairie in the point of land between the Yellowstone and Missouri. While Owen was cutting up his Cows two men crossed on a raft from the Fort below and continued the chase *on foot,* with very little prospect of success, of course. It is now evident that the Buffalo are moving towards this quarter where they have been very scarce for the last two years. We are promised one more hunt before we leave, and I am in hopes that some such chance may be thrown in our way to give us still another opportunity. Both Bell & I have been remarkably successful for beginners having killed all the cattle we have started after. Bell and his party returned from the Bighorn expedition this morning[7]—As I forgot to mention his return from the trip up the Yellowstone, I will here give some account of both.

Bell started on the 2d. instant on horseback with Owen McKenzie on a trip up the Yellowstone in search of the "Cock of the Plains" which Owen had seen on his return from carrying an express to Mr Kipps Boat on its way to Fort Alexander in the Crow Country. They reached Pellow's camp the first [night?] having shot 3 sharp-tailed Grous and saw two fine Buck Elks,

[7] That is, the expedition that had left on the morning of the seventh.

and a few Buffaloes. The next morning about daylight they were awoke by the snorting of their horses and saw a large Buffalo Bull within a few yards of them, they fired and killed him and while cutting out some meat another approached which they also killed and finding it fatter, supplied themselves with meat from it and returned to camp, where they saw a large bear a few hundred yards from them. They went in pursuit but he escaped in the bushes. After breakfast they proceeded on their journey, saw eight or ten Elk on a sand bar and Bell afterwards shot a Bull in the bushes which he thought was a Bear when he fired, supposing there was no possibility of his avoiding him. Soon afterwards Owen shot a female Elk, which they skinned and hung the skin on a tree as high as they could reach in order to take it with them on their return. They now found the Buffalo by thousands and they killed a young Bull having lost the meat they had with them. They afterwards saw Sharp-tailed Grous, old and young, 13 Elk and wounded one, then saw 5 more, also a hare but could not get a shot at him. Buffaloes all around them. After reaching their camping ground and turned loose their horses they approached a large band of Buffaloes which were traveling and passing through a ravine, they placed themselves on the bank to leeward, within 8 or 10 feet of the path in such a way that the cattle could not see them, excepting when they raised their heads to look out for a good fat cow, when the Bulls would stop and gaze at them, but as they remained perfectly still they did not take alarm, but passed quietly on—They soon selected a good cow and shot her, she ran a short distance before she fell and several Bulls collected around her and remained several minutes before they left her. After camping for the night and cooking their cow meat, they were entertained by the music of a rattlesnake very near them. In the morning Bell shot a fine female Elk which he skinned and hung the skin in a bush as before. While skinning it a Black-tailed Deer came near them which Owen wounded with buck shot but they did not get it. At ½ past 11 o'clock they arrived at the place where Owen saw the Grouse. Where they camped they saw 5 Elk lying on a sand bar, they both fired together at one of them and Wounded her so that they secured her by firing once or twice more. While skinning her the Buffaloes came within 20 yards of them and Bell remarks it in his journal as somewhat singular that this should have been the case during the skinning of each of the Elks they shot.[8] They then commenced their search for Grouse. The ground they hunted on was covered with low bushes, and literally cut up with Buffalo tracks and hundreds of these animals passing over the ground while they were hunting. The Buffaloes started a fawn which Bell shot down but it succeeded in hiding away in the bushes. After hunting for some time and seeing the utter hopelessness of hunting over such ground without a good dog they took something to eat and started for home. I would here remark that although I am tenacious about my young dog hunting with any one but myself, yet on such an occasion as this I should have been glad to have sent him with Bell who is an excellent hand with a dog, had there been any mode of carriage for poor Brag, but to let him run 70 miles and then hunt grous and return, all in the course of four days, would have been too hard on the poor dog, and he would besides have been in bad condition for hunting when he got there. They set out the same afternoon and saw great quantities of Buffaloes, some Elk and occasionally an Antelope. After camping and turning loose their horses they killed a cow, there was a Bull and a calf with her and they were obliged to wound the Bull severely before he would suffer them to approach. They started early on the morning of the 5th with the intention of reaching the Fort by night. The Buffalo were still very abundant. Bell wounded a Male Elk and while in pursuit of him found a Porcupine in the bushes, which he attempted to kill with his gun rod, but the beast ran and Bell broke his Gun rod in the bushes in following him. On overtaking him he held him fast with the gun screw[?] and finished him with his knife. They reached the Fort that night. On Monday the 7th, Bell went with Provost & Lafleur to

8 This reference is not in Bell's Journal as quoted by Audubon (*Journals*, II, 176–77). Harris's is a much fuller account of Bell's observations.

hunt Bighorns up the river on the Fort Union side, they went about 30 miles and returned this morning as stated above. They were unsuccessful in the pursuit but saw some of the animals, the existence of which so near the Fort we had not before been aware of. The most interesting part of the expedition was Bell's having seen the Hills in the *Mauvais terres* in which they were hunting, actually on fire. His account is that there can no longer be any doubt as to the cause of the Red appearance of the tops of some of the hills as well as some of the Strata of clay & Shale below. That the progress of the recent fire could be traced along the hill to where it was actually burning by such an appearance of the Bluffs (which were too steep to ascend) and that in the recently burnt parts, large portions of the burnt surface had fallen to the bottom, while in advance beyond the fire, the cliff retained its more perpendicular form and exhibited its strata unchanged by fire, and further that in advance of the fire a seam of coal was plainly visible, while in the rear it was entirely obliterated and its place supplied by Red earth & stones. This confirms the conjecture of Lewis and Clark that these red appearances were caused by the burning out of seams of coal. I should here remark that Bell's observations correspond with my own, that neither in the recently or more anciently burnt portions is there the least appearance of *Pumice Stone* as stated so confidently by Catlin, and that the Pumice stone which is seen on the river shores and bottoms and frequently floating on the water during freshets, has its source high up along the mountains.

[*Entry in Diary*] young male Magpie killed by Bell Aug 8

Saturday, August 12th. As we are now very busy in preparing for our departure for St. Louis on the 16th of this month we have done little in the way of shooting.[9] This morning however we

---

[9] One of their principal concerns was a mackinaw boat for the trip to St. Louis. On August 8 Audubon wrote: "Our boat is going on well, and looks pretty to boot. Her name will be the 'Union,' in consequence of the united exertions of my companions to do all that could be done, in this costly expedition." On August 11: "It was concluded that, if our boat was finished by Tuesday next, we would leave on Wednesday morning, but I am by no means assured of this, and Harris was quite startled at

started on our last Buffalo Hunt. Bell, Owen McKenzie and I were the Hunters and as some little confidence began to be placed in our skill, two carts (enough to carry the meat of 6 cows) were sent with us. Just before we reached the valley of the Fox river and within half a mile of the spot where we killed our first Bulls we saw a band of 50 or 60 Buffaloes. We approached in the usual manner and got very near before they started, and as we rushed into the band I selected a cow and knocked her over at the first fire, at which I was much surprised as I saw that I had struck her very high on the shoulder, but observing that she did not offer to rise I took after another which I gave an excellent shot with the other barrel directly in the lungs and I saw the blood issue from her mouth, she kept on and I followed reloading one barrel of my gun as my horse galloped along side of her, on putting the ball into my gun I perceived that it did not run down freely, and no efforts of shaking the gun or striking the breach would loosen it I was therefore compelled to halt and force down the ball with the ramrod, while doing so my cow rejoined the band, after which I galloped as soon as the ball was down, with all my efforts in riding from one end of the band to the other I could not find the wounded cow again and thus I followed them for more than a mile expecting every minute to see the wounded cow separate from the band, being now on the top of a hill where I could see the band for some distance as they ran I halted and watched but none of them appeared to halt I gave up the chase, very much to my regret and mortification. I now returned and found that Bell had killed a cow, although the horse he rode proved an indifferent animal, as it was with difficulty he could whip him up to the Buffalo. We returned to the starting point, where I found Owen McKenzie butchering my cow which he said had risen to her

---

the very idea. Our boat, though forty feet long, is, I fear, too small. *Nous verrons!* Some few preparations for packing have been made, but Owen, Harris, and Bell are going out early to-morrow morning to hunt Buffaloes, and when they return we will talk matters over." On August 12: "The 'Union' was launched this evening and packing, etc., is going on." (*Journals*, II, 139–40, 142, 146.) The skins and specimens acquired on the trip are listed in the appendix.

feet again, and he had shot her down. On examination my shot proved a very singular one. It had glanced from the shoulder and struck in the neck just behind the Horns, probably breaking the spine. Owen had killed one other, so we had a load for only one cart and had to look out for another band. Owen said he had shot down 3, but found but one of them. Bell was so discouraged with the running of his horse that he determined to return at once to the Fort and as Provost and Lafleur were in sight returning from a hunt on which they had been absent two or three days, he galloped off and joined them. Owen & I proceeded with the determination to procure 3 more cows to fill another cart. It was about half past one o'clock when we had finished butchering Bell's cow, and leaving the meat and one cart on the spot where there happened to be wood and water for camping we proceeded with the intention of bringing back our meat and remaining there for the night. We had rode about 2 miles when we discovered a band of Buffalo some of which were lying down and others feeding, as we approached two or three of the Bulls which we supposed were on the outskirts of the herd we were surprised to discover a band lying down in the hollow before concealed from our view, consisting of between two and three hundred. We were soon among them and at the first shot I wounded a cow which kept on and most unfortunately I lost her in the crowd which was so great that I held back my horse rather than risk myself in the mélée, after following for some time to see her separate I pushed my horse ahead of the band to overtake the cows, I selected the first one I met and running up gave her a shot, she separated at once from the band and struck off to the left, meeting the Bulls of the band which were now coming up, instead of joining them she rushed through the midst of them across their course, one of the Bulls came against her and almost knocked her over, I followed in the opening she had made and gave chase across the open prairie, she proved to be an old cow and low in flesh and ran remarkably fast, I fired several shots at her and was surprised to see no impression from my ball, at last I discovered that in my anxiety to kill her I had not paid sufficient attention to the level of my gun and the balls had rolled out, the first shot after I became aware of this checked the speed and I saw she was bleeding at the mouth and nostrils I checked my horse and she soon came to a walk. I now approached her to give her a death wound, she turned upon my horse and gave chase and it was not until after a good deal of manoeuvrering that I could get into position to fire effectively. This shot brought her down. This was the longest chase I had had since running Squire's Bull and as I was out of sight of Owen and the cart, I merely cut off her tail and turned back. I had some difficulty in finding Owen who had killed 3 cows and as mine was the most distant and the poorest she was left for the Wolves. The meat was soon on the cart and we went back to the camping ground about 4 o'clock where we found some ribs already cooked for us, and as we had not eaten since morning they were very acceptable, while picking the ribs we consulted as to the propriety of attempting to return to the fort or camping on the ground, the majority were for starting (about 10 miles) and we were soon packed up and under way, we had ridden out in carts but were obliged to return on horseback, and Owen and I galloped ahead as soon as he put the carts on a plain track. We reached the river about an hour before them and waited their arrival. On reaching our quarters Bell told us that he saw a Grisly Bear on his return in the Bottom opposite the Fort, but his horse was even more averse to chasing him than the Buffalo and that he was compelled to let him escape in the bushes without a shot.[10]

Wednesday, August 16th. Left Fort Union.[11]

[10] With this entry for August 12 Harris's folio journal stops. In the small diary he made a number of brief entries which give some details of his trip down to St. Louis and thence to Louisville and New Orleans.

[11] Audubon noted that they started from Fort Union at 12:00 noon (*Journals,* II, 154). Sprague mentioned in his journal that there were fourteen in all on board the *Union.* From later reference in Audubon's *Journals* these included, besides our five, Culbertson, his wife and her babe-in-arms, Moncrévier, Provost, and four boatmen who were paid off in St. Louis on October 20.

Thursday, August 24th. Found Red Stones with impressions of leaves &c &c petrified wood (according to Sprague it was this day but I think it was after we left the Mandans)

Friday, August 25th. Arrived at Mandans.

Wednesday, August 30th. Yellowwinged Woodpecker Male with black stripe *above the eye* shot Aug 30

SEPTEMBER

[1843]

Thursday, September 7th.[1] Bell killed a new Goatsucker (old male) today, probably the same seen by Nuttal in the Rocky Mountains.[2]

Thursday, September 14th. Left Fort Pierre at [blank in MS] P.M.[3] Stopped at the Farm on an Isld. 9 miles below, got some potatoes and green corn and one Pig. Sand Burrs and Ground Cherries of two species are abundant on the Island. They raise the Mandan corn and it appears to yield well. Crossed to the other side and camped for the night.

Friday, September 15th. Foggy this morning, prevented our reaching Fort George (9 miles) until 9¼ A.M. Traded one of

1 At their camping place on September 4–5 the travelers examined a beaver lodge (Audubon, *Journals*, II, 160–62). Harris makes no mention of it in his journal, but years later he described it in detail in "Remarks" he made at a meeting of the Academy of Natural Sciences on May 12, 1857. These "Remarks" will be found in the appendix.

2 Nuttall's Whip-poor-will. See *The Birds of America*, VII (1844), 350–52 (Plate 495); and Audubon, *Journals*, II, 163–64.

3 They had reached Fort Pierre at 5:30 P.M. on the eighth. They now exchanged their boat for a larger one. On the tenth, Culbertson received orders sending him to the Platte. Changes had taken place at Fort Pierre since the first of June: "The new Row of Buildings lately put up at this place with 7 Doby Chimneys in them, not only improve the appearance of the Fort, but are very substantial buildings a Carpenter Shop is also about being built anew." (William Laidlaw to P. Chouteau Jr. and Company, Fort Pierre, 8th September 1843, in the Chouteau-Maffitt Collection, Missouri Historical Society.) Laidlaw set out for Fort Union at 11:30 A.M. on the fourteenth; Audubon and his friends left for St. Louis at 2:00 P.M. (Audubon, *Journals*, II, 165.)

the rifle pistols for a hunting shirt, a pipe and two tobacco pouches, one Mink and the other young beaver. Left at 10¼ A.M. Soon after the wind raised and by 2 P.M. it blew so hard we were obliged to land. Here we killed our two pigs and we cooked one half of another that we brought from Fort Pierre.

Saturday, September 16th. Reached the Great Bend and stopped at our old Camp of the Six Cottonwood Trees at 10½ A.M. Mr Audubon & Bell started to hunt black-tailed Deer & Sprague & I went to look up fossils. Deer hunters unsuccessful. Fossil hunters found but little. Deer hunters out again in the evening with no better success. Found plenty of the seeds of the Yucca. Formation the same as we found below Beaver River—Black shale apparently vitrified in places, and soft shale of the same colour as the clay (colour of Potters clay.) In the evening a tremendous squall came from the N. W. with some rain in the middle of the night.

Sunday, September 17th. Wind has somewhat abated this morning, we started but after going a few miles it increased and we were obliged to stop. Went to look for Rabbits and started a covey of Sharp-tailed Grous of which we killed 3, Mr A. two and Bell & I one. Saw numerous traces of Indians both to-day and yesterday. They appeared to be a few days old. The wind fell and we left at [blank in MS] P.M.[4] and camped near the lower end of the Great Bend. Saw Golden Plovers today.

Tuesday, September 19th. Moved three times to-day and as often stopped by the wind, did not make more than 25 miles on the whole. Found no game to-day. Dug up a Yellow Buffalo Berry Tree and wrapped the roots in moist earth. There was a small male tree along side of it which I also packed with earth (opposite White River). Squalls in the evening.

Wednesday, September 20th. Blew hard all night and we could not leave our camp until 12½ P.M. Saw today an immense flock of Ducks on a sandbar. Supposed to be principally Pintails[5]—

[4] About 3:00 P.M. (Audubon, *Journals*, II, 165.)
[5] *Ornithological Biography*, III, 214–18 (Plate 227).

the first signs we have seen of migration, made about forty miles to-day and reached Cedar Island and cut 4 fine sticks for oars— The Island was full of recent Buffalo Tracks—Bell and I killed a Buffalo Bull this afternoon. There were eleven in two bands, all Bulls—saw 15 to-day. We have seen none since [blank in MS]

[*Notation opposite entries for September 14th and 15th*[6]] The Yellowstone formation of Sand and Clay continued below Beaver River and the great stratum of Clay of which Nicollet speaks commenced between Beaver and Grand Rivers. Just about Beaver River where we were stopped by the Wind [I] found a stratum of sandstone containing similar leaves to those found at Fort Union. This sandstone was in some parts burnt red & on the upper surface of the stratum it was vitrified, still retaining the impressions of the leaves. From the commencement of the clay stratum it continues to occupy the hills from the base to the summit until the great bend is passed when a stratum of very soft clay rock commences which does not appear to increase in thickness (from 20 to 75 feet—with frequent undulations apparently occasioned by slides of the hills) so far as we have proceeded (20th) the clay still overlying it. On the upper surface of this rock is a thin yellow stratum which frequently takes fire and burns for years, causing the rock in large masses to slide and crumble.

Thursday, September 21st. Left Cedar Island at 8½ A.M. and in about ½ an hour were stopped by rain and appearance of a blow.

Friday, September 22nd. [*Notation opposite entries for September 16th, 17th, and 18th*] Friday 22^d Below Cedar Island— the stratum of Clay stone still continues, with the Yellow portion above much wider, having increased to about 15 feet, while the grey stone is seldom more than 20 feet above the water. I can only account for this by the whole bank along the river having slid at various times, leaving the stratum somewhat irregular

[6] These dates merely indicate the page on which the entry was made—the actual date on which it was written appears in the body of the paragraph.

and undulating & much broken—There is one point we have passed about 50 miles above Cedar Island which was known to have been on fire for 6 or 7 years—the bute which was the highest when the fire commenced is now the lowest, having slid and crumbled down to the water. It appears to have subsided of its own weight, still leaving the traces of the stratification distinct though somewhat irregular. About 20 miles above Cedar Island [I] found a substance like petrolium in consistence but without smell oozing from the bank—saved a phial—[7]

[7] From the day he started packing at Fort Union, Harris seems to have lost interest in diary-keeping; certainly on the downriver trip the pleasures of travel may have palled a bit. Audubon writes on Friday, the twenty-second: "Raining; left at a quarter past eight, with the wind ahead. Distant thunder. Everything wet and dirty after a very uncomfortable night. We went down the river about a mile, when we were forced to come to the opposite side by the wind and the rain. Played cards for a couple of hours. No chance to cook or get hot coffee, on account of the heavy storm. We dropped down a few miles and finally camped till next day in the mud, but managed to make a roaring fire. Wolves in numbers howling all about us, and Owls hooting also. Still raining heavily. We played cards till nine o'clock to kill time. Our boat a quagmire." (*Journals*, II, 167.)

OCTOBER

[1843]

Wednesday, October 4th. Windbound, Stopped for the night at Cabané's Bluffs ab[ou]t 20 miles from Ft. Croghan.[1]

[*Entry on opposite page*] At a small Creek where we camped 3 miles below Cabané's Bluffs, a ledge of rocks crosses the river, making a slight rapid. This rock is doubtless the limestone which first appears above water ab[ou]t a mile above Bellevue. Cabané's is about 30 miles above Bellevue—Between that place and the Grand Sioux River a distance of ab[ou]t 160 miles we saw a stratum of soft sandstone apparently ab[ou]t 50 feet thick in places—it was seen just above the old Council Bluffs and at Wood's Bluffs. The Clay formation we lost somewhere near the Big Sioux but it probably might be traced lower down above the sandstone. At Iowa river 24 miles below the Vermilion, at the bottom of and mixed with the blue clay we discovered a vein of alum & copperas (?) about 2 ft. thick. This blue clay lies below a thick stratum of soft clay stone of 70 to 80 feet thick which we traced from the Great Bend to the mouth of the Iowa, it overlies a thick (say 20 ft) stratum of very tenacious dark blue clay. The next underlying stratum of stone was seen at Woods Bluffs

---

[1] Maximilian had visited Jean P. Cabanné at this post ten years earlier; it was near the old Council Bluffs (Maximilian, *Travels in North America*, XXII, 271–74). A few years later it was superseded by the Bellevue Post.

and traced nearly to Council Bluffs, it appeared to be a soft yellow sandstone, but we had no opportunity of examining it.

Thursday, October 5th. Wind bound at point. Walked 4 miles to Ft. Croghan,[2] off[icers] preparing to abandon post next day —Boat arrived at 4 P.M. Capt. Berguin, Lts. Calton, McCrate[3] & Noble, Dr Madison & Mr Hamilton—gave up Michaux[4] as Pilot for Mr Calton who took [takes] a Mackinaw with 16 men for Ft. Leavenworth, where the rest of the troops go by land—accident to the trooper. Bell shot a sparrow, supposed young of Harris's. Left boat B—G [?] & I at 8¾ A.M.—arrived 11 A.M.[5]

Friday, October 6th. Left Ft. Croghan (new Council Bluffs) 8¾ A.M. Lieut. James Henry Carleton, U. S. D. [*sic*] with 18 men left in Co. taking Michaux for a Pilot to Fort Leavenworth.[6] Capt. Berguin started same morning by land to Fort Leavenworth with rest of Dragoons having abandoned the Post.

Tuesday, October 10th. Arrived at Fort Leavenworth 4 P.M.

Wednesday, October 11th. Independence lower landing.[7]

Thursday, October 12th. 10 miles below Liberty.[8]

2 Audubon noted on this day: "A clear and beautiful sunrise. Started early, but stopped by the wind at eight." (*Journals*, II, 171.) To be within four miles of Fort Croghan it was necessary that they travel twenty miles or more from their night's camp.

3 James Henry Carleton (Harris gives his name correctly in the next entry) was a second lieutenant of dragoons from October 18, 1839 to March 17, 1845. His accounts of dragoon campaigns in 1844 and 1845 were edited by Louis Pelzer in *The Prairie Logbooks*. Lieutenant McCrate was a graduate of the United States Military Academy from Maine.

4 They had acquired Michaux on September 27 just above the Vermilion Post. Audubon hired him (at his own request) and agreed to pay him twenty dollars a month for the trip to St. Louis (*Journals*, II, 169).

5 The initials in the diary are difficult to decipher. Audubon said that "Bell, Harris, and Squires have started off for Fort Croghan." (*Journals*, II, 171.) Audubon's final report for the day was that at midnight Squires, Harris, and Sprague returned to their boat "after having played whist [at the fort] until that hour."

6 Carleton's boat traveled with Audubon's to Fort Leavenworth. They camped this night thirty miles below Fort Croghan. On the ninth, Harris, Squires, Bell, Sprague, and Carleton walked across the bend to the Black Snake Hills (Audubon, *Journals*, II, 172–73).

7 They left the fort at half-past six and reached Independence at sundown (Audubon, *Journals*, II, 173).

8 Probably *Liberty* should read *Lexington*.

Saturday, October 14th. [*Notation on opposite page*]
Hutchin's Goose Oct[r] 14th[9]

Bill to pinion	11½
Wing	14¾
Bill to end of tail	26
" " " " claws	27⅜
Alar extent	52¼
Weight 4 lbs 1 oz	

Thursday, October 19th. Arrived St. Louis ab[ou]t 3 P.M.[10]

[*Notation on opposite page*]

Out of Fund

New Hat	4.50	
Balls &c	.62½	E. Harris D[r]
Pocket money	1.00	

Neglected to include the above in a/c current of Nov[r] 16 sent to
M[r] Audubon.

To pay for Dog for Mr. A. $3.00—J. J. A. D[r]
for M[r] Kipp
paid

Saturday, October 21st. Cash returned to M[r] Audubon   59.55

returned   62.55

Am[t] of Pierre Chouteau & Co's a/c	1617.83
4 mo[s] interest	32.35
	1650.18

Sunday, October 22nd. M[r] Aud[ubon], Sp[rague] Sq[uires]
& Bell left in the Nautilus for Cin[cinnati] at 1 o'clock

[9] Killed by Michaux, said Audubon (*Journals,* II, 174); "the first I ever saw in the flesh." See *Ornithological Biography,* III, 526–28 (Plate 277).

[10] Their return did not go unnoticed in the local press. "Mr. Audubon with his party, arrived in the city, last evening, in good health and spirits, and brings with him a rich harvest of his labor and industry." (St. Louis *Daily Evening Gazette,* October 20, 1843.) In his enthusiasm C. M. Sawyer burst into a poem, "To John James Audubon," dated from the Glasgow House, which appeared in the *Missouri Republican* on October 21, 1843.

Sent by Mr Audubon to be forwarded from Pittsburgh by Canal to Messrs Thomas & Martin

1 Trunk Indian Curiosities—1 Box Geological Specimens
I Box of Cactus—1 Bundle of Trees
1 Box Bird Skins—

Monday, October 23rd. Met Mr F^d Rozier[11] of St. Genevieve M^r A's former partner—

Some of Sir Wm Stewart's party reached St. Louis today[12]

Saturday, October 28th. Drew on Messrs. Thomas & Martin at 5 days sight for $200.00 in favor of Mr Audubon, cashed by Pierre Chouteau & Co.

Paid $2.25 postage for Squires.

Monday, October 30th. Left St. Louis in the Belle Air, went on board at 10 A.M. & left at 5 P.M. Some of Capt Stewart's party came down in the John Aull just before we started[13]   Mr Herman[14] one of the party is on board our boat having reached town some days since. Passage to Louisville $5.   to Cinn. $6—

[Entry opposite Tuesday, October 31st] A gentleman on board the Belleaire informed me that Mr Thos. Jeff. Boggs[15] of Boonville Missouri intends going out to Santa Fee, that he would be in every way a desirable person to travel with having made the trip before—that he is acquainted with Mr Clay from whom I could get a letter of introduction.

[11] For Ferdinand Rozier see Herrick, *Audubon the Naturalist*, I, 146–69, 186–201, 233–46; and John Francis McDermott, "Audubon's 'Journey up the Mississippi.'" *Illinois State Historical Society Journal*, XXXV (June, 1942), 148–73.

[12] About twenty arrived on the *Omega* on this day (*Missouri Republican*, October 24, 1843). For an account of Stewart's expedition see William Clark Kennerly and Elizabeth Russell, *Persimmon Hill* (Norman, University of Oklahoma Press, 1948), 143–67.

[13] The *Missouri Republican* of October 31, 1843, reported the arrival the day previously of about twenty-five more of Stewart's party.

[14] According to Kennerly's diary (Kennerly and Russell, *Persimmon Hill*, 258) there were two Heermanns in Stewart's party, initials "J" and "D," both from Maryland, the second described as "clerk." Arthur (*Audubon, an Intimate Life*, 454) identifies Harris's fellow-traveler as the son of Dr. Louis Heermann. When they were all in St. Louis in April, the young man had introduced himself to Audubon and said that Audubon had given his mother drawing lessons years before.

[15] Thomas Jefferson Boggs was one of the many sons of Governor Lilburn Boggs of Missouri. He emigrated to California in 1846.

NOVEMBER

[1843]

[Entry opposite Wednesday, November 1st] James Goodwin
—Carthage

8 miles from Cincinnatti

Thursday, November 2nd. Arrived at Louisville. Found P.
Frazer at the Galt house with Mr Smith on their way to N.
Orleans by first boat. Mr Laud [?] is also here but will be de-
tained some days.—

[Entry on opposite page] Sent by Mr Herman to Messrs Bakewell & Pears[1] of Pittsburgh to be forwarded to Messrs Thomas
and Martin of Ph[iladelphi]a

1 small Leather Trunk

1 Box Bird Skins & Sundries

2 Gun Cases

1 Bundle of Bedding

Friday, November 3rd. Had made up my mind to go to Ash-
land to see Mr Clay and leave the Mammoth Cave for another
opportunity—Propose starting in a steamer to-morrow afternoon which goes up the Kentucky River to Frankfort. This
afternoon felt strong symptoms of an attack of asthma.

[1] Thomas W. Bakewell and Thomas W. Pears, with whom Audubon had been
associated in business a quarter of a century earlier in Louisville.

Saturday, November 4th. This morning my asthma has increased so much as to induce me to call in a Physician—Spent a bad night although I soaked my feet and took some of James' Pills. Dr Rogers whom I called in decided on bleeding and small doses of Lobelia to produce nausea—also [illegible] pills to induce [?] a return of the Piles—not much relieved in the afternoon, when the old D[octor]s son called and advised to finish the day with an emetic, and as I always obey orders (of the Doctor) even at the risk of breaking the owner I swallowed it, to my very great relief, passed a good night.

This attack of asthma has determined me to change my plans altogether. I now go to N. Orleans with Frazer. Start to-morrow morning on the Joe H. Daviess. Wrote D^r S[pencer] and sent him a box of books & seeds by way of Pittsburgh to the care of Messrs Bakewell and Pears. Left it with Mr Basham Steamboat agent at Louisville and pd fr[eigh]t to Pitts. $1.

Sunday, November 5th. Left Louisville—Sent box & seeds to steamboat agent Mr Basham to be forwarded to Messrs Bakewell & Pears Pittsburgh—They to forward to Thomas & Martin Ph[iladelphi]a Advise Mr Bakewell & Dr Spencer.

Mem. to write D^r S[pencer] about kinds of seeds in the box and their treatment.

Steamer Jo. H. Daviess Capt Keys Passengers
    Mr Martin & Lady of Mississippi planter
    Duncan 2 Misses Duncan their Grand Children
    Col. Waldo Arkansa (blind gentleman)
    James Wallack & Lady ⎱
    Mr Sloman [?]   ⎰ of the Stage[2]
    M^r [M^rs ?] Tuttle   ⎰
    Dr Fisher & Lady

[2] James William Wallack, Sr. (1795–1864) was at that time bound for an engagement with the Ludlow-Smith company at New Orleans. (See Sol Smith, *Theatrical Management in the West and South* [New York, Harper and Brothers, 1868], 178.) John Sloman first appeared on the American stage in Philadelphia in 1827. (See T. Allston Brown, *History of the American Stage* [New York, 1870], 337.) "Mr Tuttle" is possibly Harry Tuthill, born in Dublin, who made his American debut in New York in 1832. (Brown, *History of the American Stage,* 364.)

Passage to New Orleans $15.—

Wednesday, November 8th. Cough much relieved to [*sic*] and but little oppression in breathing.

Thursday, November 9th. Mr Martin left at 2½ P M   Col Waldo after dark—

My cough has returned to-night with redoubled violence in consequence of a heavy fog which detains us where we landed Col. Waldo, Walworth or Wallace[3]

Friday, November 10th. Heard Hutchin's Goose about 90 miles above Natchez

Had to lie by for a fog last night   did not start until 11 o'clock A.M.

Saturday, November 11th. Passed Natchez this morning. Saw a black Squirrel for sale—Its tail was injured so that it would not make a good skin.

Sunday, November 12th. Arrived at Lafayette[4] about 8 P.M. Mr Frazer and Mr Smith left us.

Monday, November 13th. It took several hours last night to get the Cattle out of the boat and she did not get to the City until some time in the night. Left the boat before breakfast and went to the St. Louis hotel in the French municipality.[5]

Wrote Dr Spencer.

Tuesday, November 14th. Subscribed to the Picayune for 3 months $3.00 pd. A man of the name of Orrin Byod [*sic*] who dined at the St. Louis to-day took the liberty of taking Brag home with him after dinner, and the rascally servant who took care of him did not let me know until after ten. I got him back by sending round to his store.[6]

[3] It is not clear whether Harris means that the Colonel's name was "Waldo, Walworth or Wallace" or that the last two were names for the place where he landed.

[4] A suburb of New Orleans.

[5] For a good description of this hotel see *Norman's New Orleans and Its Environs* (New Orleans, 1845), 157–59.

[6] Brag died at Tampa, Florida, in January, 1844. On a scrap of paper in the Harris Collection, Montgomery, is found this note in Harris's handwriting: "Poor Brag died last night. In him I lost one of my best friends, whose whole aim in his

Thursday, November 16th. Wrote to Mr Audubon, sent a/c of exp[ense]s and a/c current, enclosed a Draft on Dr Spencer 90 days after date for the balance of the a/c am[oun]t $391 58/100 —omitted to give him credit for sundries am[oun]t[in]g $6.12½ (see Octr 19th) Also to mention $2.25 which I paid for postage for Squires I neglected also to collect the $10 for the Mackinaw boat of Provost. Also to charge board at Glasgow House for Bell, Squires & Sprague $13.75[7]

Wrote to Mr Berthoud to collect the $10 of Provost[8] (see Bill)

Saturday, November 18th. Sat for Daguerreotype likeness to Maguire Camp St. unsuccessful Dined at Mr Grimshaw's, met Major Mathias

Monday, November 20th. Wrote Mrs Vansittart Nov. 16–20. Drew on Messrs Thomas & Martin at sight in favor of Mr Saml Nicholson for $500 and advised them of the draft. Wrote Mr Berthoud about price of Mackinaw Boat to be collected from Provost.

Tuesday, November 21st. Wrote to Dr Spencer advising of draft of yesterday, also that of the 16th sent to Mr Audubon.

Thursday, November 23rd. Mr Orrin Byod who took my Dog fought a duel this morning with Mr Richard Hogan, the former received a flesh wound in the calf à la Colonel Webb—Hogan was dangerously wounded—shot through both thighs and a branch of the femoral artery divided.

Thursday, November 30th. Wrote to Dr Spencer in answer to his of 16th.

short life appeared to be to please his master. The last, and not the least devoted of my companions of the Expedition has left me, and I leave him in this bright sunny spot of the South to wend my dreary way to my northern home, his affectionate fondling and bright looks of gratitude for the slightest attention, are gone forever, and I trust there is naught of sin in the tear which I shed in writing this short tribute to the memory of a truly devoted and disinterested friend. I had him buried in the garden of the Tampa Hotel and a walnut tree planted over his grave."

[7] The letter to Audubon is quoted in the introduction; the expense account appears in the appendix.

[8] Provost had become "extremely drunk" and had left them at St. Charles on October 18 to go by land to St. Louis (Audubon, *Journals*, II, 175). The ten dollars was for the purchase of the *Union*.

DECEMBER

[1843]

Tuesday, December 5th. Mr Rothwick, a lawyer from Natchitoches, told me that he met a person to day whom he had formerly known in affluent circumstances of the name of Green, now reduced to poverty, who has just been left a large Estate in Eng. on the river Trent called Armitage Park. It was bequeathed to him by a Dr Warren Mercer of New Albany, Indiana, who left Eng. many years since on account of a domestic calamity, which was known to but few of his friends. He resided many years with Mr Green. Being aware that Mr G. could not as an Am[erican] Citizen, possess Real Estate in Eng. Dr M. left Armitage Park, said to consist of ab[ou]t 2000 acres to a friend Mr Armitage Lester in trust, to be sold and 49/50 of the purchase money to be paid to Mr Green. His personality [*sic*] is also left to Mr G. and among it is said to be one item in the funds of £7000 per ann. Mr G. was reduced to such extremity that he had not the means to take from the Post office letters and papers from New Albany relating to the bequest.

Tuesday, December 12th. Sold draft on Messrs Smith, Payne & Smith's of London for £60 St[erlin]g at 6½ prem[ium] am[oun]t[in]g to $284—This draft is on two div[iden]ds of this year and one of last, on Ashton Canal Sh[are]s, leaving a

190

small balance in their hands, which I have instructed them to add to the next years div[iden]ds and advise me of the am[oun]t.

Wednesday, December 13th. Wrote to Messrs Smith, Payne & Smith's advising them of draft of yesterday

Thursday, December 21st. Wrote to Dr Spencer.[1]

---

[1] That is to say, he closed on the twenty-first a very long letter begun on the first. All of this letter that applies to his western experiences is quoted in the introduction.

Fox Squirrel

from Audubon and Bachman,
Quadrupeds of North America, Vol. II, Plate LXVIII

Prairie Dog   Prairie Marmot Squirrel

from Audubon and Bachman,
Quadrupeds of North America, Vol. II, Plate XCIX

Appendix I

Report on the Geology of the Missouri
by
EDWARD HARRIS

[*Proceedings of the Academy of Natural Sciences, Philadelphia,* II (1845), 235–238]

To Professor Henry D. Rogers, Samuel George Morton, M.D., and Professor Walter R. Johnson, Committee of the Academy of Natural Sciences of Philadelphia.

GENTLEMEN,—A plain statement of such facts as I have been able to collect in reference to the Geological character of the country bordering on the Missouri River, will perhaps be preferable to attempting a detailed reply to the questions proposed by your Committee to Mr. Audubon and myself on our departure for the upper waters of the Missouri in the spring of 1843. I would beg leave to remark that our opportunities for Geological research fell far short of our anticipations. The extent of our journey was unexpectedly limited to the mouth of the Yellowstone, and just before leaving that place, a diagram, which I had found of the strata in the hills rising back of Fort Union, was unfortunately destroyed when too late to replace it. The specimens taken from these strata will be found in the box which I have sent to the Academy. Our opportunities in descending the river were also far from being favorable. Frequent storms and high winds obliged us to lie by in places which we would not have chosen for any of the purposes of the expedition, so that by taking advantage of all the good weather to hasten our progress, we were only able to reach St. Louis in our Mackinaw boat on the sixty-third day from Fort Union.

In the whole course of the Missouri, from its mouth to the mouth of the Yellowstone, the strata are *horizontal,* and as we passed up the River, I noted the points at which each of the principal series was lost under the water by the rise in the bed of the stream. Thus—the lower series of secondary limestone disappears in a few miles above Bellevue, and at Cabaué's [Cabanné's] Bluff, twenty miles further, a ledge of rocks crosses the river beneath the water, causing a slight rapid at a low stage water. I take this to be the last evidence of that formation. From Cabaué's Bluff to the Grand Sioux River, a distance of about 160 miles the River approaches the Bluffs in but a few places, and in those places the rock, of about 60 feet in thickness, appeared to be a soft sandstone. (In no part of this formation had we an opportunity of landing to ascertain the nature of the rock, still I thought we were near enough to pronounce it sandstone.) This stratum loses itself in the River near the Grand Sioux. At this place a stratum of soft clay stone appears, which runs to within a few miles of the lower end of the Great Bend where there is another submerged ledge of rocks crossing the River. Then we have Nicollet's great bed of clay which is visible until you pass the Mandans, terminating between Beaver and Grand Rivers. Here commences what I have called the Yellowstone series, which probably continues to the great Falls of the Missouri, or until it is met by the outcropping rocks of the mountain range, if these Falls be not formed by such outcropping.

Thus we have in the ascending series—No. 1, The secondary limestone from the first Bluff on the Mississippi, above the mouth of the Ohio, to Cabaué's Bluff on the Missouri, ten or twelve miles below Old Council Bluffs. No. 2, Yellow sandstone (?) to Grand Sioux River. No. 3, Clay stone to lower end of Great Bend. No. 4, Nicollet's clay to a point between Beaver and Grand Rivers. No. 5, The Yellowstone formation. It will be perceived that the localities named as the ending of one and beginning of another series, are not in fact the beginning of the upper bed, but are the points where the superior stratum of the last series is lost sight of in the River. Hence it is evident (from the fact of the strata being perfectly horizontal) that while the lower series will never be seen higher up the River than the points indicated, the superincumbent series must have its beginning many miles lower down, according to the height of the Bluffs and the angle of descent of the stream.

Whenever we ascended the Bluffs to the High Prairies, we found them more or less covered with a Boulder drift, with frequent denuded points, leaving the larger Boulders lying upon the regular strata. As we ascended the River, the Boulders, which are much worn and rounded, increased in size (with some variations) until we reached the high hills of the *second Great Bend,* between the Mandans and the mouth of the Yellowstone, say, from the size of paving stones at Fort Croghan to rocks of several tons at the second Great Bend, after which, and at the Yellowstone, half a ton would probably be the size of the largest Boulder.

The exceptions to perfectly horizontal stratification are only found in series No. 4, and appear to have arisen from two causes —from slides of the Bluffs, and from the fact of their frequently taking fire and burning for several years, causing the Bluffs to sink and crumble down. Mr. Bell was the only one of our party who had an opportunity of witnessing the burning of the cliffs, while on a hunting excursion about 30 miles above the Yellowstone on the northern bank of the Missouri. Smoke was issuing from the summit of the cliffs, under which he was riding—there was a thin seam of coal on a line with the smoking part of the cliff, but where it was burning, and where the fire appeared (by the crumbling down of the cliff) to have passed, there was no coal visible. I am inclined, from this circumstance, and from having found remains of coal in a stratum of sandstone containing impressions of leaves, and bearing evident marks of fire, to think with Lewis and Clark, that the burning of the cliffs is to be attributed to the spontaneous ignition of the coal. The soil in No. 4 and 5 is strongly impregnated with salts, apparently sulphate of magnesia (?) so that most of the brooks and springs are saliferous. In excursions on the Prairies it is difficult to find good water. Soon after rains it may be found in small basins, but these soon become brackish, unless they are in the detritus of the drift.

Series Nos. 3 and 4 appear to contain the greatest quantity of crystallized salts, such as alum, copperas and sulphate of magnesia, and saliferous springs and streams in great numbers. Warm springs are said to exist, but we did not meet with them. We found a substance like petrolium in colour and consistence, but without odour. Crystallized gypsum (? see specimens) is exceedingly abundant in No. 4, lying in thin veins, cutting the regular stratification at right angles, Fossil shells abounded most in No. 4.

In No. 5 commence the remarkable strata which form the picturesque hills noticed by travellers, and called the Mauvaises Terres by the trappers and voyageurs. The strata vary from a few inches to a few feet in depth, and from the variety of their colours, and from the singular forms and grouping of the hills into which the great Bluff of the high Prairie is gullied by the torrents of ages, they appear in many places more like the work of art than nature. They are usually called Clay hills by travellers, but repeated inspection has satisfied me that clay occupies but a small number of the strata, at least in the vicinity of Fort Union. There are strata of sand, clay, shale, sandstone and coal alternating, but without regularity. I have frequently seen a stratum of sand completely covered by the washing from a superincumbent stratum of clay, like a coat of paint, so that its nature could only be ascertained by scraping off the thin covering of clay. I am inclined to think, however, that the proportion of clay is greater in the lower strata of this series, immediately overlying the Nicollet clay. The cause of the singular castellated appearance of these hills is the great variety of materials of which the strata are composed being acted upon in various degrees by atmospherical influences, according to their capability of resisting them; hence the spires, pyramids, cones and other forms cut out by the torrents, are frequently capped by hard sandstone, while the stratum, immediately underlying it, may be sand or clay, which being more easily affected by the atmosphere, crumbles away and leaves the sandstone projecting, and so on with thirty or forty distinct strata of hard and soft sandstone, sand, clay, shale and coal, of very marked shades of colour, and in many places reddened by the action of fire. I should have remarked that the visible coal seams which commence in the upper part of No. 4, are most abundant soon after entering into No. 5, and become small and few in number about the Yellowstone. I counted in one place eight seams of coal between the river bank and the top of the Bluff, varying from six inches to four feet in thickness. This coal is very light, and ignites with difficulty, emitting a very unpleasant odour while burning. Fossilized wood is very abundant in No. 5; I saw one specimen very much flattened by the pressure of overlying strata. Small beds of limestone are found at Fort Union.

In regard to the evidences of volcanic matter overlying the stratified rocks on the borders of the Missouri, and of the existence of red pumice in such situations, I have no where been able to discover them, although I sought them diligently in my frequent excursions into the Mauvaises Terres. The red appearance of the shale and clay, and in many instances of the sandstone, is, I believe, to be attributed to the action of fire, but may be more readily accounted for from the effects of the spontaneous combustion of the coal going on at the present day, than from volcanic agency. These evidences of fire occur in so many of the strata at such different levels, that to give them the latter origin we are compelled to suppose a succession of eruptions, but in this case what has become of the tuffa and lava? It is impossible that I could have failed in discovering some evidence of their existence. Still I do not pretend to deny that the pumice which is so frequently found floated down the Missouri, may have had its origin in these hills and may have been found there by Mr. Catlin; (I do deny that it is the cause of the red appearance of the hills) but may it not be accounted for by the action of these spontaneous fires? *May not pumice be found without volcanic action?* Some of the specimens of sandstone with impressions of leaves, in the box sent to the Academy, are evidently changed in their specific gravity by the action of fire, and your Committee will be better able than myself to judge, whether an increase of the heat, short of that necessary to produce vitrification, may not have converted the mass into the red pumice of the Missouri.

In a bed of soft sandstone at the mouth of Cannon Ball River, great numbers of those singular stones are found, which give name to the stream. The following remarks from my Journal, made on the passage up the River, were fully confirmed when we stopped at the mouth of Cannon Ball River on our return. "June 6—On passing the mouth of Cannon Ball River yesterday, we noticed a remarkable formation in this stratum" (soft sandstone) "of round masses of rock" (hard sandstone) "in the divisions of the strata, many of them apparently perfectly spherical, and from 18 to 30 inches in diameter, some as perfect as cast balls, others appear to be flattened or composed of two sections of a sphere, from a smaller ace up to a hemisphere, joined together with mathematical nicety, and surrounded by a belt or zone at the junction projecting from one to four inches, which zone lies horizontally in the line of division of two strata. I had observed traces of this peculiarity in the rock the day before, and this evening, 30 miles below the Mandans, I noticed it again. Cannon Ball River takes its name from the presence of these balls. They are said to be hollow, and to contain crystals." The last remark was not confirmed by the opening of two large specimens brought home by Mr. Audubon, which were found to be solid and of uniform texture throughout.

A somewhat analogous formation occurs in the region of the Yellowstone. It consists of a similar hard sandstone, lying also in the divisions of the strata of soft sandstone, but in form like a flattened trunk of a tree swelling out at the root, and might be taken for fossilized wood, but that it is destitute of concentric rings, and laminae can always be traced in the direction of the longest diameter of the elliptical end, sometimes in exact correspondence with, and in other instances lying obliquely to, that diameter. I have seen them *in situ* projecting ten feet horizontally and perpendicular to the face of the cliff. I have seen others of more than twenty feet in length lying at the foot of the cliff whence they had fallen. The smaller end always exhibits the appearance of a transverse fracture with edges sharp and well defined, the larger end rounded and resembling the head of an immense bone fitted to work in a socket.

If this meagre statement of facts and the few specimens which accompany it, will serve in a small degree for the better appreciation of the Geological character of this interesting region, and hold out any inducement to well qualified persons to undertake its investigation, the object of the undersigned will be accomplished.

Yours Respectfully,
Edward Harris.

Appendix II

Description of a New Species of Parus
from the Upper Missouri
by
EDWARD HARRIS

[*Proceedings of the Academy of Natural Sciences, Philadelphia,*
II (1845), 300–301. The original MS is in the Harris Collection.]
Parus septentrionalis. Young, in summer plumage.

Bill brownish black, short and stout. Iris dark brown. Feet
greyish blue. Upper part of the head, chin and foreneck dull
black; the black of the head scarcely descending to the hindneck, and that on the foreneck hardly reaching to the breast.
Cheeks and sides of the neck, a line running from the base of
the bill under the eye and almost meeting on the hindneck,
white. Back greyish, slightly tinged with yellow. Quills and tail
feathers dark greyish brown, margined with pure white; secondaries conspicuously so. Lower parts greyish white with an
almost imperceptible tinge of yellowish under the wings.

    Length $5\frac{7}{8}$ Wing $2\frac{13}{16}$ Tail $3\frac{3}{32}$ inches

A single specimen of this bird was procured on the 26th of
July, on the Yellow Stone River, about thirty miles above its
junction with the Missouri. It is evidently a bird of the season,
with immature plumage, to which may be attributed the dul-
ness of the black on the head and throat. On comparison of this
bird with *P. Carolinensis* and *P. atricapillus,* it will be perceived
that, beginning with the smallest bird, the parts which are black,
decrease, and the white parts increase in size and intensity in

ascending. In *septentrionalis* the outer web of the lateral tail feather is entirely white, except a small portion near the base, where there is a slight tinge of grey next the shaft, and the quills, secondaries and all the tail feathers are margined more broadly and with a purer white than in the other species.

I have given a table showing the comparative measurements of the three American species of this division of the genus Parus having black heads, which so closely resemble each other in voice, habits and markings; and have also added some measurements from a paper in the Archives of the Academy, by M. de Selys-Longchamps, Corresponding Member of the Royal Academy of Brussels, extracted from their Bulletin, vol. 10, No. 7. I have reduced his measurements to English inches and decimals, and have given my own also in decimals for ready comparison. It will be seen that his specimen from Iceland (*frigoris*) corresponds so nearly with our *atricapillus* as to render it probable that it is identical, while his *atricapillus* from Brisson is so near to Audubon's *Carolinensis* as to render it almost certain that the description of *P. atricapillus* by the old authors was from our small southern bird. If this opinion be correct, our *Carolinensis* should resume the name of *atricapillus*, and the larger bird be called *frigoris*, as suggested by M. de Selys-Longchamps.

The note of this bird is similar to *atricapillus*, but its voice more liquid, and less harsh and querulous in the utterance. Bill longer and stouter.

	Length.	Wing.	Tail.	Length.	Wing.	Tail.
Parus *Carolinensis*	4¼	2½	2⅜ or	4.250	2.500	2.375
" atricapillus	5⅛	2¹¹⁄₁₆	2⁹⁄₁₆	5.125	2.687	2.562
" septentrionalis (Nob.)	5⅞	2¹³⁄₁₆	3³⁄₃₂	5.875	2.812	3.093
" atricapillus (Briss.)	from the paper of			4.794		2.397
" frigoris	M. de Selys-			5.149		2.663
	Longchamps.					

It will be seen by the above table, that while in each of the old American species the wing is .125 or ⅛ of an inch longer than the *tail,* in the new bird, the *tail* is .281, or nearly ³⁄₁₀ of an inch longer than the *wing;* compared with *atricapillus,* the total length is greater by ¾ of an inch, the wing by ⅛, and the tail by $^{17}/_{32}$ or more than half an inch.

The colours in this immature specimen are only to be depended upon as showing the much greater development of the white, and smaller extent of the black markings, than in the other species. For the sake of more easy reference, the description has been made parallel with those of Audubon in his Synopsis. I would propose as an appropriate English name for this bird, the "long-tailed black-cap Titmouse."

Appendix III

Remarks on the Beaver and Their Houses
by
EDWARD HARRIS

[*Proceedings of the Academy of Natural Sciences, Philadelphia,*
II (1857), 107–109]

Mr. Harris observed, in relation to the specimens of cotton-
wood and chips cut by beavers, presented this evening, that they
had been obtained by him from the Missouri River, between
Fort Union, at the mouth of the Yellowstone, and Fort Clark,
at the Mandan Village. He added, that in returning from a trip
up the Missouri to the mouth of the Yellowstone, in company
with the late J. J. Audubon and party, in the month of September, 1843, our Mackinaw boat was moored for the night on the
right bank of the river, under shelter of timber on the bank,
which was here about twenty feet above the water at its then
rather low stage. Our guide and pilot in descending the river,
Prevost [Provost], who was an old trapper, hired by Mr. A. at
St. Louis for the trip, soon discovered signs of the beaver, and
presently a newly constructed beaver-house about one hundred
yards above the boat. It was too late to examine the premises, and
after cutting wood, building a fire, and cooking our supper, we
turned in for the night. Very early in the morning, before break-
fasting, we hastened to examine what had been the object of
more than one expedition on the Yellowstone, and which had,
heretofore, baffled our search. Prevost assured us that the noise
and smell of smoke, and cooking from our camp, must have
driven the beaver to a place of safety soon after our landing the

203

night before, and that we could only gratify our curiosity by the inspection of the building; whereas, had daylight permitted, we might, at first landing, have proceeded quietly and stopped the covered outlet from the house to the water, and thus secured the inmates, and this only by using the utmost caution in approaching without giving them the wind of us, or making the slightest noise, even the crackling of a dry twig under our feet; so religiously did he believe in their superhuman sagacity in discovering and avoiding danger. Thus assured, I took my gun, more from the influence of the habit of some months of seldom stirring from camp without it, than from any expectation of seeing a beaver. I followed the water to the outlet, while others took the bank; here I stood watching the operations of those above, who had commenced removing the branches of cotton-wood which formed the covering of the domicile. I was startled suddenly by the splashing of the water at my feet, and, looking down, I saw the dusky back of a beaver a few inches under the surface, gliding out into the deep water of the river, and before I could prepare and bring my gun into position, he was out of sight. Nothing could have been easier, had I been prepared, than to have shot him as he thus passed within three feet of the spot on which I stood. Thus, from too much reliance on popular tradition of the unerring instinct of this animal, was I prevented from adding the skin, and description, and measurements of a fresh specimen of the beaver to the trophies of our expedition. As the beaver passed down the stream he was seen to rise for air, abreast of our boat, by some of the men on board. We then proceeded to unroof the house by removing the cotton-wood branches, which covered it for several feet in thickness; they extended for a considerable width on each side, and covered the passage from the house to the water; this passage was about fourteen inches square, as neatly excavated as a ditcher could have made it with a spade; it was from twenty-five to thirty feet long, following the scope of the bank, and ending some two or three feet under the water. The branches were laid with their butts uppermost, and formed a complete thatching to the house, nearly weather-proof. The house itself was a vertical excavation into the bank, cylindrical in form and about three and a half feet in diameter; the slope of the bank, where it was cut, gave it the figure of a section of a cylinder of about four feet high on the side of the bank, and the heighth of the passage to the river, on the other, about fourteen inches. The bottom and walls of this room were smooth and hard as though they had been pressed or beaten, but not plastered. The circle was apparently perfect in form. I should have said, it was rather more than half-way up the bank. Prevost said that the house was unfinished, and that, before winter, the whole interior earth and brush of the sides and roof would have been neatly plastered with clay so as to render it entirely weather-proof. The quantity of cotton-wood branches and saplings used in this structure was enormous; I suspect the measurement would have been about three cords, or as many wagon loads, and so closely impacted that it was only after considerable labor that a breach was made. On the bank above was the area of *stump-land* where they had felled their timber, taking what was suitable from the most convenient distance. The large block presented this evening was cut from the largest log felled; the branches only were taken, leaving the trunk where it fell. Small saplings were taken entire. The smaller piece, which is cut at both ends, was the butt of a bough or sapling, which, in their attempt to drag to the bank, had become wedged among a clump of bushes in such a manner that they could not back it out again, owing to the resistance of the branches on the ground and of other bushes, so, like the sailor who throws overboard a portion of his cargo to enable him to save the rest, they cut off this piece that they might steer clear of the difficulty with the remnant of their treasure. The chips are from the larger specimen; in cutting them out they must work horizontally around the trunk, and when they have cut two grooves at the proper distance apart, they take hold of the isolated portion with their teeth, and split off portions *vertically,* and so in succession split off chips until they have girdled the tree; a second course is then removed from the bottom of this, and so

205

on diminishing the size of the chips until the tree is only supported by a portion of its heart connecting the apices of two cones—one on the stump upright, the other on the butt of the log inverted. In this manner, also, the Indians cut down the trees with their hatchets, leaving the same form of a cone on the but[t] of the log and on the stump, as their beaver neighbors have done before them.

Appendix IV

Skins and Specimens Collected on the Missouri

[The following lists and notations are to be found on several pages towards the close of the small diary for 1843, Harris Collection.]

List of Skins of Quadrupeds prepared by Bell during the Passage from St Louis to Yellowstone in Omega 1843

2 Ground Hogs
2 Red Squirrels
2 Grey Squirrels
2 Young D^o
1 Black D^o
4 Rabbits
1 Townsend Hare
1 Young D^o
1 Meadow mouse
2 Whitefooted mice
2 Young Woodrats
3 Bats
_____
23

Birds procured on the passage up the River
[*the second column probably indicates Harris's share*]

1 Wild Turkey	1
2 Blue Herons	1
13 Parrots	10
5 Yellowheaded Troopials	5

14 Lark Finches Smith's 1 new	7	
2 Chestnut-collared Dᵒ	1	
4 Rose-breasted Grosbeaks	3	
4 Bells Vireo 2 new	2	
5 Harris' Finch 3 new	2	
6 White-crowned Dᵒ	4	
6 Lincoln's Finch?	4	
12 Clay-coloured Bunting? 4 new	8	
1 Cardinal Grosbeak	1	
1 Balt Oriole	1	
1 Golden-winged W.	1	
1 Kentucky W		
1 Wormeating W.	1	
2 Small Green-crested F.	1	
1 Red-shafted Woodʳ		
1 Purple Martin	1	
1 Rough-winged		
3 Cow-buntings	2	
1 Henslows Bunting?		
1 Humming Bird		
1 Blue Grosbeak		
1 Young Woodcock	1	
2 Say's Flycatcher	2	
4 Tennessee W.	2	
3 Blackheaded Grosbeaks	3	
5 New Meadow Larks	5	
8 Arkansas F	8	
14 Arctic Towhee Buntings	9	

117 [127]

List of Birds procured at Fort Union

Lazuli Finch	9	4
Arctic Towhee Bunting	4	
New Meadow Lark	5	3
New Titlark	14	8
Chestnut Collared Bunting	3	

Cow Bird	2	
Rusty Grackle	5	2
Prairie Lark Finch	1	
Lark Bunting (grammaca)	11	11
Clay-coloured Bunting (pallida)	3	
Arkansaw Flycatcher	12	4
Say's Flycatcher	5	1
Red-shafted Woodpecker	11	
Yellow-shafted do	3	
do do do with red cheek	2	
Harris's Woodpecker	1	
Rock Wren	4	4
Shore Lark	5	2
Night Hawk	1	
Rice Bird	1	1
Black headed Grosbeak	5	3
Arctic Blue-bird	8	4
Cliff Swallows	4	2
House Wren	1	
Marsh Hawk	1	
Great Horned Owl	1	
Raven	1	1
Sharp-tailed Grous	2	2
	125	

Skins of Quadrupeds at Fort Union

Porcupine	1
Fawn	1
Townsend's Hare	1
White-footed Mouse (?)	1
13 Squirrel	1
Porcupine	1
Badger	1
13 Squirrels	5
Hare (Townsends)	1

Bat (Subulata)	1
	14

Balance of Birds [at Fort Union]

	125
Raven	1
Sharp-tailed Grous old & young	2
Magpie	1
Yellow Shafted Woodpeckers	4
Arkansas Flycatcher	1
Black-headed Grosbeaks	3
Loggerheaded Shrikes	2
Arctic Towhee Young	1
Rock Wrens	8
Henslow's Buntings { differs from that found on the river }	3
Titmouse Black capped?	1
Lark Bunting	1
	153

Birds procured on passage down the river

Hutchin's Goose	2
? New Whippoorwill	1
Troopials	7
Harris Finch Young?	1
Yellow-shafted W.	2
Prarie Finch	1
Parroquets	8
	22
	153
	117 [127]
	292 [302]

Quadrupeds on passage down

Grey Squirrels	4
Red do.	1
Prarie Dogs	3
Grisly Bear	1
Least Ground Squirrel	1
Field Mouse	1
	11
	14
	23 [?]
	48

*List of Bird Skins in Box packed by Sprague and Bell
for share of E. Harris—at St Louis*

  1 Wild Turkey
  1 White-fronted Goose
  1 Blue Heron
  1 Sandhill Crane
  2 Sharp-tailed Grouse
 10 Parrots
  1 Magpie
  8 Missouri Larks
  5 Yellow-headed Troopials
  2 Rusty Grackles
  6 Black-headed Grosbeaks
 12 Arkansaw Flycatchers
  9 Arctic Pipilos
 13 Lark Finches
  3 Rosebreasted Grosbeaks
  1 Purple Martin
  2 Cow Buntings
  1 Rice Bird
  1 Cardinal Bird
  3 Say's Flycatcher
  2 Cliff Swallows

2 Western Shore Larks
1 Baltimore Oriole
8 Sprague's Lark
4 Lincoln's Finch
1 Muscicapa?
1 Finch?
7 Smith's Lark Finch
1 Chestnut-collared Bunting
4 Arctic Blue Birds
1 Golden-winged Warbler
1 Wormeating Warbler
8 Shattuck's Bunting
6 Rocky Mt Wrens
4 Lazuli Finches
2 Harris' Finches
4 White-crowned Finches
1 Hutchin's Goose
1 White Pelican
11 Pinnated Grouse
1 Young Snow Goose
———
154
2 Bell's Vireo
2 Tennessee Warblers
1 New Black-capped Titmouse
———
159

Out of this list sent to Bell in exchange

3 Pinnated Grouse
3 Arkansaw Flycatchers
3 Lark Finches
2 Black-headed Grosbeaks
2 Arctic Pipilos
1 Young Rocky Mt Wren

Objects worth Collecting on our return
[from Fort Union]

The *Wild Potatoe* which grows in Strings and is said to be the original of the Irish Potatoe and will become the same by cultivating it a few years?
Seeds of the *Buffalo Berry* & *Dwarf Wild Cherry.*
Seeds of Plants of the *Kinnikanik* or Indian Tobacco, a very pretty flowering *Cornus* with a Red Bark. Catlin is mistaken in calling it a Willow.
Plants of three Species of *Cactus* and a *Yucca* with narrow leaves.
Specimens of *Fossil remains* wherever we can find them and particularly to search the hills at the Great Bend where fossil fish are said to be found in a very perfect state. Also specimens of the different Strata of *Limestone* and *other rocks* found on the river as well as of the *debris* covering them.
Procure shells wherever we can find them.
Roots of the pomme blanche for planting, and strings of the dried Root as prepared by the Indians.
Seeds of Maple—Seeds of narrow leaved Willow
Stop at Mouth of Little Missouri, lower side, and look for Forest of petrified wood on the hills of the first bend in the river—
Seed of Mandan corn

Appendix V

Expense Accounts

[*Notations from the pages opposite March 13th and 29th and October 21st in the Harris diary*]

Edward Harris   Cashier of the Expedition

Paid bills at Sandersons	12.45
Paid Servants at Sandersons	$1.00
Carriage Hire	1.00
Porters	2.50
fare to Wheeling 4 persons @ $13	52.—
Extra freight for baggage to Baltimore	50
Expenses paid by E. Harris to Baltimore	$69.45

Cash advanced by E. H. and J. J. A.
    which when expended will be carried out

Mar. 14. By E. Harris	$80.—	
" 15 " Mr Audubon	25.—	
" 16 " Mr Audubon	25.—	
" 18 " E. Harris	100.—	
Mr Audubon advanced J. Bell for Expenses to Balt. on the 12th	5.—	
Mr Audubon adv^d for exps at Cum^d	2.50	
	237.50	
Cash on hand on arrival at St Louis Mar. 28th	46.—	
	$191.50	191.50
Exps from Ph^a to St Louis (transf^d to page opp. March 29th		260.95

214

Exps. to St Louis bro^t over from

March 13th	260.95
Cash on hand	46.—
Ap^l 4th advanced by J. J. Audubon	90.—
″ ″ ″ ″ Do	25
″ ″ Mr Audubon's bill at G. House	9.65
Ap^l 15 advanced by J. J. Audubon	30.—
″ 24 advanced by J. J. Audubon	40.—

Carried for^d to Octr 21

Octr 21st

To pay for Dog for Mr A. $3.00—J.J.A. D^r for Mr Kipp

Cash returned to Mr Audubon	59.55
returned	62.55

Statement of Account of Expenses of Expedition to Yellowstone River in Summer of 1843. J. J. Audubon paying four fifths and Edward Harris one fifth of the same

[The draft, with the draft of the letter to Audubon, New Orleans Nov. 16. 1843, is in the Harris Collection, Montgomery]

Advances made by E. Harris

1843

Mar. 13. Exps paid by E. H. in Ph^a & to Balt.	69.45	
″ 14 Cash advanced by Do.	80.—	
″ 18 ″ ″ ″ ″	100.—	
″ paid for Gunpowder $12	12.—	
	$261.45	261.45

Advances made by J. J. Audubon

Mar. 12. To J. G. Bell exps to Balt	5.—
″ 15 ″ Cash advanced by J. J. A.	25.—
″ 16 ″ ″ ″ ″ ″	25.—
″ ″ ″ ″ ″ ″ ″ exps at Cum^d 2.50	
Apl 4 ″ ″ ″ ″ ″	90.—
″ ″ ″ ″ ″ ″ ″	25.—
″ ″ ″ paid his own bill at Galt House Louisv. [sic]	9.65

" 15 " Cash advanced	30.—	
" 24 " " "	40.—	
	252.15	
Less returned by E. H.	62.55	
	189.60	
Oct 20th Amt of settlement with Pierre Chouteau & Co	1640.18	
	1829.78	
Oct 21 Amt paid Michaux	20.—	
	1849.78	1849.78
		2111.23

Statement of Expenses to Yellowstone in the Summer of 1843

[from the original sent to Audubon, November 16, 1843, Audubon MSS, Houghton Library, Harvard University. The draft is in the Harris Collection, Montgomery]

Advances made by E. Harris			$261.45
Advances made by J. J. Audubon $252.15			
Octr 21 Less Amt returned by			
E. Harris	62.55	189.60	
Amt of N. Berthoud's A/C			
by J. J.A.		120.—	
Octr 21 Amt of Pierre Chouteau Jr. & Cos A/C exclusive of			
Cash advanced J.J.A. same day	1617.83		
4 Mos. Int on same	32.35		
	1650.18		
Less charged on A/C of J. G. Bell			
Provost $4 Skins $6	10.—		
	1640.18		
Amt of Fort Union and Fort Pierre A/Cs included in above Amt	351.43		
Less items actually expended a/c expedition	115.06		
Leaving Balance to be deducted, composed of			

items at Forts on a/c
of J.J.A. & others   236.37   236.37
                                  1403.81

Paid Michaux by J. J.A.   20.— 1423.81   1733.41
                                                 1994.86

D^r

(transferred) Edward Harris to his ⅕ of 1994.86 398.97⅕
               J. J. Audubon to his ⅘ of 1994.86 1595.88⅘ 1994.86

Dr Edward Harris in a/c with J. J. Audubon   C^r
1843   1843
Octr 21 To his ⅕ of $1994.86   March 18 By advances made by
        (trans)   398.97   E. H. for travelling
" " " "½ of $500   Exps &c   261.45
       paid to Bell   250.—   Novr 16. By draft on Dr Spencer
Sundries in Fort Union A/C   for Balance this A/C 391.58
  1 Antelope Skin   50   653.03
  1 Elk Skin   .56
  Making Moccasins
Making Mocassins
  Say   3.00   4.06
                  653.03

Index

Adams, Bernard: 142 n.

Alton, Ill.: 15, 51, 52

American Fur Company (Pierre Chouteau, Jr., and Company): 9 n., 12, 21, 48 n, 91; *see also* Fort Clark, Fort Pierre, and Fort Union

Antelope: 19, 21, 103, 104, 114, 140, 145–46, 150, 150 n., 172

Ashley, General: 87, 87 n.

Audubon, John James: 9 n., 43, 47 n., 49 n., 50 n., 53, 55 n., 66, 75, 76, 77, 82, 86, 94, 102, 103, 104, 107, 113, 114, 116, 118, 119, 122, 123, 124, 127, 130, 131, 132, 133, 134, 135, 136, 137, 138, 140, 140 n., 141, 142, 143, 144, 145, 146, 148, 150, 153, 154, 157, 157 n., 158, 163, 167, 169, 178 n., 179, 183 n., 184, 184 n., 193; considers western expedition, 2; regard for Harris, 3–4, 5, 57 n., 131 n.; plans 1843 expedition, 5–10; writes Baird of success of trip, 7 n.; described, 9 n., 14; describes voyage on *Gallant*, 11–12, 45 n.; at St. Louis, 12–16; letters to Gideon Smith, 21–23, 24 n., 97 n.; on buffalo hunt, 28; parentage of, 43; describes departure from St. Louis, 54 n.

——, quoted: 2, 3–4, 5, 6, 7, 8, 9, 10–11, 11–12, 13–14, 15, 15 n., 24 n., 44 n., 45 n., 49 n., 50 n., 51 n., 54 n., 55 n., 56 n., 57 n., 58 n., 59 n., 63 n., 64 n., 65 n., 66 n., 67 n., 68 n., 72 n., 73 n., 75 n., 76 n., 77 n., 82 n., 84 n., 86 n., 88 n., 89 n., 90 n., 97 n., 101 n., 102 n., 106 n., 113 n., 122 n., 124 n., 127 n., 130 n., 131 n., 141 n., 142 n., 150 n., 151 n., 154 n., 173 n., 181 n., 183 n.

Audubon: Victor: 10

Bachman, Dr. John: 4, 5

Badger: 8 n., 102, 102 n.

Baird, Spencer Fullerton: 5, 6, 7, 8; letter to Audubon quoted, 5 n.

Bakewell, William: 10, 11, 45 n.

Ball given at Fort Union: 101

Baltimore: 10, 43, 44

Bear: 63–64, 114, 117 n., 176

Beaver: 203–206

Bell, John G.: 6, 7, 9, 10, 14, 18 n., 30, 31, 32, 33, 34, 35, 38, 43, 47 n., 49, 50, 50 n., 51, 53, 55 n., 61, 64 n., 66, 68 n., 69, 70, 74, 77, 78, 86, 87, 93, 95, 102, 104, 105, 106, 107, 111, 114, 115, 117, 118, 119, 121, 122, 122 n., 123, 124, 125, 127, 128, 129, 131, 132, 133, 135, 136, 137, 138, 139, 140, 141, 142, 143, 144, 145, 146, 148, 152, 153, 154, 156, 160, 161, 162, 163, 165, 169, 174, 175, 176, 178, 179, 180, 183, 183 n., 184, 195; biographical sketch, 7 n.; trip up Yellowstone, 170–72; hunts bighorns, 172–73

Bellevue Post: 59, 59 n., 182, 182 n.

Berthoud, Nicolas: 14, 48, 48 n.

Bighorns: 97, 118, 124, 173

Bijou's Hills: 71

Birds: procured on passage up river, 207–208; at Fort Union, 208–209, on passage down river, 210; Harris's share of skins, 211–12; skins sent Bell, 212

Bluebird, Arctic: 107, 111, 113, 121

Bobolink: 133

Brant: *see* Geese, White-fronted

Buntings: Baird's, 157 n.; Bay-winged, 93; Clay-colored, 59 n.; Henslow's, 57; Lark, 63, 66, 105

Chickadee: see *Parus*

UNIVERSITY OF OKLAHOMA PRESS

NORMAN